THE HEART MODEL

An Integrated Faith-based and Psychological Approach to Heal from Trauma and Produce Balance in the Mind, Body, and Spirit

Dr. Benjamin Keyes

Copyright © 2023 by **Benjamin Keyes**

All rights reserved. No part of this publication may be reproduced, distributed, or transmitted in any form or by any means, without prior written permission.

Scripture quotations marked (ESV) are taken from The ESV® Bible (The Holy Bible, English Standard Version®) copyright © 2001 by Crossway, a publishing ministry of Good News Publishers. ESV® Text Edition: 2011. The ESV® text has been reproduced in cooperation with and by permission of Good News Publishers. Unauthorized reproduction of this publication is prohibited. Used by permission. All rights reserved.

Scripture quotations marked (KJV) are taken from the King James Bible. Accessed on Bible Gateway. www.BibleGateway.com.

Scripture quotations marked (NASB) are taken from the New American Standard Bible ® (NASB), copyright © 1960, 1962, 1963, 1968, 1971, 1972, 1973, 1975, 1977, 1995 by The Lockman Foundation. Used by permission. www.Lockman.org.

Scripture quotations marked (NIV) are taken from the Holy Bible, New International Version. Copyright © 1973, 1978, 1984, 2011 by Biblica, Inc.® Used by permission. All rights reserved worldwide.

Scripture quotations marked (NKJV) are taken from the New King James Version®. Copyright © 1982 by Thomas Nelson, Inc. Used by permission. All rights reserved.

Renown Publishing
www.renownpublishing.com

The HEART Model / Benjamin Keyes
ISBN-13: 978-1-960236-07-4

Praise for *The HEART Model* by Dr. Benjamin Keyes

The HEART Model is an easy-to-read guide that explores the therapeutic process of trauma. It begins with establishing rapport with clients and concludes with refocusing and returning to life. Each chapter gives a solid therapeutic approach that is dotted with personal examples. These snippets give the reader an inside look into the true-life application of the HEART Model.

I enjoyed how this book gives rationales for its positions and is not afraid to look at differing opinions. This is particularly true in the chapter on forgiveness. This chapter explores the difference between setting forgiveness as a treatment goal versus allowing forgiveness to be an artifact of good therapy. Dr. Keyes explains the Christian view of forgiveness and explains why some researchers believe that it is needed as a treatment goal. He asserts, however, that it is an artifact of good counseling. In the words of Dr. Keyes, forgiveness of self and the willingness to let go and move on is more important than focusing on the perpetrator. This expanded view of forgiveness allows for clients to "accept the possibilities that God has in store for us."

Dr. Keyes' HEART Model is consistent with current standards of care in trauma work and includes a spiritual perspective into this model. It provides a true research-based Christian model. His model does not shy away from the inclusion of the client's spiritual health. It looks at how the client views God and explores common distortions. It provides a mechanism to confront these distortions of God in the therapeutic process, bring awareness of God's presence, and receive forgiveness from God. This inner healing work provides a structure to bring healing to trauma survivors.

The title of Chapter Ten is "Refocusing and Returning to Life with New Insight, Purpose, and Hope." Is this not the purpose of all therapy? He challenges the reader to look at the difficulties clients face when attempting to reemerge with new insight into a world that may or may not like the changes. Clients face the challenge of a new way of being: to become their whole and true self, with spiritual connection to God. This permits clients to be healthy and fully alive, and to experience the deepest source of love.

Dr. Keyes encourages all counselors to be more than a technician of counseling. He advances the art of therapy.

Dr. Kim Harris
Researcher, trauma specialist, educator, and wife

To the brave clients that I have had over the years, who survived terrible abuse at the hands of those who should have known better. And to the many clients who have been trafficked here in this country and across the globe. Their strength, their courage, and their sheer persistence have all worked with the Holy Spirit of God to bring them to a place of healing.

And to my wife, Kim, who has been my rock and support for most of the time I have been working on this manuscript. Without her support, this never would have been accomplished.

Disclaimer and Warning: I have tried to write about difficult and sometimes monstrous experiences in ways that will not shock or trigger the reader. If you are prone to, or frequently experience triggering of, flashbacks, abreactions, or dissociation, please do not go any further without support, therapy, and prayer. If a trigger starts, please have a plan of care and do what is necessary to cope. Please discuss this with a therapist before continuing.

CONTENTS

Foreword by Colin A. Ross, M.D. 3

Preface 7

A Christian Perspective on Trauma Theory 9

Establishing Rapport—Creating a Safe Environment 21

Connecting to, and Anchoring, Relevant Memory 35

Processing Affect 71

Negotiation and Reconciliation Between Present and Past Ego States 83

Forgiving Yourself: Letting Yourself Off the Hook 97

Awareness of God and Processing Possible Distortions of God 111

Receiving Forgiveness from God 129

Merging the Split Parts 135

Infilling of God 161

Refocusing and Returning to Life with New Insight, Purpose, and Hope 167

Trauma and HEART Model Research 183

Human Trafficking 203

Afterword 213

Acknowledgments 215

About the Author 217

About Renown Publishing 219

Notes 221

Foreword by Colin A. Ross, M.D.

I accompanied Dr. Keyes on a series of trips to Shanghai Mental Health Center in the late 1990s and the 2000s, and I am a coauthor with him on a set of papers resulting from those visits. I have listened to him speak about the HEART Model on multiple occasions, and also about the trauma therapy trainings he has provided on different continents. I have seen his thinking evolve over decades and have always been impressed by it. He has done a great deal of work to increase the awareness of dissociative disorders internationally. Also, I have heard him talk about the need to educate Christian counselors on the dissociative disorders and their treatment. This book accomplishes that goal very well.

Over the years, Dr. Keyes has explained to me why there is a need for better education on trauma and dissociation among Christian counselors. For one thing, as in the mental health field in general, there is too little training on the topic; this is true in the entire mental health field, including psychology, psychiatry, and social work. It is true both in secular schools and in Christian-based training institutions. As a practicing Christian therapist, Dr. Keyes has long been concerned about the tendency of some Christian counselors to attempt exorcisms without considering the possibility of a dissociative disorder.

In *The HEART Model*, Dr. Keyes succeeds in integrating a Christian therapy approach with the principles and techniques developed in the secular dissociative disorders field. His thorough, detailed explanation of dissociative disorders and their treatment is integrated with an "overlay," as he calls it, of Christian and religious theory and practice. The Christian counseling approach is not just an add-on, however; it is blended in, as an essential, foundational principle. At the same time—and this is a remarkable achievement—*The HEART Model* is well worth reading for secular therapists, because it provides an excellent account of trauma-dissociation therapy.

For a secular therapist, the religious and spiritual techniques can be viewed as culturally-sensitive guided imagery and metaphor suitable for a Christian client. Secular imagery could be used instead, but the principles and techniques would remain the same.

The HEART Model has many features that make it an excellent book. It is written in a clear, readable style, without jargon and in the warm, personable tone one expects from Dr. Keyes. The many case histories throughout bring everything to life with sensitivity and empathy. Many different strategies and recovery tasks are described in detail in a way that can be used readily by therapists from different schools. Dr. Keyes's approach is a blend of cognitive, systems, and other schools of therapy, and incorporates and is receptive to many different tools and techniques. For example, one client in a case history benefited from EMDR. Throughout, an inner family systems approach is used that can be adopted across the full trauma-dissociation spectrum including DID, other specified dissociative disorder, PTSD and complex-PTSD, and borderline personality disorder.

The modern dissociative disorders literature began to emerge in 1980 and has evolved ever since, including the addition of extensive international research based on structured interviews and self-report measures, with many different types of statistical analysis. Dr. Keyes adds to this scientific literature by providing uncontrolled treatment outcome data from a series of cases, based on standardized measures used throughout the mental health field. His results provide a proof of concept and lay the foundation for more definitive research on the HEART Model.

One of the most important features of the book is Dr. Keyes's extensive discussion of the late pre-integration and post-integration treatment of DID. He provides by far the most thorough and useful discussion of the conflicts, fears and tasks of the person who now has "single personality disorder." This by itself is a valuable and noteworthy contribution to the field. For decades, there has been a large deficit in the dissociative disorders literature concerning post-integration treatment of DID. *The HEART Model* fills this gap far better than any other work I have read.

I'd also like to mention a previous book co-authored by Dr. Keyes and Dr. Sela-Smith, *E Pluribus Unum*. It provides an account, supplemented with numerous drawings, of a client's journey from full DID with amnesia, switching, and internal conflict to a stable post-integration recovery. The present volume builds on and extends that work.

I strongly recommend *The HEART Model* for Christian and secular counselors, and also for survivors. It provides a wealth of information and expertise based on Dr. Keyes's decades of experience as a therapist, speaker, author, and trainer in the field of trauma and dissociation.

Colin A. Ross, M.D.
Richardson, Texas, U.S.A.

Preface

When I was a neophyte in the field of counseling, I was told that I would probably see only one case of multiple personality disorder (now referred to as dissociative identity disorder, or DID.) in the whole of my counseling career. Within the first month, I had a client whom I misdiagnosed with post-traumatic stress disorder (PTSD) and who turned out to be suffering from a case of dissociative identity disorder.

After four months of working with this client, I referred her to a learned colleague who, after meeting her, got on a phone call with all the experts in the country on multiple personality disorder. At the time—it was 1986—she could only find eight such experts. She pointed out to me that I had referred the first, and possibly only, DID. client in my career. If I wanted anything to do with the case, I would need to meet her in Alexandria, Virginia, for a conference on Dissociation in order to recognize and treat this disorder. She also challenged me to learn all I could on the subject.

I made it my business to do just that, only to discover the huge numbers of victims whose odds of healing could be improved by more effective techniques and by doctors knowing how to diagnose the disorder properly. I came away from the experience committed to never again misdiagnosing a client. I have been in the field, continuing to learn and train, ever since.

INTRODUCTION

A Christian Perspective on Trauma Theory

We now know that memories include feelings, concepts, patterns, attitudes, and tendencies toward actions, any or all of which usually accompany a mental picture and can be stored in the brain in what is called the implicit memory. We will discuss implicit memory further in Chapter Two. Such memories can be accessed using a process of creative visualization, which may actually cause a client to abreact to the memory.[1] That is, the client may relive or reexperience with whole actions, not just with mental pictures, from their stored memories, particularly memories of a traumatic nature. When not confronted and worked through, these memories tend to draw the victim toward certain behaviors and actions that often lead to dysfunction.

It has been said that time heals all wounds. However, in the case of emotion and memory that have not been addressed sufficiently, the remaining feelings are often repressed or compensated for, in ways that will allow the person to cope with or manage the problematic situation; but, they are not actually healed. For instance, in the area of childhood sexual abuse, a child may learn to dissociate or disconnect from the actual feeling of the sexual violation in order to cope with a traumatic situation. Later, because of that disconnection, the child may continue to idolize the perpetrator. This is especially likely if the perpetrator is a close family member, because the affective memory of the trauma has been blocked effectively.[2] Over time, this can and will cause significant cognitive distortion in the child's perception of various relationships.[3]

Our minds act as protective defense mechanisms not only in significant trauma situations, but also in times of hurt, shame, and humiliation. This provides a wonderful way to protect ourselves from such difficult emotions and to preserve the essence of self. Humans have a wide variety of psychological defense mechanisms and acting-out behaviors that allow us to process and cope with our experiences. On the psychological side, these coping mechanisms might include minimizing, rationalizing, denial, forgetting, splitting, avoiding, and controlling. On the behavioral side, suicide attempts, cutting, various forms of addictions, isolation, avoidance of intimacy, and sexual acting out might be seen.[4] Sometimes, in the process of therapy, it is important to acknowledge the coping strategies we have used as a means of survival. When these mechanisms and patterns of behavior are brought into the light, they can reveal the wounds that need to be healed. Survivors of human trafficking persevere in any way they can, and all the methods listed above are often employed just to make it through another day. Breaking free of these patterns is psychologically difficult and requires quite a bit of effort, but it can be done.[5]

The process of healing is a form of counseling that focuses on the healing power of God (in Christian terms, God embodied in the Trinity of Father, Son, and Holy Spirit) in specific areas of emotional and spiritual wounding and distortion. The creative force of God's healing power allows us as individuals to create, with God, new reactions to the old material embedded in our memories. We are able to do this by exploring our emotional boundaries and new landscapes for our psychological well-being. To a considerable extent, we humans can expand our lives through creativity, insight into our conditions and problems, and faith in a Being beyond ourselves.

The HEART (Healing Emotional Affective Responses to Trauma) Model offers a spiritual model, from a Judeo-Christian worldview, that is designed to work with those who have experienced traumas and hurts, and who have difficult or painful memories of the past. The definition certainly encompasses the backgrounds and experiences of those who have been trafficked for sexual exploitation. The HEART Model is consistent with current standards of care for trauma work and offers a fresh approach toward incorporating spiritual issues into the treatment process. The standards that this model follows are those set out by the International Society for the Study of Trauma and Dissociation for treatment of the sexually traumatized and for dissociative clients.[6]

The HEART Model is a process of "inner healing" (a process of connecting to the inner self). Inner healing has been incorporated by certain Christian counseling professionals as a psychological technique, used primarily with Christian clients, to connect and abreact (that is, reexperience, or relive) memories of pain, hurt, or trauma in order to effect cathartic resolution. The purpose of the abreaction is to work through deep-seated and repressed feelings and memories and to enable the present-day effects thereof to dissipate.

The HEART Model is a step-by-step process of plumbing the depths of emotional experiences, resolving and restructuring cognitive distortions, and then reframing the affective responses. It is also a way of reframing those same emotional processes as they relate to a personal relationship with God. The HEART Model can be used to treat *any* traumatic situation, including complex trauma, such as human trafficking, ritualistic abuse, the death of a family member, severe sexual trauma, the effects of war, child abuse, perceived hurts and slights by others, family-of-origin issues, and man-made or natural disasters, to name but a few. When the emotional reactions and feelings become overloaded and overwhelming, the experience can be likened to that of a fuse blowing. To protect the essence of who we are, the fuse blows out before the full impact of the experience is felt.

An example could be an individual who has experienced a car accident that resulted in severe injury. The event itself can lead to shock and then unconsciousness. Often, when the victim wakes up in the hospital, the memory of the pain and, sometimes, the memory of the actual traumatic event have been blunted or completely removed. This amnesia is sometimes partial, sometimes complete, and it may be temporary or permanent, depending on the individual.

This same process happens with survivors of sexual trauma when conflicting or extremely painful emotions from their experience flood their being, such as when memories are accessed or triggered. Without therapeutic intervention, individuals often resort to dysfunctional coping skills. All too often, the result is that problems and feelings are submerged into the subconscious and the client unconsciously sublimates, or redirects the problems and feelings. These may later reappear as physical illnesses, unhappy marital situations, or significant psychological distress, which can spiral into recurring cycles of defeat.

Theory

Though René Descartes held a Catholic worldview, Cartesian theory separates the mind from the body and separates both from the spirit. He said, in essence, the spirit is not tangible, cannot be measured, and should belong to the church.[7] I would suggest that this theoretical disconnect between mind and body has led scientific frameworks to inadequately address the spiritual nature of human beings. Moreover, Cartesian theory has been challenged recently through the use of quantum physics and the postulation that the spiritual self can be quantified, through electromagnetic energy, as the spiritual self.[8] Regardless of whether this postulation is accurate, religions around the world—

and humanity itself—have been wrestling with the essence of who God is and the nature of our purpose in life.

I believe that the one place where the three energies of mind, body, and spirit converge is in the heart. By *heart*, I refer not to the literal body part, but to the soul, which we often call "the heart." The heart, in Jewish tradition, incorporates the wholeness of the self; it is the seat of emotion, love, and transcendence. The heart is the gateway to the higher self. The ability to love and to receive love unlocks the gifts of insight, true knowledge, and spiritual awakening. It is the heart that is the seat of the ultimate battle between the higher and lower selves, good versus evil, and heaven versus hell.

The good news, I believe, is that there is a way out of hell and out of the lower self—in other words, a way to avoid evil. The tough news is that all of us have to work *on* it to work *through* it. The hurts, pains, and traumas of our lives often hinder our continued growth, and they affect all areas of our self in various ways. The processing of the affect, or feelings, previously held back or repressed allows both release and the freedom to continue our growth.

My personal work in trauma has spanned more than forty years. It has encompassed hospital, residential treatment, outpatient, and field settings. I have worked with the entire dissociative spectrum, including borderline personality disorders, post-traumatic stress disorders, and a variety of dissociative disorders. Because of the dissociation, all instances of hurt and trauma, whether emotional, physical, or sexual, become encoded into mind and body at various levels, depending on their degree of severity, their duration, and the victim's perception. In childhood, these experiences and feelings become encoded from the psychological and emotional framework of childhood and are, thus, often frozen in time. For childhood victims, time literally stands still in an internal state, and if the trauma is not dealt with or processed at the time of the trauma, it will force the child to adapt or integrate the experience, complete with feelings, sensations, and thoughts.

Moreover, the encoded trauma results in firmly held beliefs, since they have been incorporated into the child's concept of how the world is. This childish method or approach often causes distortions of thoughts and behavior in later life. For a trafficked client, this is frequently compounded by the addition of multiple perpetrators and abusers, along with extended periods of sexual violation that may continue well into adulthood.

It is said that the kingdom of God is in the heart, and the New Testament tells us that to enter this kingdom, we must enter as children (Matthew 19:14; Mark 10:15). It is therefore worthwhile to consider both the heart and childlikeness before exploring the inner healing process.

First, if God resides in the heart, then His kingdom includes all that we are, the totality of self. It is the place where mind, body, and spirit are perceived as one. Only much later did the Greeks contemplate disparate aspects of themselves and produce a theory that has shaped much of Western thinking, resulting in the popularly held view of a division between one's physical self and one's spiritual identity.[9] By contrast, given the earlier framework of the human psyche, when we are encouraged to have a change of heart or to take heart, it means to change or take stock of the entirety of who we are.

The Greek verb *metanoia* translates as "to repent."[10] It can be described as having a change of heart or, in other words, a change of wholeness. Therefore, the inner healing process and the model we will be discussing is a journey to the core of the heart, or the depths of one's wholeness, in order to reach the place where we can experience change. When we are not complete in our wholeness—and most of us are in process—we find we have parts that are infirm or incomplete. Unexpressed hurts, traumas, and weaknesses tend to distort our ability to function. They become qualities of our personality that predispose or incline us not to become all that we are capable of being. They are weakened places in our defenses that undermine resistance to our lower or baser selves.[11]

For the second aspect, consider for a moment the world of a young child. If the child is nurtured, he or she experiences wonder, awe, and growth. If the child is shut down or receives an unloving response, that child experiences hurt, pain, and frustration. Think about the world into which you were born. Most likely, your parents planned for you and nurtured you, and you might have been breastfed by a loving mother. Your diapers were changed regularly, and you were given attention and myriad opportunities to grow and develop healthily. Such experience in early childhood leads to growth, development, and the capacity for curiosity and awe.

Now consider a child born to a mother who was addicted to crack cocaine and who engages in prostitution to support herself. Her child's most basic needs are often neglected. The child is frequently left alone; his or her most fundamental hygiene is ignored or attended to minimally. The child may be physically harmed or malnourished. It is no surprise that this child experiences the world as cold and unbending, and thus develops distrust around having core needs met.

The Greeks used two words to identify aspects of childhood. The first was *nēpios*, which literally meant "childish" and would be used to categorize an unhappy childhood.[12] It also denoted someone who was spiritually immature.[13] A healthy childhood, however, was described using the word *padion*, which literally meant "childlike."[14] A healthy child is teachable, is humble, accepts others openly, and has faith. The process of inner healing, especially with the HEART Model, can restore and transform part or all of an unhappy childhood. Blessedly, by co-creating with God, it is possible to create a healthy "adult child" who is capable of being taught and seeing the wonder in life.

Certain theories of trauma—especially that of John and Helen Watkins, who wrote extensively regarding ego state therapy—hold that most people are multiplicities at some level, whether covertly or overtly.[15] These personality segments, called ego states, represent specializations of various functions that were initiated and developed to improve the adjustment and, in some cases, support the survival of the individual. We all have ego states. Currently, I am in the role of a writer, but when I answer the phone and speak to my wife, I am in the role of a husband. When I talk to my son, I am in the role of a father. Each of these is an example of an ego state. When I experience feelings of anger, sadness, ecstasy, or joy, these are ego states. When I remember situations in my life, such as when I was seventeen and hated school, or five years old and frustrated about not attending a party because I was ill, those are also ego states. Qualities such as vulnerability or possessing a strong will can also be considered ego states.

Another way to express the concept is that we do not feel, think, perceive, or act the same way all of the time. A music fan may shout or scream at a concert but be perceived as shy or conservative at home. A laid-back mother may become fierce or warrior-like if her child is threatened. To quote John Watkins:[16]

> Such differential responses are common and are taken for granted. What perhaps is not so recognized is that these different response patterns result not only from different precipitating conditions, but also from differing internal organizing systems of feeling, motivation, and cognition within the individual. Sometimes the same internal conditions will provoke a very different response because a personality segment has been activated and for the moment becomes activated or controlled by the individual.

In layman's terms, it simply means that parts of ourselves can be, and often are, segmented, isolated, or disconnected from our conscious selves. The inner healing process is essentially designed to make it possible for the conscious self to reconnect to those disconnected places in order to achieve a greater sense of wholeness. If we are to achieve completeness, this reconnection not only requires a journey to our individual pasts, but also must be done with a sense of God. Regardless of which theological framework you might embrace (Christian, Zen Buddhist, Muslim, spiritualist, etc.), a sense of something greater than yourself is essential for complete healing and the resulting transformation.

Several years ago, my daughter read a book while she was exploring her theological boundaries. In essence, the book said, "There is a God, and you are not Him." We must connect with something beyond ourselves, even reaching out beyond other humans. When we do, we will see the total of others as being greater than ourselves. People in Alcoholics Anonymous (AA) who are dealing with alcohol addiction often start out this way, by seeing the group as greater than the individual and as being more powerful than themselves in isolation. The canvas of psychological co-creation is limited only by our creativity. As the hand of God holds us, we can use our God-given creative force and connection to God as vehicles for healing and growth.

Methodology

The technique itself is a step-by-step process that utilizes creative visualization and incorporates guided prayer to allow the individual to see and recreate the experience of the submerged memory clearly. The experience of reconnecting to difficult, sometimes horrific situations often causes abreactions. The emergence of that response will usually need to be talked out, worked out, and processed using therapeutic counseling interventions. Often, the issues of repressed anger, hurt, and deep-seated emotion quickly come to the surface. When that happens, they can be confronted, and it is possible to work toward resolution. In these situations, clients typically blame themselves, though the blame is not in any way theirs to bear.

In a spiritual context, the victim's view of God is typically distorted, and the distortion must be confronted. Without addressing the perception, survivors are likely to feel that God did not protect them or rescue them from the horrific situation. For instance, trafficked women wonder how a merciful God could allow them to be trapped in their lives. They question God's very existence. In most major Christian denominations, the Bible is interpreted to emphasize God's promise as one of presence. Essentially, God promises to be with us through difficult times, not to save us from the current horror. Nevertheless, rescue is often the immediate change for which many people long. The sure and certain knowledge that God was with us at times of trauma and hurt, and that God continues to be with us now, represents a significant paradigm shift for many individuals dealing with ongoing spiritual and psychological issues. It is, frequently, enough of a shift to foster hope and purpose in life as survivors work toward resolution of ongoing issues.

The healing process moves through the series of events to allow the adult self of the present time to reach out, emotionally and spiritually, and rescue the child or younger adult self from the time of hurt or trauma. From a Judeo-Christian perspective, since time is a man-made concept that does not constrain God, we must literally allow God to travel back to the memory with us. From there, it is possible to work toward healing that memory in order to bring awareness of change in the present. In a real sense, we are allowing the adult self to reach to the inner child.[17] As I will state later on, God literally reaches to us to help us, to move us from childishness to childlikeness. The Holy Spirit's purpose is to help us, which means in part that He unbinds us from the things that keep us trapped. He reaches to us in our childishness and moves us to a place of safety, which brings us into a place of childlikeness.

At its core, the HEART Model encompasses a process of forgiveness that focuses on self-forgiveness and the ability to receive forgiveness from God. It is the element of self-forgiveness, and the Christian overlay of the model, that set it apart from other models currently in the literature.[18] The goal in the current book is to examine clinical applications of the various stages of the model in order to give the reader the opportunity to understand both the model and its application(s) in a clinical therapeutic setting. The hope is that the practitioner will be able to apply these strategies in a variety of settings and enter the dialogue of responding to the emotional and spiritual needs of clients who have a trauma background or history.

Any spiritual process, whether from a counseling framework or as a spiritual intervention, needs to provide safety for the person having the experience. This safety should not only be physical, but must also encompass some level of trust and rapport with the practitioner, who needs to provide a place of emotional safety for the client or the one who is on the spiritual journey. Trust and safety are key elements of the therapeutic alliance, and as such are the first stage of the HEART Model. The client's process of inner healing begins with trust in the practitioner and then focuses on reconnecting to memories and becoming attuned to them. Sometimes, we are not consciously aware of those disturbing memories or the state of abreacting, or reliving the experience. It is important for the person working through this process to anchor the memory, in order to bring it into a fullness of experience by expanding and deepening the perceptual hold on it. This is achieved by using all five senses and locking into the broadest possible awareness of feelings, sensations, reactions, thoughts, emotions, and anything that is reactive to earlier thoughts and memories similar to the situation the client may be discussing. Some will find this similar to hypnosis, neuro-linguistic programming, and other regressive techniques. Nevertheless, it is essential to be clear about the various distinctions, including the use and awareness of the person's feeling-state during prayer. The use of active prayer, the second stage of the model, then becomes a guiding focus for dealing with the inner pain or trauma.

The third stage has to do with allowing the full expression(s) of, and reaction(s) and connection(s) to, past and present feelings. As unpleasant as they are, they are the current experiences that grant access to the situation, to the self, and to others who may be involved. This connection may happen quickly, over the course of a one- or two-hour session, or may take time (days, weeks, or months). David Grove describes the processing of trauma as going to a time *before* the trauma and working *through* the trauma to a time just *after* the trauma:[19]

$$T\text{-}1 \quad T \quad T\text{+}1$$

Predictably, this stage brings up a myriad of feelings, reactions, and cognitive distortions. The encoding of the trauma is like the workings of the child's brain—occurring in pictures and whole concepts—because a child has no time or ability to sectionalize, compartmentalize, or categorize.[20] This process has raised criticism from some people, who believe that the child is able to create false memory. It is essential, therefore, that the questioning process not introduce any self-ideas or have any iatrogenic quality, and that any and all information revealed comes solely from the individual's process.

The final stage of this process has to do with reconnection, or in Gestalt terms, "the sum of the parts become (the combination of the parts comprise the) whole." The feeling of wholeness can be achieved with a corresponding, pleasant affective response by combining techniques of creative visualization, creative relaxation, and visual color therapy. A full sense of wholeness requires not just a connection to the self, but also a connection to God that completes the process. While I have not defined *God* here, I have a particular Judeo-Christian bias, which is the framework within which my work is developed. In the domain of therapy, it is essential that the individual begin to experience God (however he or she understands God) as truly loving, caring, and supportive.[21] The view of a benevolent Being is critical to long-term healing because, in the course of these individuals' therapy, distorted views of God that cast a negative light and create spiritual distance may well surface. Just as personal issues must be worked through in the case of traumas, the same must be done regarding issues with God.

While this process can be effective in the course of the therapeutic session (i.e., one to two hours), it is far more common for this process to occur over an extended period of time; for severe trauma, it may take several months or years. Thankfully, smaller issues of hurts, shames, humiliations, and the like can often be worked out in a matter of sessions or weeks.

We live in an exciting and challenging time for Christian counseling, particularly in the field of trauma and dissociative disorders. It is exciting because previous therapies and regimens of this field that were once considered heretical or demonically influenced, such as pharmacology, visualization, or hypnosis, are now being reclaimed and used in a godly way for healing. And yet, it is also challenging, since misunderstandings and conflicts occur regarding treatment methods. The controversy of the false memory debate back in the 1990s, for example, had many therapists (both Christian and secular) leaving the practice to avoid legal entanglements and harassments. Now, many therapists do not want to take on a client who will require an extended amount of time in the therapy process. As usual, it is the trauma survivor who suffers the loss, abandoned by the very profession that is intended to help him or her.

Couple these problems and therapeutic biases with denominational and personal prejudices, doctrinal conflicts, and poor theological application, and one might wonder that those in the church who have survived trauma continue to seek healing at all. Because churches know so little about trauma and dissociation, they typically offer little in the way of support. Baffled or even frightened by the bizarre behavior noted in those who are suffering from any type of dissociative disorder or having a psychotic break, Christians frequently assume, particularly in very conservative spheres, that demons may need to be cast out. History is replete with documentation of cases of attempted exorcism, deliverance, or the laying on of hands for survivors of trauma and abuse. The evidence shows that about 99.9 percent of these attempts have been unsuccessful in treatment. More often, these attempts to cure the trauma survivor damage them further.

In a more benign attempt to help, the church might offer cliché sayings, such as, "You just need to tough it out"; "Trust God more and you'll be okay"; "We all have our bad days"; "You need to spend more time in the word of God, and then you'll have victory"; or, perhaps most detrimentally, "You just need more faith." This kind of misinformed counsel sends the trauma survivor into a spin of guilt and self-condemnation for not doing enough as a Christian or as a mother, daughter, father, son, etc. And now, on top of their previous trauma, they are haunted with phrases like "just trust" and "have faith," until they break under the pressure of trying to be a "victorious Christian."

Hence, the victimization cycle starts all over again.

It is time for Christians to increase our awareness of the special needs and problems of trauma survivors and to begin to offer hopeful solutions for complete, Spirit-filled wholeness. Trauma survivors often do not believe they will attain this kind of wholeness or victory. In this book, I hope to encourage both counselors and victims that it really is possible. Not only *can* it be done, but it can be done powerfully and wonderfully as a process of inner healing and freedom. The process, however wonderful, is fraught with much pain and struggle; this is undeniable. Yet, God does bring healing and wholeness, as long as both victim and counselor are willing to complete the journey. Of all the clients with whom I have worked through this journey of wholeness and recovery, those who have chosen to accept God's healing touch have the highest success rate, by far, in remaining whole. We as counselors can use the tools and techniques God gives us to walk our clients through the process, but God alone completes the healing.

It is my hope that this book will help you distinguish the facts from the fallacies about trauma. It will help you to clarify the differences between various treatments, and it will give you a faith-based model that can be overlaid on any particular counseling theory from which you work. And hopefully, it will offer ways to work effectively with the families and loved ones of those who have been traumatized.

While this book is intended to demystify trauma a bit, its purpose is not to serve as a complete "how to" manual, providing every answer to every situation faced by those who have had to deal with trauma. Trauma survivors can experience unpredictable circumstances and outcomes, since each case is as unique as any individual person. However, certain common characteristics are shared by every patient with trauma. These common threads are what we will discuss and use to proceed effectively and sufficiently with treatment.

The healing process moves through the series of events to allow the adult self in present time to reach and rescue the child or younger adult self, emotionally and spiritually, from the time of hurt or trauma. What we have examined is a way out of that trauma and its psychological consequences, following the standards set by the International Society for the Study of Trauma and Dissociation (ISSTD) and using a Christian overlay with a standard three-phase model of treatment.[22] This ten-step HEART Model incorporates the spiritual dynamic in such a way as to produce healing and balance to the mind, body, and spirit within the one place they all reside: the heart.

CHAPTER ONE

Establishing Rapport—Creating a Safe Environment

One of a therapist's most important, and sometimes most difficult, tasks is to establish rapport with the client. As many writers across theoretical applications of therapy have determined, the establishment of rapport is the key to successful treatment outcomes.[23] Rapport is built on a foundation of trust, honesty, good communication, and finely honed listening skills. Often, this connection develops in the initial minutes of the opening session. First impressions are imperative in formulating long-term opinions, including cultural sensitivity and insight into self-identified problems.[24] Because rapport is necessary for building a relationship based on trust, most counselor-training programs emphasize such skills as making eye contact, using a calm and soothing voice, and making direct statements. These and other skills can be used to put the client at ease and to convey that the counseling office is a safe arena in which to explore and disclose tightly held secrets, feelings, and beliefs. The sense of safety must include physical, emotional, sexual, and spiritual arenas.[25]

The therapeutic alliance, according to Gelso and Carter, "is related to how the client presents and aligns his or her ego for the counseling relationship and how the client's ego is or is not joined with the counselor's self or ego."[26] Occasionally, the therapist may realize that the relationship with the client is not a good fit. This necessitates an honest conversation with the client early on, to discuss alternative options or to provide referrals. Forming the therapeutic alliance is about developing an emotional bond and attaining a goal together. According to Carl Rogers,[27] the therapeutic relationship is critical to positive outcomes, as are the counselor's personal qualities.[28] There must be a "joining" together to deal with the issues[29] and to form the therapeutic approach.

THE HEART MODEL

EMPATHY AND UNCONDITIONAL POSITIVE REGARD

"Carl Rogers brought the importance of empathy to our attention. He made it clear that we need to listen carefully, enter the world of the client, and communicate that we *understand the client's world as the client sees and experiences it*" (emphasis mine).[30] This does not happen through clichéd and sometimes patronizing phrases such as, "I understand," but rather through actively listening to the client's perception of his or her experiences, the impact they have made on him or her, and the belief systems that have developed as a result. True empathy acts as a key to unlock some of the most hidden and protected traumas clients have experienced.

A deeper dimension of empathy is found in acceptance, or as Rogers coined, "unconditional positive regard,"[31] which "is an attitude of grace, an attitude that values us even knowing our failings. It is a profound relief to drop our pretenses, confess our worst feelings, and discover that we are still accepted."[32] While the concept seems easy enough to understand, the execution can be challenging when working with certain populations. It is not nearly as difficult to find a place of empathy and unconditional positive regard for a child who has experienced molestation; however, if you are working with the perpetrator, that can be a more grueling pursuit. It becomes even more complicated when the individual has been both the victim and the perpetrator and fluctuates between those two personas. Rogers reminds us that even the most difficult client has some good qualities and strengths.[33] Listen for them, and make the positives part of your listening skills.[34]

In the trafficking world, pimps will often designate a "top female" to identify, recruit, groom, and ultimately pimp out other girls. This process takes an individual who has been victimized and turns her into a perpetrator.[35] To survive this new role, the girls often must dissociate to carry out the victimization and violence toward another soul. From a therapeutic perspective, it can be humanly challenging to hear about the pain they have suffered, and then to begin to learn about the atrocities they have also committed against others. However, for the sake of the client's healing, it is imperative that the counselor find core strengths in the individual and begin to develop those. The sheer fact that victims such as this survive and are in the healing process speaks to their strength and resilience.[36]

When clients feel they have at least one person who believes in them, despite all their wrongdoings, an invitation arises for them to begin to believe in themselves, forgive themselves, and move toward a healthier version of self. Unconditional positive regard is an exceptionally powerful tool in this process.

IDENTIFYING A SUPPORT SYSTEM

Early in the counseling process, working with clients to identify their personal support systems is critical.[37] These systems could entail the healthy-enough personal relationships they have, as well as social and community clubs, support groups, and church groups. For some, this will be an easy process, but for many others, they may have few interpersonal relationships on which they can truly rely. If that is the case, working with them to identify and follow through on pursuing some new social and relational outlets is very important. As their memory work begins, they will need alternative support systems outside of the counseling office.[38] It is too difficult to establish a support system in the midst of processing the emotions of the memories; therefore, this is a step of considerable importance in Phase 1. Many free groups are offered in most communities, including Alcoholics and Narcotics Anonymous, Al-Anon, Celebrate Recovery, Bible studies, Mothers of Preschoolers (MOPS) groups, sports teams, and so forth. Part of clients' therapeutic homework can be trying out some of these during the week and then reporting back on their experience and the connections they are making. Referring to their support system throughout the therapeutic process also helps remind them they are not alone as they go through this painful journey.

COPING MECHANISMS

Along the same lines, helping clients distinguish specific behaviors to deal with negative emotions is something that needs to be discussed in the earliest stages of therapy. Everyone has different things that help him or her push through discomfort and pain, such as taking a walk, listening to music, exercise, being creative, journaling, hitting a punching bag, taking a bath or shower, having time with a friend, or taking space and being alone for a bit. Sometimes, allowing clients to identify things that have helped them in the past, or things that have brought them joy at some point in life even if they are not experiencing the joy in the current season, can be effective. These activities are natural ways the individual can redirect some of his or her emotional energy. If you get clients who claim there is nothing that brings them comfort or release, then ask them to try a few suggestions from you each week until they build a small toolbox of coping mechanisms.[39]

COUNTERTRANSFERENCE AND OVER-IDENTIFICATION

While empathy is an extremely important part of building rapport with a client, counselors must find the balance between their ability to "enter the client's world" and the need to uphold the boundaries of personal separation, ensuring they do not get too emotionally entangled in the client's issues.[40] Counselors need to ask themselves, "Do we face the very things the clients are struggling with? If so, do we have our problems compartmentalized enough to distinguish between ours and theirs? If the conversations are constantly triggering our own issues, then we are doing our own therapy at the clients' expense." This entanglement of the counselor's emotions and the client's is known as countertransference.[41] Over-identifying with the client's experience can be harmful to the client and destructive to the counselor, and can even create ethical violations.[42]

Self-disclosure is another avenue that can allow for countertransference.[43] During a counseling session, there are times when it is appropriate and effective for the therapist to self-disclose a small amount of personal information that may provide new perspective, guidance, or hope to the client.[44] A standard caution is to ensure the primary focus does not shift too much from the client to the therapist. However, there are additional precautions counselors may want to take if their clients have encountered complex trauma resulting in dissociation.[45] When we are working with someone who has a fractured or split psyche, self-disclosure can become fuel for future manipulation, bargaining, or triangulation. Counselors must remember that for many people who have lived a lifetime of abuse and trauma, dysfunction is their "norm." Traumatized clients, therefore, are not looking for another person who has been abused or had similar circumstances for the sheer sake of "identifying" with them. They can usually find plenty of others, within their own circles, who have had similar experiences. The client is looking for *health*. Ensuring the information that the counselor discloses is intended to bring the client closer to health, rather than closer to the counselor, is an important healthy practice when utilizing self-disclosure.[46]

Attunement to Nonverbal Communication

We know that eye contact and visual connection are important, as reflected in the work of Grahe and Bernieri.[47] Moreover, Grahe and Sherman found that situational context (e.g., physical surroundings and the counselor's body language) was often a significant contributing factor in the attempt to establish rapport.[48] The therapist should be attentive to the environment and should provide some degree of physical and aural comfort. Many counselors use devices that create white noise just inside or outside the office door to help mask other noises and prevent the divulgence of confidences from being heard by others. If all goes as hoped, counselors are successful in answering the client's questions, allaying fears, and forming the necessary bond to begin working with deeper issues in the sessions to come. However, miscues, or misinterpretation of body language or statements made, can sometimes interrupt the bonding process, which then may go in a different, undesirable direction.

The need for cultural sensitivity has been well researched and documented.[49] Most often, when we think of cultural sensitivity, our first assumption is that it means an understanding toward racial differences and the cultures associated with specific ethnic groups.[50] Race and culture undoubtedly create a foundation for one's worldview. For example, we mentioned earlier the need to establish rapport using direct eye contact. In Western culture, looking someone directly in the eyes shows a level of honor and respect and is an unspoken cue that one is intently listening.[51] For the most part, this nonverbal behavior is appropriate for the counselor, and a reciprocation of eye contact would make the counselor assume the client is engaged. This nonverbal interaction additionally provides the counselor with cues as to the client's comfort level (as the old proverb says, "the eyes are the window to the soul," which is derived from Matthew 6:22–23). Yet, in an Asian culture, eye contact may have the completely opposite meaning: extended eye contact is often taken as a challenge of authority, while avoiding direct eye-contact is a sign of respect and honor.[52]

Furthermore, a counselor must be sensitive to subcultures including, for the purposes of this book, those of trauma and trafficking. These subcultures have differences due to specific world cultures; however, as we have learned from survivors from various countries around the world, there are some standard behaviors within the global trafficking subculture and trauma subculture.

Following the example above, of how eye contact can have different meanings and intentions in various cultures, those being sexually exploited also have very specific "rules" when it comes to eye contact. A victim is groomed to give direct eye contact *only* to her pimp. Any other eye contact is an invitation for physical and sexual punishment. Buyers, on the other hand, may force a victim to look them in the eyes, leaving the victim feeling as if her or his very soul were undressed before this stranger.[53] It is critical that the counselor be aware of this subcultural norm when working with the client since, without understanding the client's lack of eye contact or the triggers that could result from eye contact, the counselor may misunderstand and assume that the client is disengaged in the therapeutic process.[54]

Connecting to the Client vs. the Information

> Early in my days of private practice, Mary came into my office seeking counseling and direction regarding a childhood trauma related to sexual molestation by both her brother and her father over an extended period of time. I kept myself busy taking copious notes and attempting to get a detailed social and family history. I wanted to learn all I could so as to understand her story in all its developmental contexts. At the end of the session, when I asked her when she could return, she politely shook my hand and asked me for a referral to a female therapist. She went on to say that my note taking had distracted her and that, as a consequence, she did not feel that she was heard. She thought that perhaps a female therapist might be more sensitive to what she needed in the moment.

Needless to say, Mary's experience would have been very different if I had taken the time to assess her affective responses instead of following my own set intake protocol. Specifically, when one is working with victims of sex trafficking and other complex trauma, taking notes in general can be very off-putting, because the client often feels immense fear connected to disclosing the trauma.[55] Even if the therapist is getting the client's bio-psycho-social history, having those details put on paper can create suspicion and mistrust. When possible, it is best to remember the details during the session and make notes immediately afterward. If the therapist does not feel able to do this accurately, then allowing the client to review the notes and explaining why they are being written can help establish trust in these beginning stages.

RISKS OF ASSUMPTIONS

A colleague was directing a home for juvenile victims of sex trafficking. A frequent mistake she found among her team was that the staff often interpreted all negative behaviors to be the result of a trauma trigger. The clients would get extremely upset when assumptions were made, which negatively affected their trust and rapport with staff.

> Maria, a fourteen-year-old girl, had recently moved into this home, which was on a large ranch. Part of the program consisted of both equine therapy and horse-riding lessons. Maria was from a big city and seemed unsure of the country lifestyle. One day as the equine therapist was preparing to do a group with the clients, Maria refused to go out to the barn. Her refusal was quickly followed by outward expressions of anger that escalated abruptly to aggression and threats of violence. The staff member remained calm and empathetically explained that Maria did not have to go near a horse or into the barn, but asked if she would go outside, close by, so she could be in the staff's line of sight. Maria continued to escalate.
>
> At this point, the staff member assumed something bad must have happened to Maria in or near a barn, for her to be responding the way she was. The staff felt compassion and responded by explaining they would never require clients to do anything that made them uncomfortable. This statement only infuriated Maria even more. With tears streaming down her cheeks, she got within centimeters of the staff member's face and screamed, "Nothing about a barn makes me uncomfortable! My best memory with my father was in a barn and you guys aren't going to take that away from me!"
>
> While this staff member did a great job at remaining calm and speaking with empathy, her mistake came in assuming that Maria's refusal to participate was connected to trauma. The staff member's response indirectly insinuated that they would not want to re-traumatize the victim. Maria was not reacting from a trauma trigger, but rather out of fear and anger that a new positive experience would somehow interfere or diminish some of the only good memories she had with her father—and, frankly, that was too big of a risk for her.

As counselors, we must remember that we have expertise in psychological frameworks and tools, but the client is the expert on his or her own.[56]

NOT AT FACE VALUE

Another form of assumption-making is building rapport solely with the person presented to you during the therapeutic sessions. For those who have endured complex trauma, and sex trafficking more specifically, a common survival skill victims are forced to learn is to scan another person instantly and identify quickly what that person is asking of them. Sometimes, this is merely a survival technique that the victim can easily turn on and off, as one buyer might want a compliant encounter while another buyer might request the contrary. This constant changing of persona keeps the victim from being beaten or physically harmed by both the buyer and the pimp.[57] However, sometimes this switching of persona is one result of a much deeper level of fracturing within the psyche, creating multiple ego states.[58] This deeper fracturing means that you may experience a client who presents as passive one day but, moments to weeks later, seems to be a completely different person.

The clients are often entirely unaware of their changes in behavior or their presentation of dissociated parts.[59] When possible, it is incredibly helpful for the therapist to have a release of information with the caretaker of the client, particularly if the client is a minor or is in a safe-home. A systematic approach between therapist and caretaker is necessary for building consistency and accountability, as well as for the ultimate goal of integration. Such an approach should be taken only if the home and caretaker are considered safe by the client.

CREATING SAFETY

A colleague who teaches in an adolescent psychiatric facility described her first interaction with a fourteen-year-old teenager, a new admission to the sexual predator's unit. He wore size 16 shoes, was six-foot-five, and weighed in at about 350 pounds. Unbeknownst to her, the night before, Chris had done over ten thousand dollars in damage to his room, bathroom, and furnishings. The walls he had kicked through were concrete block. He had wrenched the metal door completely out of its frame and used it as a battering ram at the nurses' station. Chris had also ripped some of the plumbing out of the wall, pulled up the toilet, and thrown it down the hall.

When Chris arrived at the classroom, he was accompanied by three mental health technicians (one of whom was seven feet tall, a former professional football player) who refused to go inside, preferring instead to stand outside the door and keep watch in case they were needed. The teacher did not even have the chance to welcome Chris to her class, because he stormed in, leaned forward onto her desk on his fists, and announced that he was going to kill his new roommate. Chris was sweating and breathing heavily, obviously in a highly agitated state.

The teacher said, "You sound pretty upset. Say, does it seem hot in here to you?"

"Yeah, I'm hot. I'm gonna kill that kid!" he yelled.

"When I'm hot or mad, I usually go over there and stand by the air conditioner."

Chris strode across the room, flipped open the control cover, and jabbed the "on" button on the air conditioner. Meanwhile, with a foot, the teacher slowly pushed a chair over, to within Chris's reach. He grabbed it, sat down, and leaned over the vent with his eyes closed, letting the chilled air blow on his torso, neck, and face.

A minute later, when he opened his eyes, he looked down into the vent and spied the thermostat wire. He said, "Hey, somebody left a coat hanger in here."

The event was over, danger had passed, and his anger had evaporated. The psych techs breathed a sigh of relief and left. Only then could the teacher begin to work with Chris on more subtle tasks like establishing rapport and academic pursuits.

The veteran teacher was intimately acquainted with behavioral theory and classroom organization techniques, and she had taken myriad de-escalation trainings. However, when the angry giant stormed into the room, she had no advance warning. That was no time to sift through various theories and go over her training sessions to figure out which would be the best in the situation. Instead, she dealt with exactly what walked into the room: a furious, mentally unstable teenager with poor impulse control, whose calming medications had long since worn off. She did not try to figure out what had set him off or ask questions about his background. She paid attention to all of Chris's verbal and nonverbal cues, most of which were overt. She stayed calm and addressed only Chris's agenda. She dealt with exactly what Chris had brought into the room, not with classroom routines, academic testing, or the English lesson. After a few days, Chris announced that she was his favorite teacher because he felt like he could relax and be himself in her classroom.

THE HEART MODEL

In the example above, the teacher "read" Chris and responded appropriately, which allowed him to become calm and guided the tenor of their interactions from then on. The teacher's ability to remain calm and to create an avenue for external safety allowed Chris's internal world to become safer. Many clients have yet to develop enough coping mechanisms to regulate their emotions and feel safe during heightened emotional states.[60] They begin to rely on those around them and their external environment to gain a sense of safety.[61] When clients begins to believe that you can handle them at their "worst," trust begins to develop, they glean from your confident security, and they thus begin to develop their own coping mechanisms.[62]

When working with traumatized clients, however, rapport sometimes looks a bit different, because such clients often appear, and actually are, detached or dissociated: body language does not always match up to the words that are spoken, and the visual cues on which therapists typically rely are often a defense mechanism from the original trauma.[63] As a result, the practitioner's normal ability to "read" the signs through conversation and body language in the session can be hampered significantly. Even so, these clients will often respond positively, in their own way, and the therapist must be tuned-in enough to recognize the connection, thus building rapport, because the quality of the relationship is critical to effective outcomes in treatment.[64]

CLIENT DISCLOSURE OF MISTRUST AND THERAPEUTIC REDIRECTION

Sometimes, the return to the office week after week provides these clients with a non-threatening place and avenue for disclosing what they must if they are going to get better; therefore, it can also be an expression of placing their reserved trust in the therapeutic process. The two critical factors of building trust are (1) the quality and depth of connection between the client and the therapist and (2) the ability of the client to interact in the process of his or her own healing. These factors give the therapeutic relationship the impetus to succeed in moving a client toward healing.[65]

> Dory began being trafficked when she was fourteen years old. Years later, after she had broken away from the situation, she began seeing a therapist. She wanted to begin focusing on childhood sexual abuse issues and then the ravages of her trafficking. Dory had the following dialogue with her therapist.

> Dory: I don't really trust you, you know. I guess I've never really trusted any of the counselors I've been with.
>
> Therapist: It's quite normal for you to not trust me. We are just getting to know each other, and you are not sure whether it is safe here or not.
>
> Dory: I don't know if I'll ever trust you. I want to, but I don't seem to be able to.
>
> Therapist: What seems to get in the way of your trusting others?

By refocusing the conversation back on the issue, the therapist was able to get Dory to explore blocks that she put up, as well as the emotional walls that functioned to protect her and insulate her from being hurt. To deal with her handlers and pimps, she had shut down emotionally on the inside. She presented a strong, gruff exterior, which she had developed to help her navigate the pitfalls of her outer life. After this session with the therapist, Dory not only made the next appointment, but also saw this therapist for two more years. Despite the professed lack of trust, her actions clearly indicated trust in the therapeutic relationship.

OTHER FORMS OF SAFETY

In the previous section, we discussed environmental safety as an important factor that allows clients to engage in the therapeutic process. Environmental safety is a component of physical safety; however, other forms of physical safety also apply in the therapeutic environment. Sexual trauma survivors, especially those who have been trafficked, are often fearful that they might be physically or sexually attacked by a male therapist in particular.[66] It is important to address physical and sexual safety, especially with female clients. They need to know the therapeutic room is a safe environment for them to explore their deepest thoughts, and their most enduring pain and betrayals, in the dialogue that eventually leads to healing.[67]

> Robbie was a forty-eight-year-old schoolteacher, married with two children, who came to my care after losing a relationship with her previous therapist, who had violated the therapeutic boundaries to start an ongoing sexual relationship. Robbie had been in therapy for eight years and had been diagnosed with dissociative

> identity disorder. One of her altars, named Helen, had been a promiscuous twenty-five-year-old, who had made a living through prostitution in order to survive. The therapist had aligned with that part of her psyche (alter) and begun a relationship with her, while the other parts of herself maintained the secret and had limited or no information regarding the affair. What made this easier was that she had been in a sexual relationship with her psychiatrist two years earlier, also with the same part of herself. Both the psychiatrist and counselor lost their licenses when the facts were presented to their perspective licensing boards, but neither was charged criminally, and both are working outside of their respective fields. It was important to assure Robbie during the first session that such activity would not happen in the office she was in and that I would never enter a sexual relationship with any part of her.

Aside from physical and sexual safety, emotional safety must also be addressed.[68] The client must understand that the counseling office is a safe place in which to air any thoughts, experiences, or behaviors and that the therapeutic process would be free of judgment or condemnation.[69]

Lastly, it is important for clients to understand that the counseling environment will maintain spiritual safety. This means that anything pertaining to the client's spirit—thoughts, actions, or deeds believed to be unspiritual, denominational issues, religious or sacrilegious practices, demonic or satanic thoughts or practices—could be shared and talked about, without concern. It is also important for the client to know that the therapist will not proselytize the client with any of the therapist's own beliefs and that the client always has choice.[70]

INVITING THE HOLY SPIRIT INTO THE RAPPORT-BUILDING

From a spiritual standpoint, rapport is the heart-to-heart connection with another person that seems to take on a mystical quality all its own. The connection transcends the self, and God is invited into the exchange. The scripture that says, "For where two or three gather in my name, there am I with them" (Matthew 18:20 NIV), captures the essence of this connection. Sometimes this is done without formal acknowledgment—it can be as simple as an awareness that the client or the therapist may have—or it might be invoked with a formal prayer or some other spiritual discipline or ritual. Regardless, God becomes the third party in the process of therapy and in healing. For some who come from a strong spiritual background, their ability to trust God may be enough to override their hesitancy to trust a new person and may make inviting God into the process more comforting. For others, their belief in God may be present while their trust in a good God may be very broken as a result of their pain.

A colleague was working specifically with young girls who had come out of ritualistic abuse. All of her clients had dissociative identity disorder (DID), and within her caseload, each girl had a range of two to ten distinctly different personas.

> One evening, Amaya, a fourteen-year-old girl, was struggling with anxiety and asked the staff to read her a psalm out of the Bible while she laid on the couch and tried to breathe deeply. About three minutes into the reading, the child flung her body off the couch and toward the staff member, grabbing the staff's neck and screaming, "Stop saying the fucking name of Jesus!" Amaya had just experienced a switch from her scared fourteen-year-old self and into an angry and rebellious twelve-year-old, who made sure she let everyone know how much she hated God.

A commonality among DID clients is their strikingly different views of God within themselves.[71] They often have at least one part of them that believes in and trusts in a higher power, and their faith is a source of comfort and strength.[72] However, a different part of their identity holds equally strong hate for God, faith, and religion. As a counselor, part of building the rapport is honoring the belief system of all parts of the client and allowing each to have a voice.[73]

The therapeutic alliance is born of authenticity, acceptance, open-mindedness, competence, psychological adjustment, and the therapist's ability to make sense of the complexity of the client's world.[74] This connection is constructed through consistent respect, thus inviting the counselor into some of the most sacred and vulnerable places of the human heart and mind. The journey from here on out becomes one of even greater privilege, requiring increasing levels of courage and commitment. In this writer's opinion, the client is allowing the therapist into the essence of his or her soul, and this needs to be treated as an invitation to sacred and hallowed ground.

Chapter One Notes

CHAPTER TWO

Connecting to, and Anchoring, Relevant Memory

All encounters in life are experienced through the five senses.[75] The consolidation of these five senses is what helps our brain create memory files. Throughout each moment of the day, the hippocampus and the amygdala (which is located just in front of the hippocampus in the temporal lobe of the brain) work together to consolidate the sensory input, create a memory, and file the memory.[76] However, when a traumatic event occurs, sensory input floods the brain, which overwhelms the normal data-processing mechanism and jams the memory consolidation and filing process. Because traumatic memories are outside of ordinary human experiences, they cannot be organized on a linguistic level; instead, they are assimilated directly as a somatic-sensory event (a body sensory event) and not integrated with other memories.[77] This can create numerous challenges in recalling and processing these traumatic events.

NARRATIVE MEMORY

Narrative memory is memory put into language regarding the totality of one's life experience.[78] It functions in direct correlation with the degree of arousal of the amygdala. If the amygdala in the brain is totally nonresponsive (as in sleep), the hippocampus records no data. If the amygdala in the brain shows little arousal (as in familiar, expected, or uninteresting events), the hippocampus pays little attention and records little data.

If the amygdala in the brain is strongly aroused (as in interesting or important events), the hippocampus pays more attention and recognizes the need to record it. The more stimulated the amygdala becomes, the more data the hippocampus records.[79] If this is the person's first encounter with this kind of data, the hippocampus will create a new file, but both the quantity and quality of the record will be limited. The amount of information will decrease as more and more experiences come into the file. The quality of the data will also decrease because the files will have greater amounts of information in them. If this is not the first encounter with this kind of data, the hippocampus will add to its existing file and record a greater quantity of data with greater accuracy.[80]

IMPLICIT MEMORY

If the amygdala in the brain is *excessively* activated (as in highly traumatic or overwhelming situations), the transmission of data to the hippocampus does take place, but the memories are stored only as isolated sensory imprints or affective states.[81] Dr. Bessel van der Kolk calls this "chronic dissociative amnesia."[82] In this case, the memory is isolated from the normal stream of consciousness and cannot be voluntarily recalled. It can, however, be triggered in situations reminiscent of the original trauma. This is what is called the implicit memory:[83] sensory data is recorded in highly volatile states and can be accessed only if it is triggered.[84] This response is more typical in cases of repeated, severe traumatization that occurred in early childhood. The trauma memory gets imprinted and put in the file, but if the event is repeated over and over, the intensity of the memory decreases. These memories are stored in a place the person does not want to access because all those feelings (of fear, pain, hurt, and betrayal) are overpowering. These emotions get sectioned off so the person does not have to feel them all the time.

One of the most challenging realities of this process is that because these memories are stored as raw data—just as they were received from the five senses—they do not get stored in the narrative memory. This sectioning off is the body's adaptation to traumatizing events. In extreme cases, it can result in dissociative identity disorder.[85] Implicit memory can affect one's perceptions, emotions, behavior, body functions, and sleep patterns without the individual knowing why. It is often the primary indicator, and sometimes the only indicator, of early childhood trauma.[86] Implicit memory is a capacity shared by both animals and humans.[87] In the same way an abused dog can be differentiated from a well-cared-for canine, a traumatized child will live out the effects of the abuse suffered, in many non-verbal forms. Implicit memory is particularly significant in supporting the validity of "recovered" traumatic memories.[88]

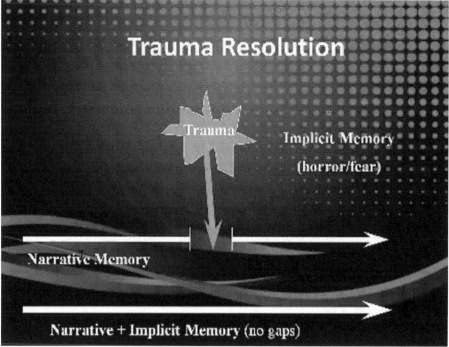

Figure 1: Trauma Resolution[89]

BODY MEMORIES

We know that memories can be stored in different ways. Scientists now recognize that there is a memory apparatus in virtually every cell of the body, something that is being demonstrated strikingly in transplant recipients who start manifesting characteristics of the donor.[90] Van der Kolk says it well: "The body keeps score."[91] He also claims that "the mind is suggestible, but the body is not."[92] Trauma memory must go somewhere, often being stored in the body itself. Body memories, therefore, are extremely reliable and lend strong support to "recovered" traumatic memory.[93]

Sometimes, the physical symptoms associated with the original abuse reappear in the forms of welts, bruises, abrasions, burns, pressure, or pain in virtually any part of the body. These symptoms usually occur when the memory is activated in some form. We sometimes refer to this as *stigmata*.[94]

> Several years ago, I had a client who was having an abreaction during a session. Her father had used her in child pornography for about ten years, from the time

> she was about four or five years old on. Whenever she was cranky or didn't want to do what her father wanted her to do, she was tied up and placed in a trunk. The trunk was then set in a hole in the backyard, where she would be left for hours. During one of our sessions, she began to process this memory and quickly began to have an abreaction. In between crying, she was trying to explain what was being done to her. As she is explaining this, I can see the rope burns starting to appear on her wrists. Her body had reacted in such a way that one could see where the rope had been.[95] This is often also referred to as stigmata—where there is a physical reappearance of things that have already happened.
>
> I had my own experience of this many years ago, in 1979.[96] I was having body therapy done in which they were moving my tissue facia. As they were working on my collarbone, I immediately had a flashback of injuring my collarbone as a young child. The memory was so vivid, I could tell you every toy that was on my bedroom shelf when I was four years old. My parents told me how I had fallen out of bed at four years of age and had broken my collarbone. Right as the therapist was working on the tissue in that part of my body, all the memory resurfaced because it was encoded—what I saw, heard, and felt from that particular event. It is hard when your own body tells you that what you are remembering is real.

This phenomenon may also show up as psychosomatic symptoms. Though these might technically be included in implicit memory, they involve the physical body. These symptoms are more chronic in nature but are directly related to an unresolved psychological issue or trauma. They usually involve inexplicable, ongoing pain in a particular part of the body or in persistent malfunction of a body system, often the digestive, genital, musculoskeletal, or respiratory system.[97] The physical response could be a deep, sinking feeling in one's chest or abdomen, a physical jolt, sudden anxiety or panic, or any unnatural expression of fright.

Genuine traumatic memories are often experienced physically: a person might undergo actual sensory replay when remembering; the memory might surface in response to a trigger; the experience of the implicit memory might be accompanied by body memories or body responses; content might be revealed that could not be known otherwise and comes as a surprise to the person remembering.[98] Arguments in favor of the existence of implicit memory are supported by the fact that effects in the person's life are consistent with the content of the memory, and significant change can occur in the person's life when healing is brought to the beliefs imbedded in the memory.

Early Memory

We also have spirit memory.[99] There seems to be evidence of a certain degree of awareness occurring even in the womb.[100] The most likely source for this may be the spirit of the person. We have heard reports that a child in the womb can learn to recognize musical scores and voices.[101] They can also be affected by discord in the environment or sense attitudes of rejection and displeasure toward themselves.[102] They absorb death wishes or become ambivalent about life when abortion is considered.[103] Later, a child can also act out trauma that occurred during the birth process, such as having the umbilical cord wrapped around the child's neck or having his or her mouth forcefully suctioned out.[104]

Sometimes we have to take into consideration the function of science when we discuss the formation of memory and how the interplay works within the brain. The following quote identifies certain memories that can be talked about from a client's perspective at early ages but are often distorted because of those ages: "In early childhood, memory is limited to non-verbal forms. Both because language skills are not yet developed and because myelination of the hippocampus (which creates a form of insulation)[105] is not complete until sometime between ages 3 and 5, narrative memory is not possible before that time. Therefore, any memory recorded in early childhood is either in the form of body memories or implicit memories."

Narrative Memory Recall

Narrative memory, or memory of an event that has been processed, sorted out, and stored appropriately in the brain, can be triggered spontaneously or recalled voluntarily. The ability to recall depends on the extent and quality of what was recorded to consciousness. So, if I have had numerous experiences of the same thing, the first event was recorded, but little was recorded over the original event. According to Dr. van der Kolk, this process of selective storage is determined by the familiarity of the event, the degree of mental attention paid to the event, the subjective assessment of the event, and the degree of distortion occurring *after* the memory is recorded.[106]

Memory has certain forms of distortion. Pierre Janet, in 1889, described the normal integration process that takes place with narrative memory: "Once a particular event or bit of information becomes integrated in a larger scheme, it will no longer will be accessible as an individual entity, and hence the memory will be distorted."[107] If an event becomes encoded in its purest original form, then when the memory is triggered later, it is as clean as it can be, like when it occurred. However, if the memory becomes part of a wider narrative picture or story, then it is liable to be modified in some way, because now it is affected by its larger context.[108] Social modifications take place and get reinforced in retelling a memory. The more we talk about an event, the greater the chance of distortion.

IMPLICIT MEMORY RECALL

Implicit memories cannot be recalled voluntarily.[109] They must be evoked automatically, or triggered, in situations that are reminiscent of the original trauma.[110] Something—such as a song, a poem, or a smell similar to one present during the moment of trauma— reminds the person of the original trauma and, suddenly, the original trauma is triggered.[111] Because the memory was never processed by the hippocampus but was stored in its raw sensory and affective form, it can be recalled only as a virtual replay of the emotions and physical senses of the original event. To the survivor, it will feel as if the event is reoccurring in the present. This is an abreaction, or a full reliving of the traumatic event.

Dissociated traumatic memories are inflexible and invariable.[112] They are stored as isolated sensory imprints, which remain fixed in the brain. Unlike narrative memory, nothing gets added or integrated into dissociated traumatic memories, so there is no distortion.[113] (They do not serve any social function and are not subject to distortion through this means, either.) But once the memories are spoken aloud, processed, and stored in narrative memory, then they are subject to normal decay and distortion.

CAVEATS REGARDING ACCURACY

The inflexible accuracy of dissociated traumatic memory applies only to the original, vividly relived sensory experience of the event.[114] It is a one-time occurrence. Once the traumatic memory is put into words and told to others, it becomes subject to the typical distortions of narrative memory. As it is repeated aloud to others or in one's mind, it can be modified and then reinforced in its modified form, creating more distortion.[115]

The traumatic event was most likely imprinted as a collection of snapshots rather than a complete video.[116] Therefore, errors can occur in the way the mind tries to make sense of the snapshots. For instance, our brain can misinterpret the snapshots or use imagination to fill in the gaps between snapshots. And that, of course, comes across as distortion. Dissociated traumatic memories come undistorted from the brain; what the mind does with that information is subject to considerable suggestibility and imagination. Suggestions that can be incorporated to create a narrative may be gleaned from questions, cues, responses, expectations of others (including the therapist), books, lectures, movies, or other survivors' stories.

Many years ago, I worked on a hospital unit for dissociative disorders, and we would not allow the clients to tell their trauma stories to each other. This was because clients would pick up other stories from other clients and possibly incorporate them into their own personal narrative.

THERAPEUTIC PRECAUTIONS

Because implicit memory is susceptible to suggestion, the therapist must take important precautions. First, never feed the client any preconceived ideas or hunches concerning what you think has happened in his or her life. It is inappropriate to confirm to clients that what happened to them is exactly what they said, because their narrative likely could be a misrepresentation or have misrepresented parts. What the therapist must believe is that the client believes the material. The therapist was not physically there and, so, does not have access to the exact details but must work with the story the client tells. Do not ask leading or presumptive questions, as this will only further distort the client's memory. An appropriate way to dialogue with a client about this is to say, "Tell me more," or, "What else can you describe from the picture?" Those are neutral ways of getting information without leading a client in any particular direction.

I was once watching an interview with a therapist demonstrating his abilities in working with dissociative identity disordered clients, and he demonstrated the use of hypnosis. The client was a woman who was all the way under hypnosis; she was picturing a scene in which she was in the living room. She saw something or somebody shift or move. The therapist asked, "What does it look like?" She said, "I'm not sure. It could be a man." The therapist then replied with, "What did that dark man say to you?" Neither the descriptor "dark man" nor the detail that he had said anything to the client was part of the narrative until that moment. The client picked up on these narrative elements and said, "Well, the dark man is behind the chair." This is one example of how a therapist can lead and distort a client's experience.

Avoid bringing accusations against supposed perpetrators based solely on "recovered memories." Legal cases in such instances have proven to be problematic, not least because the client may recant and retract the allegation. It is better just to work with clients about their process and progress through therapy rather than support any kind of legal action or interventions. That said, it would be appropriate to report child abuse, even child abuse that happened many years prior, because there is no statute of limitations on child abuse. As therapists, we are mandated reporters and must report suspected child abuse, regardless of the timeframe, unless the abuse has already been reported.

Introduction to the Dissociative Continuum

When talking about disorder or pathology, I remember my college professor, Dr. Murry Landsman, who worked at the University of South Florida in the Rehabilitative Counseling Program. He had a concept that he called the continuum theory. In the diagram below, you can see the arrows on either side of the continuum and then two straight lines along the continuum. The space between those straight lines is what he defined as "normal," which changes from culture to culture. "Abnormal" behavior is when people are functioning outside of the lines of the cultural norm.

The significance of these assertions is that we are all on the line. This is not an "us and them," but rather an "us and us." In other words, we all possess elements of every disorder in the DSM. This is the only way we can connect with what is going on with others. We have all experienced being sad, though only some become clinically depressed. While we may have similarities, it is not exactly the same. We all may get anxious for a test, but the anxiety lifts when the test is over, unless we have an anxiety disorder. This is true with trauma as well. Have you ever been so confused, you were unsure what to do? That is what someone with schizophrenia deals with all the time. Have you ever daydreamed? Then you have dissociated. But chronic dissociation can cause a disconnection and splitting of the psyche.[117]

Figure 2: Continuum—in which normal would be defined as what occurs between the two lines of a particular culture.

Dissociative Continuum

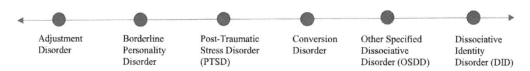

Figure 3: Dissociative Continuum[118]

Buddy Braun has talked about dissociation being on a continuum.[119] In fact, this is one of the things I think the DSM-5 got right. Dissociation can now be a symptom of any other disorder. It shows up in schizophrenia, trauma disorders, and anxiety disorders, among others.

> I remember working with a twelve-year old boy in one of my practicum experiences in my first doctoral program, where I trained for nine months in a technique called developmental play therapy. This is a therapy that is Gestalt in orientation, by working to get to the deepest feeling. Then that feeling is incorporated into the child's world in a way that is healthy and allows them to express the feeling without guilt or resentment. The boy saw his mother shot and killed by his father in their living room. He immediately went blind and mute. He was taken to all kinds of specialists who said there was no medical reason for either development. It took my instructor nine months of working with him before there was a breakthrough, in which the boy started to cry. As he started to cry and experience the feeling, he was no longer blind or mute. Just the child's experience of connecting to the cathartic part of self and allowing the emotion to be felt was enough to bring him out of the need for the conversion of symptoms. Conversion disorder is definitely on the continuum.

Ego State Continuum

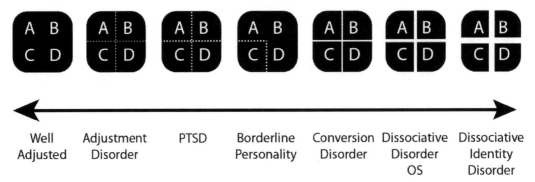

Figure 4: Ego State Continuum[120]

What you see above is referred to as the ego state continuum, based on the work of Jack and Helen Watkins.[121] We are all made up of ego states, or parts of self. Those parts can be the roles we experience, such as, in my case, husband, father, son, professor, author, or trainer. All these roles are fully integrated into my psyche, but my approach to each is slightly different. The same thing may be true for situations in life: I remember being seventeen, for instance, and what life was like back then: I had long hair, was a bit rebellious, and identified with the flower children of the era. I can remember how I felt, and my sense of urgency, about things like the environment and the Vietnam War, issues prevalent in the '60s and '70s. I can also remember graduating high school and things beginning to change.

I can remember being seven years old and being disappointed for missing a costume party because of appendicitis. Those memories can crystalize as times, events, situations, or emotions. One part of me feels sad, while another part feels peaceful or happy. If I am well adjusted, all those feelings and times are integrated. As we go further down that ego state continuum, I begin to have less access to parts of self.

My grandmother illustrates the next stage, which I call the neurotic well. She came to the United States through Ellis Island from Russia. It was tough times; they were trying to stake out a livelihood. My grandmother would never talk about these times. As an adolescent, I asked her questions, but she refused to discuss the subject. She had access to the memories, but because it was such a difficult time, she would do anything not to access the thoughts and feelings. She wanted to push them away by refusing to connect to them.

Further out on the continuum is borderline personality disorder. Notice that the lines in the figure are getting darker but are still perforated, meaning the information is still accessible but getting progressively harder to access. You can see, in the figure, parts are occluded for other specified dissociative disorder, (OSDD), unspecified dissociative disorder (UDD), and dissociative identity disorder (DID): A does not know B, or C might know B but not know A, and so forth. All parts do not know each other, because the break in psyche has made some of the material inaccessible. The lines thicken as you go down the continuum, representing a greater degree of amnesia, known as the amnestic barriers. A simplified therapy is to wear down the amnestic barriers by getting the parts to begin to share with each other. The more this happens, the more the amnestic barriers become unnecessary because the parts begin to integrate material and experience.

The lines, or amnestic barriers, diminish in the same way no matter where they are along the spectrum, meaning that a lot of the therapies designed today are made to work throughout the continuum. It used to be that all the different disorders needed separate techniques; for instance, DBT (dialectical behavioral therapy) was designed specifically for borderline personality disorder. But we are finding that DBT also works well for PTSD, DID, and addiction. It has functionality in a wide range of disorders.

Working with DID patients, David Grove came up with a methodology used today in exposure therapy.[122] Exposure therapy is great for adjustment disorder and PTSD; in this therapy, the client visualizes the trauma step by step, to work towards resolution. The client is asked to visualize a time just before the trauma and just after the trauma, and to talk step by step through the memory and feelings. The client is guided on both sides of the trauma to a place of calm. After the trauma, the client may still experience agitation, but the trauma itself has calmed down a bit. It is bookended.

Imagine we were talking to an adult woman who had the experience of her adult stepfather having intercourse with her from the ages of ten to fourteen years old. These experiences would occur at night after her mother had fallen asleep. The time right before the trauma would be right before she went to bed, anticipating him coming into her room, with her eyes closed. We would then process the trauma, all the way through to her stepfather walking out of her room and her crying quietly. We would have the client practice visualizing a safe place, or since some clients have difficulty imagining a safe place, a place of comfort or rest. The goal is to have the client bookend the memory in safety so that if she rewound or fast-forwarded the memory, she would have a safe place. It is a containment exercise that emotionally protects the client when doing this type of exposure therapy.

BEGINNING MEMORY WORK

Before beginning any kind of memory work, it is crucial that a solid client–therapist trust relationship be in place, along with a sufficient degree of stabilization and internal communication, as discussed in the previous chapter. The client needs to feel safe with the therapist and with his or her environment, and must have a strong support system in place. The lack of this kind of groundwork can be seriously detrimental to therapy. If the therapist tries to move too quickly into exploration of past traumas, it is likely to produce increased dissociative symptoms, such as fugue episodes, suicide attempts, internal homicide behavior, and other crises situations, which disrupt therapy and are harmful to the client.

Flashbacks, dreams, and abreactions of past traumas can be extremely painful for the client and typically create a great deal of distress. When an abreaction takes place, it brings buried feelings, memories, and experiences into the client's consciousness, and often it involves a sort of reexperiencing of past traumas.[123] This can be upsetting and frightening. If clients are not stabilized enough in their coping strategies, or if their relationship with you is still rocky, they are likely to react to the stress caused by the memories and abreactions in counterproductive ways. They may want to run, commit violent acts, halt therapy, create a serious impasse to further progress, or attempt suicide. However, once the groundwork of DID therapy has been sufficiently laid—once the client–therapist rapport and the client's support system are both well established, typically three to six months after the start of therapy[124]—the memory work can begin in earnest.

Repressed Memories

Working with specific memories can be fraught with difficulty. Frequently, clients are looking for acknowledgment that their experiences from the past were real and not imagined.[125] As therapists, we can lend support as our clients work through their issues, but we cannot verify the authenticity of the experience because, quite simply, we were not there. Michael Yapko's book *Suggestions of Abuse: True and False Memories of Childhood Sexual Trauma* directly addresses the issue of the authenticity of memory, explaining that some therapists use inappropriate techniques—including checklists of symptoms such as depression, low self-esteem, headaches, obesity, arthritis, and acne—to diagnose sexual abuse that never actually occurred.[126]

The discoverers of false memory syndrome did the field of mental health and therapy a service. In essence, they forced the industry to clean up its act regarding therapeutic technique and application. They asserted that early childhood memories of clients could not be confirmed without corroboration from someone who was actually there. Anecdotal descriptions or symptom manifestations were insufficient in terms of evidence. However, that distinction does not mean that our clients' memories are not accurate and based in reality. It does mean that the clients' awareness of their experiences is such that they believe the content is accurate and is, therefore, their reality.[127]

Repressed memories have a quality similar to implicit memories, and they often come to light when clients are working with specific issues. The term "repressed memory" is derived from the term "dissociative amnesia," which is defined in the DSM-5 as "an inability to recall important personal information, usually of a traumatic or stressful nature, that is too extensive to be explained by ordinary forgetfulness."[128] While the accuracy of these memories may be questionable, they nevertheless seem to have a protective quality about them. In other words, the memories were repressed as a way of protecting the core of the self. Much has already been researched and written on repressed memories,[129] and this chapter will not try to recount the many pitfalls and dilemmas such issues bring up. Suffice it to say that repressed memory, as a phenomenon, has been shown time and again to be real and that clients who suffer from it have demonstrated amazing resilience in working through their issues with the help of a competent therapist.[130]

Structuring the Process

When you feel it is time to begin the memory work, start by trying to bring structure to the chaotic process of abreaction. Work at clarifying and establishing the significance of the chain of events. The idea is to enable the client to work through the recovered material to bring resolution, as well as to allow the client to relive the experience and work through the trauma with a new outcome, if appropriate. While this process entails assisting the client in dealing with each memory as it surfaces, it does not mean that you must deal with every single memory of trauma or abuse. You would be at this forever, in some cases, if you were to try to go back to every single event of trauma. Remember, the real issue here is dealing not with the specific information but with the underlying affect and how it relates to what the client is experiencing.

The goal is to empower clients to get themselves out of the traumatic reexperience of memories by using simple exercises that anchor them to the present. When you are working with the memory, go back to the memory just before it becomes traumatic. David Grove, in his work with trauma cases, calls this going back to T minus one [T-1] (just prior to traumatic memory).[131] What was going on just prior to the trauma? Where was the client in the room or locality? What was going on with the family internally? What was happening in the house? Or, if the perpetrator was from outside the family, what was the environment? How did the client feel? In doing this, you allow the person to experience the entire trauma. At this point, you can begin to examine the affective response. For instance, there were probably fear reactions, anger reactions, pain reactions, and all kinds of other emotional complexities involved. In the case of DID, many of these responses are expressed in the form of alter identities; but, if the person experiences dissociation without the division of personality states, then the entire experience will be relived, along with all the emotions involved. It is important that these emotions get worked through in the therapy process.

$$T-1 \longrightarrow T \longrightarrow T+1$$

Figure 5: Trauma Processing[132]

There are many and various types of emotional reactions to the abuse, and each response is complex.[133] If one of the responses is anger, for instance, survivors may be angry at the perpetrator, or may be angry at their mother who knew about it and did nothing about it. They may be angry at themselves for letting it happen or for getting into that situation. They may be angry at God. In a later chapter, I will talk about the problems and cognitive distortions caused by internalizing that anger.

It is usually pent-up, unresolved emotions that create destructive (including self-destructive) reactions. During the therapy session, clients should be allowed to vent feelings of anger and grief over the painful memories. Steer them toward productive, rather than destructive, ways of venting:[134] Encourage clients to release their pain and anger rather than transferring it onto someone else. Help them to understand the difference between productive release and destructive projection. Productive venting may include talking about their pain, crying, writing in a journal or diary, writing an unsent letter to the perpetrator and then tearing it up or burning it, finding a safe place to scream, punching a pillow, tearing up a paper, or crushing something that will injure neither themselves nor anyone else. Each person may find different things that work for him or her.

Rituals for closure are often helpful. The rituals do not need to involve clients' abusers directly. They may for instance, find it helpful to draw a picture of the offender, then yell at the picture, smear it with crayons, or rip it up. Or, they might vent all their feelings in a letter to the abuser and seal it by tearing up the letter and claiming liberty from any unforgiveness. Help them to recognize that the feelings of forgiveness and freedom may take time to come (see Chapter Five).

ABREACTIONS

Recall that an abreaction is when clients relive and reexperience the feelings, ideas and/or memories of a past trauma that had been locked away in their unconscious mind. This can be upsetting and frightening to a client; however, once an abreaction has begun, it should be allowed, whenever possible, to run its course. Although spontaneous abreactions often occur, they do not normally bring about resolution and are therefore more of a stress for the client than a relief. Nonetheless, the abreaction is a common part of the healing process.

Often, certain traumatic memories must be abreacted several times before full resolution is reached. If there are contradictory versions of the trauma (e.g., one alter sees it one way while another alter sees it another way), these versions must be reconciled before the client can experience the full benefit of resolution. It is best when abreactions are combined with therapeutic assistance to help clients work toward managing and resolving the effects of memories. Once clients have learned effective management techniques and resolution strategies, they can often deal with spontaneous abreactions on their own, but during the early stages of traumatic recovery of memories, most clients are not prepared to handle abreactions themselves.

It is important to understand that abreactions in and of themselves do not necessarily bring about inner healing. In fact, they can sometimes create more problems if they are not handled correctly. The idea of allowing the client to relive the trauma through an abreaction is *not* to just let it rip, but rather to introduce interventions that enable the client to cope more effectively in non-dissociative ways and to intercept old patterns of behavior in reaction to the trauma.

INNER HEALING

Some of these interventions will be covered in the following sections, but first I want to raise an important point: as a Christian therapist, I have found again and again that the most effective and enduring resolutions come when the client allows the Holy Spirit to bring about inner healing. Professional counseling techniques do have their place in the healing process, particularly as we enable the client to understand what is going on and to learn to apply coping strategies. However, even the best therapy in the world can never seal a person's healing the way the Lord can. We therapists may be able to expose the wounds, explain the events, and help the client to manage affect in more functional ways, but only God can fully heal the client and set him or her free from the trauma's effects.[135]

Our job as Christian counselors is to bring clients to the place where they are ready to receive healing from the Lord. Not every client is ready to accept God's intervention. Many times, you may need to take them through a long period of working through their memories and issues before they are in a place where they dare open themselves up to any kind of relationship with God. In fact, you need to be careful about the kind of terminology you use with trauma survivors: for example, the phrase "a touch from God" could terrify them if they have been "touched" in unholy ways by an abuser. Be sensitive to the client's needs and what they are ready to accept.

The client can be working through various issues and using coping strategies while also allowing the Holy Spirit to do His work.[136] It is important to keep in mind that everyone is at different levels of spiritual receptivity. While it is true that *the Lord* can most certainly heal in an instant, most people—especially emotionally wounded people—have too many emotional and mental barriers that block a full and instant reception of healing. Until some of these barriers are removed, they cannot receive what God wants to give them. Many of these barriers involve wrong thinking and distorted beliefs, which I will talk about later in this chapter.

Containment Exercises

Flashbacks and abreactions can sometimes start coming one right after another, leaving the client overwhelmed.[137] This is called *affective flooding*. Therapists can teach clients exercises to help them manage the memories.

Guided Questions

The guided questions involved in anchoring memory are extremely important. The counselor wants to be sure not to ask leading questions or questions that could obstruct the process. For example, after a basic memory has surfaced, a counselor may ask the client a follow-up question like, "What else happened?" This allows clients to continue articulating whatever else they recall in the fragmented memory. However, if that follow-up question is crafted slightly differently—"What happened *next*?"—the client could get stuck in trying to remember the correct order of how the memory unfolded. Because of the overwhelming nature of trauma, the memory of the event is stored in bits and pieces, as fragments of visual images, smells, sounds, tastes, or touch, not in a sequential timeline of events.[138] If clients feel they need to share it in the order in which it actually occurred, they could get stuck in the timeline when they hit a blocked area in their memory. However, asking them, "What else happened?" gives them room to share all the parts that are surfacing, regardless of when they transpired or in which order they occurred.

When working with clients, I often ask them, "What do you remember?" Sometimes, the answer can be quite specific, as when referring to a childhood experience. But sometimes, the answers they give are vague generalities or merely fragments of feelings, memories, or symptom clusters. Frequently, the simple suggestion to think about a time in life when they felt or experienced the feeling, symptom, or memory is enough to allow them to bring into conscious awareness the connected period of time during which these things happened. The process of visualization, guided prayer, internal meditation, or another technique for calling up what is covered often brings back details of a memory previously outside of their immediate conscious awareness.[139]

> Julie was a young professional who had been in treatment for several months for her difficulties and the attendant feelings related to low self-esteem. She was plagued by the many early messages from her father, who often told her that she would "never amount to anything" and that she was "incapable of doing anything correctly." These and other negative messages, primarily from her father, delivered loudly while he loomed over her, were almost a physical assault on her child's psyche. The epithets had found their way into Julie's business life, where she was a sales manager, even though she had difficulty closing deals. Julie clearly lacked confidence in her ability to sell and was afraid that she would lose her job as a

> result. I asked her to think back to a specific time when she remembered her father making one of those negative statements.
>
> "I was eight years old and had entered a science fair competition," she replied. "I had researched very hard and did a project on photosynthesis. The problem was that I forgot to include the final paper, which had my conclusions written out. The project was disqualified for not being complete, and all my father could say was, 'What the hell were you thinking? Can't you do anything right?'"
>
> She went on to say, "I was mortified because he was yelling at me and my whole class and teacher were right there!"
>
> After she verbalized her early distress, Julie was able to recount the entire event in graphic detail. She described who had been there, what they were wearing, the specific words that were spoken, and the torrent of feelings that she experienced at the time. By closing her eyes and visualizing the memory scene, she was able to reconstruct the entire experience.
>
> Julie stated that, until she had deliberately visualized the event while in a safe environment with her therapist, she had never been able to remember many of the details. She realized that the full memory had eluded her because she had never been willing to focus completely on the memory of that incident, as well as others like it, because they were so upsetting.

Memory can have a huge impact on the direction and choices we make in life. Out of those early choices, we sentence ourselves to various things in life, such as loneliness, the inability to trust, and resignation to a life of emotional disconnection. During the course of counseling, Julie came to see the influence of those memories and to discern the decisions she had made as a child who was reeling from the experience. She was then able to make other decisions regarding her abilities and self-worth. As an eight-year-old, she had made a simple mistake and then suffered extremely unpleasant consequences at the hands of a less-than-sympathetic parent. The consequences of the conclusions Julie made about herself, and the decisions and self-evaluations that ensued, had emotionally crippling effects on her as a child and had carried over into adulthood.

As an adult, she was able to see that she had choices regarding her decisions, evaluations, and behavior in the present. Over time, and with support, Julie was able to see that her advanced education and experience on the job were things that could add to her confidence, despite negative messages drilled into her during early childhood. The visualization alone allowed her to see where and when she began to question herself, her actions, and her value as a human being. As a result, she was able to refocus and reframe the original experience.

Autobiographical Memory

We know that emotion plays a significant role in autobiographical memory.[140] Cultural differences appear in the types of issues that are remembered,[141] and content seems to cross cultural differences as well.[142] Swanson has found that working memory—in other words, memory used for or with a task—is stored differently than short-term memory and may have an impact on crystallized intelligence.[143] These findings have significant impact on memories concerning early childhood sexual abuse as emotional memories. The emotions of fear and hurt significantly influence how those memories are encoded. For a child, the task of sexually pleasing an adult can produce a sensory overload to the extent of a fragmented personality, or what the DSM-5 refers to as dissociative identity disorder (formerly multiple personality disorder).[144]

In the context of the HEART Model, I simply ask clients to connect to a memory that represents the difficulties and symptoms they are experiencing. For instance, if we are working with issues of shame, I ask clients if they remember some incident from childhood in which they experienced shame. If the issue is sexual abuse, I ask if they can remember some incident of such abuse. I am careful to avoid dropping any hints about what sort of experience they may have endured. All memory is theirs, and nothing is created or introduced iatrogenically. *Iatrogenic* means, literally, "brought about by a doctor," i.e., something suggested from the outside that is now part of the inside. In a visualization exercise, I ask clients to use all their senses—touch, sound, sight, smell, and taste. I refer to this process as *anchoring*. I ask participants to get a sense of the colors, sounds, smells, and quality of the air (temperature and humidity) around them in the target memory. I then ask them to identify as many of the specifics of the room or outside area as they can visualize.

It has long been suspected that the sense of smell is connected to memory.[145] However, despite the beginnings of inquiry into "olfactory modality"[146] and the related psychological effects, the relationship between olfaction and memory has largely been ignored until recently. G. Neil Martin has embarked upon a host of scientifically based studies intent on discovering the effects of odor on mood, memory, and cognition,[147] followed much later by Simon Chu and John Downes, who found that odors can trigger strong reactions to both emotional and autobiographical memory.[148] Of the five senses, smell is the sense most closely connected to the hippocampus, one of the brain structures responsible for our memory. The sense of smell is also connected to the limbic system, which is the emotional center of the brain. The rest of our senses (sight, hearing, taste, or touch) must travel down a long path to reach the parts of the brain responsible for our memory and emotions. As a result of the olfactory system's connection to the limbic system and emotions, the stimuli (odors) get processed on an unconscious, nonverbal level, which grants the olfactory system the ability to connect to, and anchor with, the past in the present time and in a unique manner.[149]

Anyone reminiscing about the aroma of newly mown grass on a hot summer day can relate to the practical power of olfactory memory in the therapeutic process. For many people, just talking about a scent can stir up a broad range of memories, which can allow the client to delve deeper into various emotions in therapeutic conversation and to connect to the experience more directly, intimately, and fully.

Each of our five senses plays a powerful role in the retrieving of memories. Given that the brain first registers color, followed by shape or pattern, and then the more intricate details of small drawings or text, the memory of predominant colors and shapes can drive up memories that need processing. Sometimes, in a workshop, as well as in private therapy, I might ask participants to draw a memory after visualizing it, because I want them to recognize it, to attach to it, and to glean as much detail from it as possible.

> Cindy, a naïve sixteen-year-old girl who was the victim of date rape by three fraternity brothers, managed to block out the experience and deny its veracity, even though she had called a girlfriend who had come to her rescue. The friend arrived, bringing with her a change of clothing and, after helping her to clean up cuts and bruises and dispose of the soiled clothes, took her in for the night.
>
> Cindy refused to talk about the gang rape and, over the following weeks, denied that it had happened. Some years later, while on a trip with a friend, Cindy went into the hotel bathroom, whose floor was made up of a pattern of small, black and white checkered tiles. After a few moments in the room, she began to cry and to scream, "They hurt me, they hurt me! I couldn't get away—I tried to, but I couldn't get away!" The screaming abated, but the crying went on for hours.

Understandably concerned, the friend found a trained minister-therapist to help her. When he arrived, Cindy was still sitting on the floor, slapping it and the similarly patterned wall with one hand while holding a towel to her mouth in an effort to muffle the sounds of her anguish. After calming her down enough to talk, the minister-therapist discovered that seeing the black and white pattern on the floor triggered her memory of the rape. She recalled that during the assaults, she had focused on the pattern of the floor tiles in the adjoining bathroom. She tried to divert her mind from what was happing to her body by attempting to count the tiles and memorize the pattern. When the picture memory exploded into her consciousness, she was flooded with sights and sounds. Cindy was able to describe, in detail, her inability to move and the flashes of light as bodies moved between her and the lamp that was missing its shade. She remembered the smell of the dirty rug and the scent of Aqua Velva on one of the assailants and noticed the beginnings of a youthful beard on another. Cindy described the visualization like "something from an inconsistently exposed movie, like an old one made by someone unfamiliar with those early video cameras."

During subsequent sessions with her local therapist, Cindy was never able to remember calling her friend for help, but she was able to acknowledge that she had played a part in her own self-preservation and that the assault was not her fault. She was also able to track her own progression from assault to numbness, to guilt, to denial, to repression. The assault had been followed by years of disconnection and emotional isolation before her violent reaction to the unexpected trigger of the patterned floor. Once the dam burst, she was able to describe what had happened. Even though she was emotionally wrung out, Cindy described her predominant feeling as one of relief. She reported recognizing that she was exhausted from all the energy she expended trying to keep her awful, hurtful secret.

In this case, we can see the power of visual memory and the importance of including an attempt to evoke visual memory in the therapeutic process. Having clients draw what they remember can be a powerful tool, but it can have drawbacks. When drawing, adults who are not artists can easily get sidetracked from the task at hand, which is to draw the setting in which something happened that was then converted into a memory. Sometimes, the focus can get diverted to a criticism of the quality of the art, and little is derived from the exercise. In such cases, it may be useful to ask the client to draw using the non-dominant hand[150] in order to disengage the critical, executive function of the brain that is more concerned with artistic accuracy than it is with driving up or connecting with memory. Nor is the dominant side of the brain concerned with capturing an experience that it has been busy avoiding over an extended period of time.[151] Either way, whether the client uses the dominant or non-dominant hand, drawing or diagramming the scene further anchors survivors to the time and place of the event and brings up associated thoughts, feelings, sensations, and memories.[152]

> Susan, a young professional, was attending a workshop and learning about the HEART Model. Along with the other participants, she was asked to connect to a distressing memory from childhood that was related to an issue of concern. In Susan's case, it was the issue of childhood physical abuse she had sustained at the hands of her stepfather on a regular basis. To begin with, Susan described what she saw when visualizing the living room of a home in which the family had lived when she was nine years old. At first, her descriptions of the room were general, and she did not appear to be connected to the experience more than superficially: "I see the furniture, the kitchen in the distance, a front window looking out on the front lawn."
>
> When asked specific questions targeting the senses, the response was much different. "I see the brown color of the furniture sitting on the braided multicolored rug. There was a quilt my grandmother had done lying on a rocker in the corner," she said. "In the kitchen, Mother was preparing chicken soup; the aroma from the kitchen permeated the whole house. While I sat waiting for my stepfather to finish lecturing my mother in the kitchen, before turning his attention to me, I noticed that the texture of the curtains was coarse."
>
> As the session progressed, Susan was able to reconstruct many details of many such events that apparently had happened in that room. Later, after drawing a picture of the scene, she was able to pray specifically for the wounded child (herself) in the picture and about the cruelty of her stepfather.

USING THE FIVE SENSES TO ANCHOR INTO THE PRESENT

Teaching clients how to use their five senses to ground them to the present reality is essential in processing memory.[153] Focusing on their five senses will help to anchor them to their environment rather than getting lost in the memory.[154] A key to remember is that they cannot be present and dissociated at the same time.[155] Teach them that they can pull themselves back to the present by using their eyes to focus on something in the room. Get them to look at the color of the drapes or the wallpaper or at a safe object in the room. Ask them to think about what they can touch. Can they feel the texture of the carpet, the smoothness of the table, or the softness of the chair cushion? Can they hear the sound of the air conditioner, the birds singing, or people shuffling down the hall? Usually, I will have my dissociative clients carry peppermint candy around with them. Why? Because they can pop a peppermint lifesaver in their mouth and taste the peppermint. They can smell it and feel it tingling on their tongue. It brings them back to these senses and out of the dissociation. By teaching them to focus on their five senses in this way, they learn to get back in touch with their body—to what is going on in the present.

Creating Safe Spaces

An example of a containment exercise is to have clients think of some place that is safe to them or a place where they are comfortable. Then they put the mental picture of that safe place at the beginning of the memory, as well as at the end of the memory. You can then teach them that they can either "fast forward" the memory to get to the safe place or, if they like, "rewind," speed it up, slow it down, or whatever they want. They can do all kinds of things with it. By helping them think of the memory as a sort of tape over which they have control, it eases much of the stress of handling something for which they are not ready. It is a way of containing the memory.

The "Remote Control" Technique

This technique, like the "fast forward" technique above, uses the image of a remote control to allow the client to take charge of the way the memories come. With this exercise, clients can change channels, press the mute button, turn the volume down, or turn the flashback off in the same way they would control what they watch and hear on TV. When affective flooding of memories begins, for instance, they may be ready to deal with only one memory at a time, in which case they would tune out the other "channels" and switch to the channel (memory) of their choice. Or, if they are not prepared to deal with any of the flashbacks at that time, they can use their "remote control" to turn the flashback off.

In many cases, these techniques work together to help clients contain or manage the memories, giving them a sense of power in what was previously a powerless experience. Some clients many have their own ideas for techniques that work better for them. I like to encourage them to be involved in finding and using whatever helps them the most.

Empower Clients to Help Themselves

It is important that you empower the client to get themselves out of the abreactive memories, rather than allowing them to become dependent on you to help them through it. You cannot always be there when the flashbacks come. They need to learn to do the exercises and gain control over them on their own. In teaching them how to do it, you may need to walk them through the process initially, leading them through a memory. But, ultimately, they will have to take what you have shown them and do it by themselves. I do not know how many times I have heard a client say to me, "I really want to thank you for getting me through this." Invariably, I say, "I didn't do the work. You did the work. I was the conduit, but *you* did the work."

PIECING TOGETHER MEMORY FRAGMENTS

In cases of DID, the memory of a particular experience may be divided into several fragments across a number of different alters. One alter, for instance, may carry the actual details of the event, while several other alters may carry the resultant feelings and behaviors of the event without knowing where they are coming from. Let us say, for example, that the sight or smell of a basement triggers a sudden, uncontrollable trembling and a strong sense of unexplained horror in the host. When the prospect of having to enter a basement is mentioned, the patient begins rapid switching of alters, each of whom expresses a different affect, such as fear, anger, pain, disgust, and numbness. The fearful alter has a phobia about bricks and holes, while the angry alter wants to kill her stepfather without knowing why, and another alter experiences physical symptoms of abdominal pain, nausea, dizziness, and a searing sensation from her hips downward. Another alter may feel deep disgust every time she sees a man with a ponytail, while another is completely numb to any feelings at all. None of the alters has the full understanding of why they feel or react the way they do; yet, because the affect of each of these alters is evoked by any contact or mention of basements, you can start with the common thread and work toward assembling the fragments into one complete memory.

Let us say that in this case, the completed memory involved the client having been dragged into a basement where she was repeatedly raped by her stepfather, then forced to lie in a hole in the basement and covered with dirt and bricks, which crushed the lower half of her body until the pain was almost unbearable. Her ponytailed stepfather would then look down at her, urinate on top of her, laugh, and threaten to cover the rest of her if she ever told anyone what he had done.

Helping the patient reassemble the various fragments into one solid memory can take a fair amount of time and patience. It may involve meeting some alters with strong affects that have no rhyme or reason, and others who have odd bits of details about an event but are unable to piece the details together into anything that makes sense. Finding the bigger, chronological picture is much like piecing together a jigsaw puzzle. As with a puzzle, you have to start by taking one piece at a time and trying to match those with common background or links. Then, when you come up with a number of smaller segments, you can fit some of them together to form a rough outline. From there, you may be able to fill the gaps to come up with the complete picture. So, in other words, you can start with your patient's fragmented memories, images, and affects and gradually piece them together one at a time. You might begin by watching for switches in affect (as in the example of horror to fear to anger, etc.) in order to trace each affect through various alters to their common roots. Then, you can add to the picture recollections of images and flashbacks. Once the common threads are connected, you can work toward reassembling the whole picture and bringing about resolution.

COGNITIVE RESTRUCTURING OF ERRONEOUS ASSUMPTIONS AND CORE BELIEFS

Cognitive restructuring entails changing cognitive distortions that clients have regarding themselves, the abuse, others, and the whole schema of what has happened to them in the various situations of trauma they underwent. What we are trying to do is create and substitute more accurate and alternative beliefs to replace those current distortions. If an abreaction is experienced without being followed up with cognitive restructuring and new coping skills, it can lead to further re-traumatization for the client.

Core beliefs can be logical propositions or erroneous syllogisms. False propositions often begin with a moral injunction that illustrates a classic cognitive error, such as all or nothing, personalization, or overgeneralization. An example of this is the belief that good children love their parents. When adult survivors of trauma admit that they do not love their abusive parents—in fact, they cannot stand them, or often themselves—they begin to believe they are bad for not loving them. Meanwhile, the child part of them is saying, "I hate them! I'm afraid of them." Because of these feelings that conflict with their core belief that all *good* children love their parents, they determine that they are *bad* and deserve to be punished. This paves the way for their subconscious choices to repeatedly get into, or stay in, abusive relationships, since they determine that they are getting what they really deserve.

There are eight core beliefs or assumptions out of which cognitive distortions arise. Some are specific to DID; others appear across the whole spectrum of dissociative disorders:

1. Different parts of the self are separate selves (e.g., each alter is an identity of its own).
2. The victim is responsible for the abuse; it is his or her fault.
3. It is wrong to show anger, frustration, defiance, or a critical attitude.
4. The past is present.
5. The primary personality cannot handle the memories.
6. "I love my parents, but *he/she* (another alter or part of them) hates them."
7. The primary personality must be punished.
8. "I cannot trust myself or others."

These tend to be the core personality distortions in DID. Derived from these assumptions is another set of distortions or erroneous assumptions that make up a particular way of thinking. Let us look more closely at these distortions.

Distortion #1: Different Parts of the Self Are Separate Selves

The previous name for what is currently known as DID was multiple personality disorder (MPD). We believed that those with MPD had a number of separate alter personalities, each distinct from the others, within the same body.

Today, we consider this disorder a separation of ego states within one core person, hence, the current name: dissociative identity disorder. Patients with DID have not integrated their personality into one whole, but rather have dissociated from different parts of themselves so much that alternative identities develop within the same person. These alternative identities are sometimes referred to as different personality states, ego states, or the widely used "alter personalities." While each alternative identity has a distinct personal history, self-image, character, name, and function, they do not and cannot survive separately from the whole system and one body in which they exist.

Many DID clients believe that each alter identity actually has its own body.[156] When you begin to meet and work with the alters, you will see that many of them are convinced that they can wound or kill another of the alters, without hurting themselves. You will hear them blame other alters for irresponsible behavior, saying, "Well, her behavior is her problem, not mine." Others will say, "The abuse didn't happen to me. It happened to her." I had a client who was having all kinds of affairs while married. The alter who was the most promiscuous said, "Well, so what? I didn't marry him. *She* did. So, I don't have to be loyal to him!"

Some alters deny that they have the same parents as the other alters. Oftentimes, when some alters insist that their parents are not the same as those of the other alters, it is because they have internally created ideal parents. These ideal parents were created to take the place of the actual parents who were too far from the ideal that alter needed.

It is common for persecutor alters to believe they are separate. One alter may call me up and say, "She's gonna kill me! She's gonna kill me!"

And I will say, "Well, can you put her on the phone? Can I talk to her?"

In talking to the other alter, I will usually say something fairly blunt like, "Do you realize that if you kill her, you kill you?"

"What do you mean?" the alter asks. "No, I didn't know that." Such alters genuinely lack an awareness that they are linked together with the others and that if they kill one, they will kill all the others, too. Now, if they do not care if they die as well, then you have a situation that may require hospitalization. I may say to them, "Do you really want to die, or do you just want to stop hurting?" More often than not, they tell me they want to stop hurting. At this point, we can begin to explore other ways to stop the hurting.

The delusion of being separate from the other alters is different from psychotic delusions in that DID delusions are rationally derived from erroneous assumptions and are comprehensible in the context of abuse. It may be an inappropriate way of coping, but the thinking process—unlike that of a schizophrenic—is a step-by-step rational process.

THE HEART MODEL

In the case of psychosis or schizophrenia, there is often no rationality to their thinking at all.

Distortion #2: The Victim Is Responsible for the Abuse

Some of the cognitive errors that come with this distortion are thoughts like, "I must be bad or this wouldn't have happened to me. If I'd been more sweet, more obedient, or more perfect, it would have never happened." Or, "I deserve to be punished for getting angry. If I were perfect, I would never get angry."

In the case of someone with DID, one of the alters may blame another alter in the personality system. A persecutor alter, for instance, might say something like, "I never get angry. *She's* the one who feels angry. She deserves to be punished for being angry." Or, they might blame another alter for allowing the abuse to happen.

This set of cognitions is linked to self-destructive and obsessive/compulsive behavior. One alter tries to commit suicide, for instance, while another tries to be perfect. This can be understood as a dissociative strategy for simultaneously maintaining incompatible conditions. They do not go together, so this is the way to act them out. Creating different people inside is a short-term solution to the abuse problems.

Distortion #3: It Is Wrong to Show Anger, Frustration, or Other Emotions

Feeling guilt over angry feelings is particularly common in Christian or religious circles.[157] We are often taught from the pulpit not to be angry: "If you get angry, you must be sinning, and if you're sinning, you deserve to be punished, or at least reprimanded." What I teach, especially in recovery groups, is that anger is just an emotion. The emotion of anger itself is not wrong; what you do with that that results in something either good or bad. It is the same with any emotion. Jealously, fear, grief—each of these can be used righteously or unrighteously, and constructively or destructively. The Scriptures say that God is a jealous God. Jealousy by itself is not a bad thing; it demonstrates how much we love someone. It is okay to feel jealous if your husband has an affair. That is how God feels when we seek other idols above Him. But, jealousy can become destructive when we let it control or overpower us.

Fear, too, is not a bad emotion. Many victims despise themselves and constantly degrade themselves because they know they are fearful and they associate fearfulness with cowardice. While the Bible tells us not to be afraid, it also tells us to fear God. Is this a contradiction? I do not think so. We are to have a healthy respect for who God is and how great His power is. God put a healthy respect (fear) in each of us in order to preserve us. It is this fear that enables us to either flee or fight in the face of danger. If we succumb to bondage to constant or unreasonable fear, we often begin to act and react in destructive ways. Unreasonable and uncontrolled fear can be both self-destructive (e.g., ulcers or other physical problems) and destructive to others (e.g., sexual problems; restrictive involvement in activities, situations, and relationships; etc.).

Because of the destructiveness associated with aggressive anger, this is one of the most widely attacked emotions.[158] Throughout history, controlling anger has been admired and promoted, even at the risk of suppression—which sooner or later leaks out, in some other form.[159] Too often, when we see the bad results of something like anger, we blame the anger itself and toss the baby out with the bath water. Although many Christians still believe it is wrong to get angry, God has never said it is wrong. In fact, God Himself gets angry. Since we know that God cannot sin, and since we know that God gets angry, how can we say anger is a sin? Jesus not only became angry, but He also acted on His anger (Matthew 21:12–13); and, in His anger, He did no wrong.

Distortion #4: The Past Is Present

When you are working with clients with DID, you will sometimes see them behaving or talking as though they are currently being abused or fearing abuse that is not actually happening. A client may, for instance, come into your office one day acting like a scared eight-year-old because she thinks her doctor is going to hurt her and no one will protect her. She is scared because she feels the abuse all over again and cannot distinguish an abreactive experience from the present reality. Clients *feel* like an eight-year-old, and they *act* like an eight-year-old, because disturbing memories are surfacing and they are reliving the abuse. As this begins to happen, you will see how their core beliefs are directly linked to their abreactive experience and how that affects their present and past behavior and emotions.

Distortion #5: The Primary Personality Cannot Handle the Memories

Many times, you will come up against alters who insist that you cannot tell certain things to the host/primary personality. Often, some of the alters want to hide their existence from the host. "You can't tell her about us," they say. "If she has to remember this stuff, it will make her crazy!" Or, "She's too weak. I'm the strong one. I can handle it. She can't." Or, "If she remembers, she won't like us. She won't talk to us anymore."

On the other hand, either the host or some of the other alters might deny the painful memories. "That kind of stuff never happened! They [the other alters] must be sick to think those things ever happened!" Or, "Well, my parents aren't like that."

Again, what is important here is that these are all internalized messages that can come out of the core belief system that assumes the primary personality cannot handle the memories. It is this set of beliefs that drives amnestic barriers. The more communication between the alters, the more the internal network is established and the more you begin to erode those amnestic barriers. Intimate adult relationships can become difficult when amnestic barriers are present, because only a part of the person is available to engage in the relationship. The DID client needs to have some sense of what is going on—some continuity of time. The only way this can happen is for the alters to begin communicating internally across the barriers.

Distortion #6: "I Love My Parents, but She Hates Them"

This distortion implies that the primary personality or certain alters are bad, while the others are good. This sets up a lot of internal conflicts. "*She's* the bad one," an alter may say. "You need to get rid of her. No one could ever be friends with her. Nobody could ever like her. She's no good." This set of core assumptions cannot be made prior to the existence of the different alters.

Distortion #7: The Primary Personality Must Be Punished

The basic core assumption in this instance is the belief that the client is unloved. Because clients believe they are unlovable, they believe they deserve to be mistreated or punished. Many times, various alters will join in the accusations. "Everything bad that happens to her is because she's bad and she deserves it," they might say. Or, "She suffered enough already. She'd be better off if I killed her." Sometimes, the primary personality or alter will have hopeless or suicidal thoughts like, "No one would ever want to get close to me. No one will ever be able to love me, so I'll do something to hurt myself. I'll be better off dead."

These cognitions are usually held by persecutor alters, who are likely to attribute the cause of an event to the wrong thing. The errors are entrenched in the martyr-victim response. The various alters then play off one another to keep this faulty assumption going. For instance, a persecutor alter might attack the primary personality or a child alter, and then a protector alter will come in to protect the child alter or primary personality. Various alters may play against each other to defend their own beliefs and continue acting out their functions within the system. As long as each believes it is separate from the rest of the system, there will be internal chaos and conflict.

Distortion #8: "I Cannot Trust Myself or Others"

This assumption is based upon clients' experience of being repeatedly abused or victimized. They realize that they have always ended up choosing abusive relationships or getting hooked into an abusive situation, so they assume they cannot be relied upon to do the right thing. Or, they remember trying to trust someone and having that trust betrayed. You may hear different alters join in with accusations like, "She got herself into situations she can't handle." Or, "Don't let anybody get close to her. They can't trust her. She'll just let them down or scare them off;" "Whenever people get close to me, they leave;" "It's no use. I tried trusting before, but I just got hurt."

This set of cognitions is more likely to be said by protectors than by persecutors. Trust is a major issue that carries throughout therapy. Not only is it important for the whole system to trust you as the therapist, but the alters must also learn to trust one another and the primary personality. The DID client must learn to work with and negotiate trust relationships internally, within their personality system, to establish cooperation and consistency. And you, as their therapist, must prove yourself trustworthy with the information they share with you. As I have said previously, your trustworthiness as therapist may be tested repeatedly, sometimes to the limits of your client and beyond. What I like to say to my DID clients is, "Don't give me any information that you don't want the rest of the system to hear."

The best thing to do when you are working with the alters is to allow any of the alters to go to a "safe place" if it wants to be protected from the information about to be exposed. There have been times when I have forgotten to ask the child alters to go to their safe place before traumatic information is brought out, and they say, "We don't want to be a part of this!" Then, I will say, "Oh, I forgot. Anybody who wants to be protected, go to your safe place."

I have found that most child alters do not want to hear the information unless it is directly related to them. Even then, they often do not want to deal with it, although sometimes they will get involved because they trust you and know you are working with them.

Sometimes, when I am talking with the host personality or one of the alters, I will make it clear that I understand the others may be listening in, especially if one of the alters is being talked about. In that case, I might say something like, "I know that so and so may very well be listening in now, so it's okay if they hear what I'm going to say."

TRANSFERENCE ISSUES

Transference occurs when the client (or one of the alters) responds to you, as the therapist, as though you were actually someone else from their past.[160] In other words, during therapy they unconsciously transfer the reactions they had to past abusers or significant childhood figures, such as parents or siblings, from them to you. These displaced reactions can range from appropriate responses to stimuli to extremely inappropriate responses that are not reality-bound.[161]

Just about anything could trigger a transference reaction: what you wear during a therapy session; objects in the therapy setting; the way you style your hair; the cologne or perfume you wear; or the manner in which you handle therapeutic procedures, including basics like billing, discipline, interruptions, or taking vacations.[162] Sometimes, all it takes is a reaction to the gender of the therapist.

Because of the complexity of multiplicity, these transference reactions can trigger conflicting responses from different alters. For instance, a physical touch (anything from a handshake to a hug) can trigger in one alter a transference experience of a nurturing, comforting person from their childhood, while this same touch can trigger negative experiences, such as memories of rape or abuse, in other alters. These conflicting responses can occur simultaneously, in rapid succession, or in a mixture of both. In addition, some reactions may serve to mask or repress other reactions.

Transference reactions can occur either within the therapy setting or outside. If they take place during therapy sessions, it gives you the opportunity to analyze and deal with it then. If, on the other hand, they occur outside of the therapy setting, it may be more difficult to determine or deal with. Transference reactions that take place outside of the therapy setting usually involve some form of acting out in inappropriate ways, which often sabotage treatment. Examples include promiscuous, aggressive, violent, or self-destructive incidents. The affected alter or host might tell others distorted information about you that misrepresents you as a therapist or professional.

Dealing with Transference Reactions

Since transference reactions are usually disorganized, you will probably have to deal with them one piece at a time. Your focus in attempting to work through these reactions should be on the reality content of the material and its impact on the client rather than on the reaction itself.

The first thing you will need to do is try to locate the root cause of the reaction and the person(s) from the past to whom the client is truly reacting. The second thing you will need to do is determine the time period in the client's life during which the original experiences occurred. Determining the time period of the experience is important in order to establish the client's level of functioning and ability to comprehend, based on his or her level of maturity or development at the time of the event.

Unless transference reactions present major obstacles to therapy, you should avoid emphasizing or referring to them. Remember, your focus is not on the reactions themselves, but on whatever caused the reactions to begin with, and how they affected the client. Treatment should involve whatever interventions you would normally use in order to resolve the root issues that caused the reactions.

Allow Time for Rest, Relaxation, and Play

Always allow sufficient time for recovery from each abreaction before engaging in or encouraging new memory work. Let the client set the pace.[163] Often, after working through a memory with someone, I take some time to talk about the underlying issues before moving on with any further memory work. Taking maybe three or four weeks, sometimes longer, to pace things out, we talk about restructuring the previously uncovered memory, reframing it, identifying the distortions, and anything else that might need to be worked on, before we do more uncovering work.

All too often, I have seen therapists start working with trauma only do uncovering work. The client gets overwhelmed and decompensates quickly. They stay in an emotional mess, become suicidal, and end up hospitalized. As I said before, pace is very important. When in doubt, go slowly. Do not rush. Do not get into the "I'm going to fix it right now" mentality. It does not work in the long run, and it can be damaging to the trauma survivor.

Do not underestimate the pain of therapy. This kind of work is extremely difficult for the client. One of the things I have always encouraged therapists to do is experience being on the other side. If you have not been through therapy work yourself, do it. Many therapists, especially those fresh out of college, have never been on the other side and have absolutely no idea what it is like to deal with the emotional turmoil that comes up in the therapeutic process. So, if you have not had the experience of being on the other side, please do it—if not for the sake of your profession, then for your own personal growth.

Most therapists who have been doing this kind of therapy for some time go in and out of therapy periodically. Sometimes, it is to address their own issues, but many times, it is to deal with countertransference issues. When I was just starting out as a therapist, I thought to myself, "What countertransference issues?" However, when I learned about all the different kinds of responses we therapists have with our clients, the light went on!

One of the things that can help is peer supervision, or getting together with other therapists to talk about our countertransference issues in order to encourage us in our work with the client. It helps us personally. It also helps our client, and it helps our therapy practice.

Moreover, you must know when you need some time out from therapy. Do not feel obligated to get to the end of the "memory puzzle" before taking a vacation. It may well be that both you and the patient need some time away.

REMEMBRANCE

The Bible refers to memory or remembrance approximately 250 times. From a scriptural standpoint, remembrance is of high importance. Through the work of the cross and the sacrifice Jesus made, God remembers the whole of the persons we are and forgives other actions, particularly those of sin. Memories include feelings, concepts, and patterns. They also include, and give rise to, attitudes and tendencies toward actions, both ours and those of others in the memory. These undercurrents accompany the pictures on the screen of the mind—the entirety of actions and attitudes, not just distorted, disconnected pictures. When the Bible tells us to "remember the LORD" (Deuteronomy 8:18 NIV), we are not intended just to get a mental picture of God, but of whole and complete thoughts and deeds toward God. When the Bible says to "remember the Sabbath day, to keep it holy" (Exodus 20:8 NKJV), we are encouraged to do more than just remember Sunday as a spiritual day. In biblical times, it meant to prepare completely—physically and spiritually—for the day. Food was made ready, clothes were laid out, plans were made for worship and rest, and the entire day's sights, sounds, and experiences contributed to the consciously, deliberately created act of remembrance.

When we work with memory, we need to deal with the whole person, not any one arena alone, since all are interconnected. The interconnectedness of all the facets of a human being makes it such a challenge to get at a single area in distress: the damage is obscured behind and beneath the camouflaged clothing of defense mechanisms developed over a lifetime of hurts and disappointments.

Another of the challenges associated with self-protective walls is that they are omnidirectional. While we may think they work (or hope they will, at least to some degree) to keep out the unpleasant and the painful, they perform another function, possibly more damaging than letting in the demons would be. They serve to keep us prisoners behind our own self-defense mechanisms. Consider, for a moment, the possibility that to the exact degree we are busy working to protect ourselves from assaults (both external and internal, such as wretched memories), we are also preventing the fresh air of self-expression. Denying and repressing painful memories eats up our own freedom in great gulps, leaving us little space to live our lives as survivors of injury and allowing us virtually no freedom in which to thrive. What is required boils down to allowing those "bad" things to surface and looking them in the eye.

Session Wrap-Up

A key to successfully wrapping up a session focused on memory anchoring and retrieval is bringing clients back to the present moment. Just as the five senses were used to engage them in their memory, the counselor will want to use all senses to help bring them to a place where they can reconnect to the present. This is done gently, asking them to let that memory fade, open their eyes, and experience the five senses within their current context. This is an important step in bringing them back to "safety" and not allowing them to stay stuck in an overwhelming memory.

God said to Jeremiah, "Before I formed you in the womb I knew you, and before you were born I consecrated you" (Jeremiah 1:5 ESV). The message here is that God knows the totality of who we are. The healing process of our memory includes the awareness that God was present at the time of our trauma, hurt, or distressing experience. It also includes the collateral realization that God is present with us now—but I am getting ahead of myself.

Chapter Two Notes

CHAPTER THREE

Processing Affect

The way we compose our life stories is closely related to our self-understanding and identity, according to many theorists.[164] Thus, if a trauma memory is seen as a central turning point in our life story, it would most likely be regarded as a central component of our personal identity, too.[165] It is often hard to separate what has happened to us from who we are as individuals. Trauma, in particular, leaves a tremendous imprint on the mind, emotions, spirit, and body of a person, which can make it seem as though the person is now the trauma itself.[166] The trauma experience often creates mindsets and belief systems that can transform someone's entire identity and, time and again, create a domino effect of pain and suffering in the individual's life. A critical part of the healing journey is observing the emotional affect of the individual and the cognitive beliefs and distortions with which they have aligned.

EMOTIONAL CONNECTION TO CHILDHOOD MEMORIES

Memories often bring with them powerful emotions, which are connected to the event(s) or to our understanding and perception of the events. A significant concept in dealing with memories from childhood is the fact that they are encoded into long-term memory as whole experiences—that is, complete with feelings, body reactions, sensory input, and emotional connections.[167] The brains of young children are not developed enough for them to separate the young self (inner child) from a trauma that occurs, nor even to manufacture a rationalization that could in some way enable them not to shoulder the blame for the trauma themselves. Children have a habit of blaming themselves for whatever happens to them.[168] While the self-blame is irrational, it does not stop the child from believing that he or she is the cause of all things negative that have happened in the child's life. This is often applied to home, school, friends, etc.

This self-blame is one of the cognitive distortions that will be addressed in the next chapter. As a result, guilt can take root and begin affecting individuals' entire life story—or at least until their life story runs into resolution. Lev Vygotsky emphasizes that a child's learning tends to be affected by the environment,[169] by the memory of something that has been repeated over time, including in the child's immediate environment, and by psychologically strong figures in the child's life.[170] This shaping happens before children are necessarily able to manage their own learning and memory acquisition. Once memories have been established, the young brain immediately hurries to cloak or obscure what is painful as best it can.

While adult memory is often intimately connected to emotion, memories formed during childhood are usually more viscerally emotional because a child experiences events without the layer of distance allowed by rational processing. These feelings are especially difficult to work through, particularly for people who have been sexually traumatized early in life. Complex suffering creates a significant mix of emotions. Survivors might feel any combination of these complex emotions:[171]

Shame: hurt, guilt, betrayal, fearful, afraid, overwhelmed, forced, unloved, abused, degraded

Anger: rage, bitterness, vindictive, repulsed, disgusted, numb, controlled, abandoned, cheated, in the way

Miserable: belittled, inadequate, helpless, vulnerable, insecure, weak, intimidated, empty, blamed, victimized

CONNECTING TO MEMORIES AS ADULTS

When individuals reconnect to these memories as adults, the reconnection may bring with it all the sensory input of the original experience: they may experience an abreaction, or reliving, of the trauma.[172] Consider the flashbacks, sometimes debilitating, experienced by combat veterans, sexual abuse survivors, and natural disaster survivors, as well as those who wade in to provide relief following catastrophic events. Such flashbacks are examples of the visceral, emotional, and affective flooding that may occur with memory retrieved or focused upon in a therapeutic context.[173] Overwhelming memory reactions may also be triggered by sensory input—for example, the aromas of coffee coupled with cigarette smoke, the feel of a damp wool jacket and the smell of stale beer, or notes from a specific piece or genre of music. Subjective recall of issues previously prayed for, or that have a current and ongoing focus, can often evoke the same reactions when things are brought to mind even in the context of spiritual disciplines.

> Jean, a young woman of twenty-two years, entered counseling to deal with the sexual abuse she had endured as a child. She had been molested by a close uncle from the time she was eight until she was ten years old. Both during the initial interview and in subsequent meetings, she often referred to this uncle in a monotone voice. Jean displayed little affect connected to the retelling or the memory of the episodes. Even when recounting, for the first time, a particularly unpleasant incident when she was nine years old, her emotional response was muted and blunt.
>
> When I sensed an emotional disconnection, I asked her to close her eyes and call to mind the mental image or picture associated with the original event. What she envisioned was the first time she could remember her uncle molesting her. Once the specific event was called to mind, Jean was able to paint a rich verbal picture of her childhood bedroom, which was furnished with toys and colorful curtains at the windows. A brightly painted picture occupied a corner; there were lots of books, as well as various awards and trophies from school. As the process developed, she slowly began to cry. Over the next hour, the tears flowed freely as she recalled her fear and the intense feelings of betrayal she had toward her uncle. She knew that what he was doing was somehow wrong, but she felt frozen in her position as the victim. Jean was unable to take any steps toward action that could possibly have removed her from the situation. It was not until sometime later, in therapy, that she was able to see how she had blamed herself for the events, as well as for her inability to react.
>
> The child ego in Jean knew something was terribly wrong, and she felt guilty for her part in the sexual activities, but she had not yet developed the intellectual faculties capable of rationalizing or reasoning away her part in them. Even her fear of, and disappointment in, the formerly trusted family member was not enough to let her childhood self off the hook. Overwhelming feelings of fear, betrayal, and self-condemnation exploded into her conscious awareness, simply as a result of

> connecting to the memory from the past while in the relative safety of the present moment.

People who have experienced unimaginable trauma often lose trust in themselves, because on some level, they feel they might have betrayed themselves at an early age. This is especially true with trafficked survivors, who often blame themselves for their plight, the untold horrors they endure at the hands of those who control their actions. They may feel that they are deserving of blame because of their participation and compliance. They may also feel deserving of punishment or being stuck in their current situation because of some action that led to the trafficking. The feeling of unworthiness, in turn, adds to the burden of shame.

INNER CHILD

When humans are outwardly focused to the detriment of the true self (the inner child), they are fragmented, crippled, and codependent.[174] For those who experienced trauma in their early years, childhood was often so difficult that it became necessary to shut out large parts of their inner life in order to survive. There might have been few healthy role models to teach them about life and how to handle its challenges, though even one caring adult can make a significant difference.[175] Comfort that might have helped was also unavailable from society or peers who were in the same situation, resulting in the child being left to navigate overwhelming emotions without guidance.

As a consequence, the child might have learned rigid rules and negative messages about feelings, such as, "Don't feel"; "Don't get angry"; "Only Mommy and Daddy get angry"; and, "Your feelings are not important." Those negative messages get encoded, and the child then believes them.[176] When discovering and healing the true self, it becomes apparent that many of those old rules and messages simply were not true. As a result, it is possible to become increasingly aware of inner life and its major component, feelings, as a powerful part of human life.[177]

Practically speaking, for a young person being trafficked, the messages can be brutal and life-threatening: "If you don't meet your quota, you will get a beating." Even after a severe beating, the girl will then go right back to the trafficker because his voice echoes in her head: "Nobody else will want you"; "You are lucky I will even keep you"; "If anyone really cared about you, they would have looked for you." His words continue to crush the little self-worth that remains. Most trauma situations purposely directed at the child end up the same way—with the child feeling helpless, worthless, and unable to blame anyone but himself or herself.

INWARD FLIGHT

We have all heard of the "fight or flight" syndrome, but we sometimes forget that the third response to distress is paralysis: to freeze or to do nothing effective, presumably as a corollary of dissociation and initial denial or numbness.[178] In essence, this is an "inward" flight response. The "deer in the headlights" phenomenon may possibly be a function of the inability to process events in the moment because of their overwhelming nature. It can certainly characterize the inability of young people to remove themselves from dangerous, invasive situations, especially when perpetrators are the very friends and family upon whom they were or are currently dependent for their lives—for food, shelter, and safety.[179] Such paralysis, their inability to take evasive action or to tell someone in authority about their abuse,[180] is one of the main experiences that vast numbers of survivors cite as the primary origin of their feelings of guilt. That becomes part of the growing abuse picture, since a child's developing brain remains egocentric: children's thoughts, beliefs, actions, and feelings are centered on their own lives, and they believe that if something happens, it is because of them; thus, abuse must be their fault.[181]

EMOTIONAL COCKTAIL

Many emotions, born of memories about unpleasant events, can easily be pent up, sometimes for years, lying dormant until the client feels that it is safe to bring them out in the open for examination and evaluation.[182] For some, this time never comes, or else it is so long in coming that maladaptive symptoms and behaviors start to show up in many forms: physical illness, hypertension, migraine headaches, and acting-out behavior, to name but a few.[183] As a general rule, it is healthier to process distress as soon as possible.[184] The greater the amount of time that elapses between an upsetting event and the processing of that event, the less control the individual has over how the emotions come out—and they will manifest in one way or another, or in many ways.

Many people have experienced grief and anxiety over childhood abandonments, dysfunctional family relationships, perceived slights, hurts, and outright abuse. Allowing for the grieving process, which is essentially processing the affect, becomes a necessary component of freeing these trapped emotions. Unexpressed or unprocessed grief acts as poison limiting the capacity for joy, spontaneity, and life itself. It is important to allow our clients the time, security, and permission to grieve in all areas of their hurt and pain.[185] In particular, survivors of complex trauma need to grieve lost childhoods, lost innocence, abandonment, and usually multiple versions of abuse and neglect.

Anger is another emotion that brings with it strong connotations to people healing from past hurts and traumas. From the Christian credo to "love and forgive," societal norms include seeing anger as bad, harmful, and even evil.[186] Therefore, anger that has repeatedly been repressed and turned inward can express itself in various outward ways or directions.[187] Sometimes, those patterns can be destructive, such as getting into fights or breaking into homes, outlets that often result in the person's incarceration.[188] Anger can also be expressed inwardly, resulting in self-harm such as cutting, addictions, and suicide attempts. Many people grew up in stormy family situations, in which arguing and fighting were constants, and anger was used as a weapon for survival. Trafficked women and other complex-trauma survivors often resort to drugs and alcohol to mute or blunt their anger in order to cope with, and survive, their dismal life situations. However, anger can be healthy if used in a constructive way, one that is transformative and powerful.[189] When clients feel angry about the injustice done to them, they feel passionate about justice. Anger moves us to feel passionate about the things that are important; but, most of us have not been taught how to use anger in that manner.[190]

Anger as a natural response to many situations is often stifled in children. Rather than focusing their anger at parents, teachers, or the abusers, children tend to focus anger inwardly, toward themselves, again as a result of the undeveloped brain's inability to view the world in any way other than egocentrically. Anger focused inwardly may cause children, then adults, to see themselves as bad or wrong; it may cause clients to criticize themselves relentlessly or to devalue themselves. Some clients attempt to satiate the yearning for healthy love and acceptance with food; others use sex, drugs, or alcohol; still others manifest various somatic illnesses. After having been taught to blame oneself—or, not knowing any other way, resorting to self-blame—victims tend to stay angry at the child ego state within themselves, at the child who was vulnerable, injured, and unable to protect himself or herself, and who desperately needed affection and attention. It is the job of therapy to help clients see that this child did nothing wrong and does not deserve the burden of anger.

Charles Carver and Eddie Harmon-Jones found clear links between anger, fear, and anxiety.[191] Trauma sets off significant fear reactions, which can easily lead to repressed anger if not processed and dealt with. The mere perception of responding affectively to trauma may cause emotional reactions, such as guilt, shame, or embarrassment, and those emotional reactions, if not dealt with, can easily be repressed.[192] Typically, the fear comes first, followed by the overlay of anger. We tend to fear anger because it can become all-consuming, such as the righteous indignation or the rage that can lead us to lash out at others. Then the fear ends up consuming the anger in a self-destructive, self-recriminatory spiral. Both feelings fester when repressed but can explode nearly uncontrollably when exposed. The scripture that comes to mind is, "The truth will set you free" (John 8:32 NIV), but as a therapist friend of mind once said, "The truth may first tick you off".[193]

> Daysha was in counseling a mere two sessions when she started to complain of severe migraines. When I asked about the history of her symptoms, she reported that they had started just after our first session. In exploring the details of our first session, she acknowledged that discussing issues related to her father was emotionally difficult for her. She revealed that when she was growing up in a small village in a third-world country, she often came home after school to find her father quite intoxicated and usually angry. She had reported that her father would often yell and scream about everything that was wrong, and sometimes everything that was right. There was no rationale. There was only anger and loud, out-of-control behavior. Her father's rage and inconsistency were, for her, as powerful as, and much like, a physical assault. Daysha's extreme discomfort drove her to seek a new life in a different country and, consequently, sent her into the hands of traffickers.
>
> I asked her to get a picture in her mind of her early years at home and to revisit the period of time in her life that included her father's ranting and raving. At first, when she closed her eyes, she was calm. Then, she suddenly began raging, yelling, and screaming, accusing me of hurting her and demanding to know why I would want her to suffer this way. As I carefully coaxed her back into the experience, she was able to see that her headaches were physical manifestations of the pent-up anger and rage she had felt toward her father for many years. As the processing continued, Daysha began to see how this pent-up anger found its inappropriate way into other relationships, particularly into her home, with her husband and five-year-old son. As part of the processing, she began to get an idea of how much energy it took to keep the anger under wraps and what it cost her in her current, most closely held relationships. It became clear to Daysha that pushing through

> the process, even when it was unpleasant, would be worth the effort in light of the freedom she began to imagine on the other side.

Strong childhood emotions such as anger and rage are often stifled by well-meaning parents, teachers, and others in authority.[194] One well-meaning Christian parent, hoping to quell his child's anger, twisted her statement, "I'm mad at you!" into, "Mad means crazy. If you are insane, then you need to be locked up in an asylum, away from your mother and the rest of the family." The parent's fear about his child's strong expression of anger catapulted her into the process of repression and a subsequent need for expression in the therapeutic arena.

Another emotion I will touch on here is panic: "Panic is what you feel when you get scared by your own emotions and do not have the skills to calm yourself down."[195] It can also arise when someone is trying to suppress feelings or memories. Although panic may seem to come out of the blue, there is almost always a trigger, often based in childhood or somewhere else in the past.[196] When the Scriptures talk about emotion, it is often in the context of resolving situations or of encouraging us to embrace the experience of the emotions and to trust God in the process, thanking Him for the emotions themselves and the trials that might have set them up (2 Corinthians 7:8 NIV).[197] What a hard thing to embrace, the trials that set up negative or painful emotions. Yet, Scripture shows time and again that the process of healing is to work through the emotions and not to run away. Only this sort of healing brings us into a place of congruency that, in effect, may bring us to a place of both salvation and overcoming (1 John 5:5 NIV).

The Scriptures talk a lot about emotions. "When I am afraid, I will put my trust in You. In God, whose word I praise, in God I have put my trust; I shall not be afraid" (Psalm 56:3–4 NASB). Anxiety is discussed in Matthew 6:25 and Philippians 4:6. Tears of grief can be found in Isaiah 25:8. And anger can be found throughout the Old Testament. Feelings are necessary and indicate pain and pleasure. But, we must remember, feelings are only that—*just* feelings—and they will change frequently.

Last, positive feelings can also be scary. The idea of feeling good can seem threatening to many clients, because they feel a loss of control over the positive feelings bubbling up unbidden from deep inside, or perhaps hovering around the edges like butterflies looking for an open window. Being liked, appreciated, and held in high esteem by others can make one feel vulnerable and can bring up feelings of shame—shame over feeling good in spite of the long-held low opinion of oneself, shame for real or imagined dirty secrets not yet revealed, or shame over feeling relieved for having survived when others may not have.[198] Peace, calm, and a sense of well-being may be so unfamiliar that clients do not know how to relax and enjoy the phenomenon of just being. Here are some common

positive emotions that can, in reality, be complicated for trauma survivors to experience:[199]

> **Happiness**: joy, deserving, fortunate, loved, accepted, caring, safe, peaceful, satisfied
>
> **Kindness:** comfort, compassion, forgiving, encouraged, cared for, supported, warm, comforted, relaxed
>
> **Competent:** capable, respected, confident, successful, worthy, positive, lighthearted, comfortable, alive

Reframing

For purposes of this model, the processing of affect becomes extremely important in the total healing and health of the client. As with most therapeutic modalities, the process of releasing repressed feelings and emotions grants clients the space to develop a new perspective and the ability to reframe events in their lives. It encourages increased awareness and promotes greater ease in their ability to reach back to past hurts, particularly those in childhood, and let go of the baggage that they may have carried most of their lives. One possible trickledown effect of releasing old hurts can be the newly found delight of being comfortable within one's own skin, perhaps for the first time. It clearly leaves one better equipped for solitude and can lead to improved quality in relationships.

> In trauma survivors, Van der Kolk notes, the parts of the brain that have evolved to monitor for danger remain over-activated and even the slightest sign of danger, real or misperceived, can trigger an acute stress response accompanied by intense unpleasant emotions and overwhelming sensations. Such posttraumatic reactions make it difficult for survivors to connect with other people, since closeness often triggers the sense of danger. And yet the very thing we come to most dread after experiencing trauma—close contact with other people—is also the thing we most need in order to regain psycho-emotional solidity and begin healing. Van der Kolk writes: Being able to feel safe with other people is probably the single most important aspect of mental

The HEART Model

health; safe connections are fundamental to meaningful and satisfying lives.[200]

Approximately one man in six, and one in every four women, will have been the victim of sexual abuse by age eighteen.[201] Since the numbers of people victimized by the age of eighteen are so high, it is little wonder that the need for competent therapists is so pressing. "In discovering and healing our True Self we learn that many of those old rules and messages were not true, and we become more and more aware of that powerful part of us: our inner life, and its major component—our feelings!"[202] About half of our inner life consists of feelings; the other half of the equation comprises the cognitive distortions. I am reminded of the old quip, "Sometimes I sits and thinks, and sometimes I just sits."[203]

Chapter Three Notes

CHAPTER FOUR

Negotiation and Reconciliation Between Present and Past Ego States

Categorically, this concept is probably the most difficult to articulate. The basic idea is that the adult of present time negotiates with the child of the past in an attempt to mediate unresolved conflict and emotion. Many times, clients attribute adult thought patterns to their childhood events and have lost the essence of what it was like to be young and small. The inner child process is similar to the chair work of Gestalt therapy,[204] in that the discordant split between the adult self and the hurt child represents two distinct poles of response and behavior. Each therapy session is seen as an experiment, an existential encounter in which the therapist and client engage in calculated risk-taking that involves exploration of unknown or forbidden information, feelings, or territory.[205]

From a Gestalt standpoint, reuniting the two parts, or "completing the whole," becomes the process of therapy.[206] Each split is characterized by the nature of the two parts, the relationships between the parts, and the client's subjective experience of the split.[207] The process of therapy, therefore, is about identifying and resolving the separation between the two parts and establishing contact. It also involves owning responsibility on both sides of the split, attending to personalized issues and feelings, and heightening the sense of awareness and outward expression of each part.[208] The idea is for both parts to resolve their issues and be reunited as one. The nature of the client's process from each alter's position in the dialogue is examined in terms of each part's depth of experiences, voice quality, and willingness to cooperate in resolution. The technique of reuniting the alters produces a more direct experience of the internal conflict and encourages the client to engage in a form of self-confrontation that helps to create a resolution to the

THE HEART MODEL

conflict.[209]

Many survivors have a difficult time with the concept of the child within, even though forgiving that child is an essential part of healing. Too often, women blame that inner child, hate her, or ignore her completely. Survivors hate themselves for having been small, for having needed affection, and for having "let themselves" be abused.[210] Often with men, this process is displayed as anger and, sometimes, behavior that is reckless or violent because of that anger. Women often end up in counseling centers. Men, unfortunately, often end up in jail or prison.

It is helpful to know why survivors find it so difficult to open up to the little girl or boy within. To begin with, survival depended on covering up or hiding the state of being vulnerable, and that façade is a protection difficult to relinquish. It requires remembering shame, vulnerability, and pain. It means acknowledging, consciously and deliberately, that the abuse actually happened.[211]

From an ego state therapy standpoint, the process of therapy is focused on taking two discordant and fragmented ego states and working toward the elimination of (1) barriers and/or (2) amnestic states to allow a fluid flow of information between those ego states.[212] The end result using either process is a free flow of information and an integration of parts or ego states. The calming of the internal conflict, followed by integration, emerges as a key factor in resolving intrapsychic splits.[213]

Tina had been working in counseling for months, stabilizing a family situation with her husband, but as time went on, it became clear she had unresolved issues with a childhood trauma with her father. At age five, Tina had been left alone with her father while her mother went out for the evening with friends. While she was playing in her room for most of the day, her father was in the living room, quietly working his way through a case of beer. Sometime in the late afternoon, her father had come into her room and started to play with her. The play centered on wrestling, grabbing, and roughhousing but slowly progressed to undressing her and digitally penetrating her. Tina at first enjoyed the attention and the play in which she and her father engaged. And she didn't mind losing her clothing, thinking that it was just part of the game. While she knew her father's inappropriate touch was somehow not right, she continued to enjoy the nice things that he was saying to her and the way he referred to her as being "his special girl."

In the process of therapy, I asked Tina to recreate the experience in picture form. As she recounted the events, Tina became angrier and more upset at the little girl she saw in the picture. At one point, I asked her if she would like to say something to that little girl. She replied, "You horrid, wretched creature. Why didn't you run away? Why didn't you tell someone? Why didn't you do anything but lay there?" Then I asked if the child in the picture (her internal response) made any comment back or responded in any way. To her surprise, she responded that the child inside simply cried. Over the next four sessions, I facilitated a dialogue between the two discordant parts discussing the adult's unreal expectations of the five-year-old and an awareness of the child's innocence and naïvety at the age of five. For a homework assignment, between one of those sessions, I had Tina visit a Sunday school class for kindergarteners and observe the play of five-year-olds for twenty minutes. She reported in the next session her amazement at how simply and freely they trusted those in their environment. I asked her to apply that to the situation within herself, dealing with her father. By the end of the fourth session, the adult Tina had developed enough empathy for the hurt and confused child that she offered to take the latter out of where she was, figuratively, and be brought into present time. The child part of her wanted love and contact. The child freely agreed, and the two parts were "integrated."

The process described above in the example with Tina illustrates basic Gestalt chair work done in the form of visualization, without the inconvenience of switching back and forth between real chairs. Shifting between the two ego states or splits has been shown time and again in research data to affect positive treatment outcomes.[214] The process not only provides a structure for resolving conflict but also affords that same structure in the resolution of repressed emotions and affect. Gestalt therapy emphasizes contact with unwanted and disowned aspects of the self.[215] True reconciliation internally occurs in the space of reclaiming what has been disowned and healing the split.

Bonita presented in therapy with a laundry list of items that she used for self-deprecation. She had grown up with a physically and emotionally abusive father and a mother who remained silent so as not to incur the wrath of her father on herself. She clearly had considerable repressed anger and an ongoing frustration at not being able to stop herself from compulsive activities, such as pornography, alcohol consumption, and sexual promiscuity. When I inquired into her recollection of an event that symbolized her out-of-control behavior, she immediately went to a time when she was nine years old and had stumbled upon her father's

> pornography collection within the deep recesses of her father's closet. She knew that she would get in trouble if her father spotted her; however, she could not help but be mesmerized by the images and spent three hours in her father's closet looking through magazines. When her father returned home and headed for her bedroom, Bonita could not move fast enough to return all the magazines back to their location and was discovered before completing the task. Her father unloaded a tirade of abusive language and name calling, and he proceeded to take his belt and beat her until she was marked from her mid-back to her mid-thigh.
>
> When I asked Bonita to visualize that event and to see herself at age nine, she recoiled in disgust and anger saying, "It's all your fault. You should have known he would have been back. Why did you ever stay there?" It took several sessions for Bonita to understand that a nine-year-old's curiosity caused her to freeze in the moment and that her subsequent acting out through adolescence and adulthood were reenactments of this earlier event. When she was able to express her shame and embarrassment, along with the sheer terror of dealing with her father, she was able to move herself to a place of compassion for what this nine-year-old child had endured. The release of the feelings, the resolution of this split, allowed the two parts of self to come together in one whole. It was another three or four months before Bonita was able to release her compulsive behavior regarding pornography. But, the insight allowed her both the motivation and the ability to come to terms and resolve the issues.

EIGHT ERRONEOUS CORE BELIEFS

Eight core beliefs and erroneous assumptions provide the breeding ground out of which cognitive distortions derive:

1. *Different parts of the self are separate selves (i.e., each alter is an entity of its own).* When I first came into the field of trauma in the 1980s and '90s, it was believed that each alter or part of self was a separate identity within one mind, if the person were considered to have multiple personality disorder. As of the publication of the DSM-IV in 1994, the psychiatric community renamed multiple personality disorder as dissociative identity disorder. It had been discovered, through research, that the separate identities were separate parts of one psyche. The psyche had fragmented as a way to protect itself from overwhelming trauma.[216]

2. *The victim is responsible for the abuse; it is his or her fault.* In exploring the accusation, it becomes apparent that the adult is attributing adult qualities to the child victim.

3. *It is wrong to show anger, frustration, defiance, or a critical attitude.* This is an especially prevalent distortion if the client is brought up in a Christian (or highly structured, religious) home. In an abusive home, showing anger was dangerous.

4. *The past is the present.* Victims believe that they are still going to be hurt by the perpetrator, even if that perpetrator has passed away. They still believe that by releasing the secrets to anybody, they are going to be harmed; or, they believe that what they were threatened with (that their mother would get hurt, a sibling would get hurt, etc., as a consequence) would come to pass. The alters, especially in the case of DID clients, still believe they are in the year in which they are frozen in time. I keep a newspaper in my office because it has the current date on it and clients may need to be oriented to the present. Sometimes, I take them out into the parking lot to have a look at the cars, which are very different from the 1960s or '80s.

5. *The primary personality cannot handle the memories, which is why alters exist: to protect the host alter, because the host alter has to deal with the world and ordinary functioning.* The other alters' job has been to protect the host alter from the hurt, shame, and memory of the trauma; often, the host does not have much memory of what happened, because another part came out to handle whatever situation was at hand. Suicidal ideation is often a way of coping: "I've always got a way out, even if it is suicide." It is a survival mechanism the client has been using for years, but it should be continuously assessed for lethality.

6. *"I love my parents, but she [another alter/ part of self] hates them."* Clearly, in statements of this sort, one part is in direct conflict with another. These conflicts create further distance between two parts and could also leave the individual vulnerable to revictimization (if abuse was done by the parents) because boundaries are unclear and inconsistent.

7. *The primary personality must be punished, according to the system the alters have set up; they protect their own parts.* The twisted thinking is, "I am going to protect the system by hurting it so that nobody from the outside can do it." They are, nevertheless, protector parts. They cut and burn, and they terrorize the smaller parts in a DID system; but, it is a twisted mechanism. I often call working with DID "family therapy with one person," because it is necessary to form alliances with all the different parts, especially the

main ones.[217] The persecutor parts will harm the system, but I eventually confront them with, "What if I could teach you better ways to do what you do?"

8. *"I cannot trust myself or others."* Traumatized clients learned a long time ago that they could not trust people around them, and they have been told for so long that their opinion does not matter and/or what they think is not right, they learn to distrust themselves. However, they function well overall. They size people up better than any other group of people I have met, because they are always scanning for safety. They have to know whether you are safe to approach or whether you are going to hurt them. If you talk to teens who have been trafficked or are in the business as prostitutes, they size people up quickly, because their income, safety, and sometimes their very life depend on this ability. This constant scanning for safety creates a state of hyper-arousal and ongoing sensory vigilance.

SIX COGNITIVE DISTORTIONS

Based on these core beliefs, cognitive distortions (or twisted thinking) develop. On some level, all sexual trauma survivors deal with six basic cognitive distortions derived from the core assumptions previously listed:[218]

1. *It is the victim's fault or responsibility.* It takes a lot of work to shift the responsibility for the abuse to the perpetrator. Victims believe that the abuse is their fault, regardless of their age, and blame themselves as a result. It is essential for survivors to learn that abuse by adults was the responsibility of the adults and not theirs, as the child.

2. *Secrecy is necessary.* "The secret must be kept as long as I am alive, because if I let go of the secret, I'm going to get hurt or somebody is going to get hurt. I have to keep the secret—no matter how long." The perpetrator has often set up false beliefs in the victim that if they tell, nobody will believe them, a parent may lose their job, nobody would want them anymore, or other lies. In many instances, the therapist is the first person to whom victims disclose the secret.

3. *Seductiveness, and its adult qualities, is attributed to the child part of the self.* This, in spite of the extreme youth of the child (seven years old, for example). But the victims still believe themselves to be responsible.

4. *Physical pleasure leads directly to self-blame.* God designed our bodies so wonderfully—to respond to touch, to care, and to be responsive, even when the touch is inappropriate. If victims have any kind of emotional or physical pleasure or, heaven forbid, orgasm, the blame is then doubled or tripled. "I liked it," "I responded," "I brought it on myself," and so on, are claims that increase the shame and guilt.

5. *Emotional pleasure leads directly to self-blame.* As with physical pleasure, the child feels guilty for basking in the emotional pleasure of the favor and focused attention of the perpetrator.

6. *Exoneration of the perpetrator occurs when the child is busy defending the perpetrator by citing all the good things she or he has done, despite the emotional, physical, and/or sexual abuse.* Victims may state their love for the father who did lots of wonderful things for them, but who also molested them. The perpetrator could do no wrong because of the positive side of the equation, which is often part of the grooming. Victims of sexual trauma in familial situations are frequently groomed (by the father or stepfather) to be "Daddy's little girl," a replacement for the victim's mother, or my "special daughter (or son)." It is part of what they crave: the attention, or the feeling of being special. Although they felt the touch was somehow wrong, they also felt the burden of shame, because they liked it.

COGNITIVE DISTORTIONS IN COMPLEX TRAUMA

The abovementioned distortions are difficulties that sexual trauma survivors must work out, resolve, or cognitively reframe and refocus, all while they are dealing with the emotional feelings that come from the memory and from the impact of the situation. In trafficking situations, the cognitive distortions are combined with the number of perpetrators trafficked women encounter, as they deal with pimps, travel across borders, interact with customers, and suffer physical, emotional, and sexual abuse by their handlers and pimps.

Dealing with multiple perpetrators equals multiple traumas. When we speak of multiple traumas, we often refer to it as *complex trauma*. Complex trauma often occurs as the layering of multiple abuses over time.[219] The cognitive distortions are then complicated and multiplied many times over by the sheer number of traumas and different types of perpetrators involved in their abuse.

DYSFUNCTIONAL COPING TECHNIQUES: HONORING WHAT YOU DID TO SURVIVE

At this stage in working with survivors, it is important to honor what they did to survive—how they made it through. Consider all the things Judith Herman wrote about regarding immature psychological defenses:[220]

- minimizing
- rationalizing
- denial
- forgetting
- splitting
- control
- avoiding
- suicide/cutting
- addiction
- isolation
- avoiding intimacy
- sex

Minimizing the abuse or rationalizing why it happened is a method of easing the pain and decreasing the feeling that the injury was against the survivor specifically. Denying and convincing oneself that the abuse never occurred is an effort to keep away all thoughts and emotions connected to the trauma. In early childhood, significant repression of memories can take place because we want to protect ourselves from the overwhelming emotions experienced during the trauma. We do not want to connect to being overwhelmed or hurt. The splitting, the actual dissociation, is a protective mechanism. I often try to reframe it as a coping mechanism: "This is a way you learned how to survive, to keep your own ego and integrity and keep a sense of self."

All the coping mechanisms are ways of dealing with feelings and keeping the emotions at bay. Cutting is a way of trying to connect with feelings after victims have spent so much time numbing out, avoiding their feelings.[221] To help them feel, we teach them various methodologies. One is the rubber band technique.[222] When a client wears the rubber band and the urge to cut arises, he or she simply snaps the rubber band, which produces the same sensation as a slight cut; it produces the sting without the destruction of body tissue. Obviously, if a client is cutting deeply, he or she needs to be hospitalized, because that is getting too close to lethality; but, if the cutting is only surface-level, it is a coping mechanism.

Every trauma survivor with whom I have ever worked has held suicide as a last resort. Trauma survivors hold to the belief that if it gets so bad, they can take themselves out, yet most of them find every reason and every way to stay alive. It certainly causes a lot of dual feelings, or feelings that are at odds with each other. I am not quick to take this coping strategy away from them. In fact, this is usually the last dysfunctional coping strategy I work to remove. The client who is apathetic is a client I worry about regarding suicide. The one who simply does not care is the one to be concerned about, because that person might actually follow through.

Drugs and alcohol are used to numb pain, which often leads to addiction.[223] If a client is actively dealing with any kind of substance addiction, this needs to be addressed along with the trauma.[224] I have often found that as the trauma is addressed, the substance use also gradually diminishes. Unless the addiction is getting in the way of therapy, it is often something I will tolerate while we focus on trauma work, because I know it will eventually go away. In situations where addiction is getting in the way, I usually refer them to residential treatment that deals with dual diagnosis of trauma and addiction.

Isolation is another way of surviving.[225] Often, women who have experienced sexual trauma will either avoid sexual intimacy at all costs or be completely promiscuous. Both practices are coping strategies, or ways to resolve the internal feelings regarding sexual and emotional intimacy.

STAGES OF HEALING

This leads us to the stages of healing. I will often ask clients to read the book *The Courage to Heal*, by Ellen Bass and Laura Davis.[226] They talk about these different stages of healing, beginning with making the decision to heal. They believe that most of these stages are necessary for every survivor, but a few stages are not applicable to everyone. These are not linear stages, where one has to follow the other, but circular, meaning a person may go through a stage, and on to the next, but later relapse into a previous stage.

The HEART Model

The decision to heal is based on the belief that once survivors acknowledge they have been abused, they make an active commitment to go through the healing process.[227] We know that deep healing happens only when someone chooses it and when the survivor is willing to do whatever it takes, for however long it takes, to work through the trauma.

The emergency stage is when an individual begins dealing with the memories and flashbacks, because these can turn a person's life into utter chaos. We often try to remind clients that this is only a stage and the emotions will not always be this intense.

The next stage is remembering.[228] Many survivors have repressed the information so far back that during this stage, when reminded, they are sometimes flooded with these memories. If the memory had been intact, they may have forgotten how it felt at the time the trauma occurred. Remembering is the process of getting back both the narrative memory and the feeling or sensation of the abuse contained within the implicit memory. The feelings and sensations need to be connected and worked through.

Many survivors have a hard time believing that the abuse actually happened. According to Bass and Davis, this stage deals with the client accepting the reality of the abuse and the pain associated with it.[229] Believing the experience is a vital part of the healing process. Often, perpetrators try to talk survivors out of their own experience: "I know you think that, but that's not really true"; or, "You know that's not true." These are forms of coercion that drive the betrayal even further. At some point, the survivor must break the silence.

Most adult survivors kept their childhood abuse a secret, so the next stage—breaking silence—is a powerful healing force that can begin to work against the shame they held as a victim. Telling someone else your story is another layer of healing. As counselors, we are often on the front line of that. We may be the first person they tell.

As counselors, we want to help clients understand that it was not their fault. As we mentioned in the previous chapter, children are egocentric.[230] Their thoughts, beliefs, actions, and feelings are centered on their own lives, and they believe that if something happens, it is because of them. This is true of how a child perceives parental relationships with their partner or spouse. If there is a breakup, children often believe that it was because of something they did or did not do. Abused children, as a result of being egocentric, usually believe that the abuse was their fault. The counselor must then help them put the blame where it belongs—on the perpetrator.

Many survivors have lost touch with their own vulnerability.[231] Getting in touch with the child within is the focus of the next stage. This allows survivors to begin to feel compassion for themselves, anger against the abuser, and a greater ability to connect to others. This brings up cognitive distortions and twisted ways they might think about themselves and others.

The next stage is learning to trust themselves. Survivors are able to read signs from other people because they learned to be keenly attuned to the needs of their abusers in order to meet those needs and not get hurt. However, they often do not trust their own gut instincts.

A lot of grieving and mourning must take place. As children being abused, and later as adults trying to survive, most have not truly felt their losses. "Grieving is a way to honor your pain, let go and move into the present." [232] The grieving stage entails work at a deep level.

The next stage is anger. If I have a client who is angry, I am ecstatic. I know this client will get well, because anger is energy, and that energy provides the drive to get well. It can be described as the backbone of healing. Anger contributes to breaking the inertia of rest that preserves or perpetuates the status quo; it gives rise to the feeling, "I am sick and tired of being sick and tired," and spurs a person into action. Directing the anger toward the perpetrator, or those who knew and did not protect, is pivotal for healing.

The stage of disclosures and confrontations is not something we recommend anymore. Back when Bass and Davis were writing, the psychology field encouraged the survivor to confront the abuser. However, what we have found is that this often creates secondary trauma, as the perpetrator will deny or minimizes the abuse, which in turn revictimizes the client all over again. There are rare cases in which a survivor will confront an abuser and the confrontation leaves the client feeling cleansed and empowered. But, those cases are much less common.

Forgiving the lonely, hurting inner child is an essential component to healing. It allows him or her off the hook for not responding in a way the adult would have preferred. In contrast, forgiving the perpetrator is not essential to the process; however, it is the one most emphasized, particularly in religious circles.

Spirituality and a connectedness with God are often essential to healing, allowing or creating the room for a survivor to resolve problems and move forward to craft a new life. Sometimes people find this connection through traditional religion, meditation, nature, support groups, or friends with similar beliefs. While the journey is unique to each person, having a connection with God offers a road map for clients working through the process.

The last stage is coming to a place of resolution and moving on. As clients move through the stages again and again, they eventually reach a place of integration and self-

THE HEART MODEL

forgiveness, are able to recognize the responsibility of the abuser, and resolve that they can move forward in life with greater compassion and deeper understanding of God, self, and others. While no one can erase the history, clients will come out with new meaning and understanding for their life. More importantly, they have the opportunity to come to a place of wholeness and completeness.

It should be noted here that when the book first came out in the 1980s, it was panned by many Christian communities for two reasons. The first was that both Bass and Davis are lesbian, which many Christians found repulsive. The second is because of their statement that the only forgiveness necessary for healing is self-forgiveness—that forgiveness of a perpetrator is not necessary for healing. I happen to agree, but also believe that forgiveness of a perpetrator is an artifact of doing good therapy. I maintain that individuals will come to forgiveness (spoken about in a later chapter) in order to let go and move on.

God does not want to see us hurt, nor does He want us to struggle with the baggage we may carry around in life. "I have come that they may have life, and that they may have it more abundantly" (John 10:10 NASB). We have what might be called *infirmities.*: "Infirmities are unchosen factors, hurts, traumas. Infirmities are weaknesses, crippling our spirit, not sin but qualities of our personalities which predispose and incline us toward sin. They are weakened places in our defenses which undermine our resistance to temptation and sin."[233]

God wants us to be free emotionally and to resolve the places where we might be infirm: "He has sent me to bind up the brokenhearted, to proclaim freedom for the captives" (Isaiah 61:2 NIV). Romans 8:26–27 assures us that the Holy Spirit has been sent to help us with our infirmities, our weaknesses, and all areas in which we are crippled. While we must look to God and our faith in Jesus, the Messiah, we must also do our own work to resolve our internal conflicts. Only then can we be open to the full glory of what God would have for us.

Chapter Four Notes

CHAPTER FIVE

Forgiving Yourself: Letting Yourself Off the Hook

Forgiving a perpetrator or non-protector is an artifact of good therapy.[234] It is not and should not be a targeted focus of therapy. It is my sincere belief that forgiveness of others will happen as a byproduct of good therapeutic technique. Forgiveness, as a goal in therapy, becomes quite difficult if not pursued by looking at self-forgiveness. Many sexually abused women and men blame themselves for the abuse they have received.[235] The repressed anger and hurt directed at a variety of perpetuators is often set loose when the client becomes ready to move past the hurt and pain.[236] Forgiveness then becomes a willingness to let go of the repayment—whether that repayment is an apology, an acknowledgment, revenge, or even legal action. Letting go of the repayment and then moving on with life is a lesson shown to us by Jesus when He talked about the king forgiving a man of ten thousand talents of gold: "Then the master of that servant was moved with compassion, released him, and forgave him the debt" (Matthew 18:27 NKJV). Do you think the king forgot about the money he forgave? Do think he ever did business with this man again? Probably not. It is does not mean you must "forgive and forget." It does not necessitate a restoring of the relationship. Forgiveness is letting go of the *repayment*.[237]

When our sexual trauma clients are willing to let go of the acknowledgment, the apology, the jail term, or whatever it is they were looking for in the way of retribution or repayment, and are ready to move on in their lives, they have forgiven. That is why I assert that forgiveness is an artifact, outcome, or result of good therapy. Regardless of whether it is possible to restore the relationship, such as with a family member, the willingness to let go and move on is forgiveness. It is the client saying, "I am not willing to hold onto this resentment because doing so hurts me. I am letting go to be able to move on." For that reason, I assert that forgiving the perpetrator or non-protector should not be the focus of therapy. The real goal is for clients to let themselves off the hook, first and foremost. The client does not need to hold onto the trauma or emotional attachments any longer; this happens as a result of the therapeutic process.

Forgiveness consists of two distinct parts. The first involves ceasing to feel resentment toward an offender or non-protector. The second is to give up claim to requital, or reparation of some kind, from an offender—in other words, to grant the offender relief from repayment (for his or her sins). The second part is what is necessary to be able to move on. Giving up repayment in any form is forgiveness. This stance allows for anger and does not pardon or excuse the abuser. It is not about "forgiving and forgetting." Healing depends on forgiving self. Forgiving also opens clients to God's healing and forgiveness.

Even though many people in treatment are Christian and have experienced sexual trauma, they believe that because they are Christians, they have received God's forgiveness; yet, they have no connection to God. The reality is that they often do not have a connected relationship, because of unresolved shame and self-blame, which cause them to close in on themselves. Once they forgive themselves, they are free of the shame, the blame, and the cognitive distortions and able to move into a deeper spiritual connection.

Victims of abuse need to forgive themselves for being little children, for being small, for needing attention or affection, for needing to be acknowledged and valued, for coping as best as they could, and for being unable to avoid the abuse.[238] Sometimes, this is an issue for which others have blamed the child ("You were asking for it"; "You deserved it") despite the child's powerlessness in the situation. When the accusations are leveled by a close, valued adult, it can lend even more weight to the child's feelings of guilt. For the adult self, it becomes essential to forgive oneself for the limitations that have confined and narrowed the potential for self-expression in life. Forgiveness encompasses healing from the state of victimization, needing time to heal in the present, and self-forgiveness for how one might have dealt with others, including one's own children, subsequent to the trauma. This type of forgiveness is essential to the healing process.

Much has been written in the literature about forgiveness.[239] An esteemed colleague of mine, Everett Worthington, Jr., who teaches at Virginia Commonwealth University, has much to say on the subject.[240] His contention, which is in accord with most of the literature, is that complete healing does not come until we have forgiven those who have violated us in some way. He has divided this process into two stages: (1) the intent to forgive, and (2) the congruence of the emotions with the intention.[241] While I understand Worthington's position, I fundamentally disagree with him regarding the process. For any true healing to occur, individuals must forgive themselves first. Then, and only then, they can open up to the possibility of forgiving someone else completely, as well as have the ability to receive complete forgiveness from God.

For true healing, it is not necessary that clients develop compassion and forgiveness for an abuser or a member of the family who did not provide protection, although that could be something for which to hope or aim in the future.[242] However, if the much longed-for, deep healing is to occur, it is necessary for clients to forgive themselves and to resolve the unfinished work and conflict that may rage inside. As individuals seek healing, they have to look at their own hurts and release resentments.[243] They must say what needs to be said, feel what needs to be felt, and assume personal responsibility for who they are and what they do.[244] We, and certainly our clients, need to release the bargaining process that became known as "foxhole Christianity": "If You will just get me out of this danger, I promise I will...." For victims of abuse, the bargaining is more along the lines of, "If I forgive, then God will give me...."

Forgiveness is both a crisis and a process. In other words, it means owning up. It means we must take personal responsibility for our actions and work toward understanding our underlying motives. Then, it is being able to release resentments and hates that clearly bring us to a place of crisis. This process can be somewhat onion-like: it may return in layers. When it returns, or when another facet comes to light, we must take responsibility for that new facet as well, remembering that being responsible for the way we have responded to the pain is not the same as taking or placing blame.[245] We may struggle with feeling the need for ongoing affection, and we may struggle with resentments that strike out and punish others, but that often come back on us ourselves. The cycle of deep-seated bitterness continues to circulate and rebound within us.

We often set ourselves up with a false idolatry and set our standards higher than God's. Thus, the greatest battle of all is forgiving ourselves, particularly because many of us strive toward perfection. Robert McGee, in his book *Search for Significance*, talks about self-esteem and puts forth the idea that most of us have bought a lie regarding who we are. He believes that most people base their self-worth and self-value on how well they produce, such as monetary worth, family life, and so forth.[246] This point is further emphasized early in life when children are told to get good grades in school, and in adulthood through production requirements in the work environment.

The other part of the lie has to do with believing what other people say that we are. McGee goes on to say that to get out of this dilemma, people must see themselves the way God sees them, having great worth and value. In fact, we need to believe the famous verse, "For God so loved the world that He gave His only begotten Son, that whoever believes in Him should not perish but have everlasting life" (John 3:16 NKJV). Jesus referred to us as brothers and sisters (Hebrews 2:11–15). He said that we would be joint heirs with Him (Romans 8:17) and that we would do greater things than He did (John 14:12). Either we believe that or we do not. If not, then we have missed the message of the gospel. Are these verses talking about something or someone of little value? The problem, of course, is that when people have not resolved their own issues, they tend to devalue who they are; they often let their unresolved difficulties get in the way, not only of ourselves, but also of our relationship with God.

The first step to forgiveness is honesty about one's feelings, acknowledging the hate and anger. In some sense, this step might be referred to as spiritual surgery, because it entails shining light into the malignant places of one's life. Trying to hurry up the process so that clients can get to the place of forgiving those who have brutalized and hurt them is one of the easiest ways to short-circuit the healing process. No one forgives by trying; it is futile. If forgiveness of others is to be part of healing, it will take place only when the client has gone through all the stages of "remembering, grief, anger, and moving on; it is not the grand prize—it is only a byproduct."[247] If forgiveness of those who perpetrate against someone does come about, it is important that the focus of the forgiveness be for the sake of the victim. The client cannot absolve others for what those people have done in the client's life. Those other people must own personal responsibility and make amends for themselves. We can only deal with our own pain; the perpetrators will need to work through theirs and come to a place where they not only resolve their difficulties but also, possibly, forgive themselves. I agree with Bass and Davis when they say:[248]

> The only forgiveness that is essential is for yourself. You must forgive yourself for having needed, for having been small. You must forgive yourself for coping the best you could ... you must forgive yourself for the limitations you've lived with as an adult. You must forgive yourself for repeating your victimization, for not knowing how to protect your own children, or for abusing others. You must forgive yourself for needing time to heal now, and you must give yourself, as generously as you can, all your compassion, and understanding so that you can direct your attention and energy toward your own healing. This forgiveness is what is essential [to healing].

Jesus' mission, in reductionistic terms, was to set us free from our bondage and return us to our right relationship with God. But before we can truly have a right relationship with God, we must be free of that bondage. Forgiveness of self becomes essential for opening up to the possibilities of what God has in store for us. Until that time, we remain in bondage.

> Several years ago, Rhonda, a woman in her mid-thirties, presented in therapy describing significant sexual abuse she had endured from her father. She believed that her sexual abuse extended as far back as three years old but did not have any conscious memory of abuse until she was seven. She related that it started with "games" that her father would play with her such as, "what am I touching, where am I touching, how far in am I touching." It included roughhousing and massage, which over time included genital touching as her father taught her to manually masturbate him and to perform oral sex. This continued until she was nine, when one day her mother walked in and saw what was happening. Rhonda had no recollection of anything directly happening to her, except that there was coldness from her mother regarding any interactions between them. The sessions with her father stopped abruptly, with no discussion or explanation. At age twelve, her mother passed away of cancer, and shortly afterward, her father began to play the "games" all over again. By the time she was thirteen, she had become a sexual surrogate and replaced her mother in her father's bed.
>
> When she was fifteen, Rhonda told some of the story to a close friend, who immediately told their parents, who in turn called Child Protection. Rhonda was removed from the home, and her father was arrested and subsequently convicted of sexual child abuse. Rhonda had carried the guilt of her father's arrest for fifteen years and, during the course of therapy, was coming to terms with what had been done to her. She truly believed that she had in some ways been seductive to her father, blaming herself for anything that had happened, as well as for her mother's scorn.
>
> It took many sessions and months of therapy for her to see herself at various ages and stages of her life, both in early childhood and in adolescence. Eventually, Rhonda came to see that the responsibility for the behavior was not hers but her father's, and to understand that it was because of her father's lack of boundaries and utter disregard for her as a person that she became her father's sexual object and, eventually, his love interest. She realized how it had distorted her perceptions

> about relationships. She was able to deal with the many repressed emotions related to self-blame and guilt, and to mourn the loss of both her father and her childhood. At that point, with Rhonda as the adult having compassion for herself at the ages of seven, ten, eleven, and fifteen, she was able to forgive the child(ren) for simply having been in the situation, for coping in the best ways she knew how, and for enjoying to some degree the love and attention her father gave her. The child part of her was able to forgive the adult self for the prior condemnation and waiting so long to be rescued.

SELF-ESTEEM: CHANGING INTERNAL MESSAGES

Therapists need to help clients change the internal messages that affect their self-esteem. Victims of abuse and trafficking carry internal messages that have been repeated and reinforced, often for decades—for most of their lives, especially if the abuse began in early childhood. The unyielding negativity of such messages, which may have first come from significant adults, would be difficult to resist:

"I hate myself."

"I don't deserve it."

"I can't do it."

"It has to be perfect, or else I have failed."

"Whatever I do will never be enough."

"It's not even worth trying."

"What I want doesn't count."

All kinds of messages feed into the cognitive distortions of survivors, and these messages have to be unraveled and come to a place of resolution. I do this unravelling formally, almost ceremonially, when I work with clients, because I want it to be clear. Often, more conflict or issues come up when people are internally confronting whether they forgive themselves: "I can't totally forgive myself because of...." When that happens, it is the signal that there is more to work on.

I like this short story, especially in relation to sexual trauma, because it illustrates what therapy is about. Portia Nelson wrote a piece, "Autobiography in Five Short Chapters," about her take on self-esteem and personal power.[249] In the poem, the narrator progresses from repeatedly falling into a deep hole in the sidewalk, at which she expresses helplessness and struggles to get out, to taking responsibility for the habit and getting out quickly, to choosing to walk down a different street.

That is the essence of therapy. It illustrates what people need to do to change their focus about who they are, saying, "I have the capacity to make changes that take me in another direction."

CREATING A POSITIVE SELF-IMAGE

We have to work with clients, especially those who have suffered sexual trauma and trafficking, to create a positive self-image. When standing in the new place of having forgiven oneself and having acknowledged God's healing forgiveness, it is time to create the next phase of life deliberately—on purpose. A positive self-image opens the door to a life that is not merely driven by circumstances; it is above and beyond merely existing and struggling to get through yet another day. It means standing on the threshold of living a brilliant life. Sometimes, even a change on the outside can contribute to an improvement on the inside.[250]

> When Annie had felt down in the dumps for days on end, she finally called a friend. The friend advised her, "Walk out the door, buy some new underwear, and get your hair color touched up. Then take yourself for lunch at a nice restaurant and smile at everyone." Annie followed directions and was treated like a queen by the wait staff, both male and female, strangers who responded to the woman they saw. For Annie, it was an eye-opener.

Live for Yourself

Survivors need to learn how to make choices and live for themselves. They have been "doing" for everybody else for most of their lives—their traffickers, their pimps, or their parents. They have been doing, doing, doing, in order to survive.

Do Things You Are Proud Of

It is time survivors get a turn—that they make choices in favor of themselves and live for themselves, doing things of which they are proud. For some clients, cleaning the bedroom is a monumental task. Getting one's own room clean can be a substantial source of pride. Clients who are terrific chefs can bake a cake or a gourmet meal. If they are gardeners, they can attack the weeds and plant some posies.

Affirmations

Affirmations can help change self-image, too. Just as when extinguishing old behavior or establishing a new habit or way of being, it takes about twenty-eight days for affirmations to make a difference. If clients repeat them over and over, the messages will sink in and begin to make a difference in the realm of changing behavior. The idea is to select a new affirmation every month (*not* every week), one that comforts and heals a new place or an old sore spot. I have clients stick messages on the dashboard in the car, on their mirrors, and on the window above the kitchen sink. Some examples include:

- "I am capable of being loved."
- "I can learn to think for myself."
- "I can learn to make choices for myself."
- "I love and approve of myself."
- "I trust myself."
- "I matter, and what I have to offer this world also matters."
- "I forgive myself for all the mistakes I have made."
- "Wonderful things unfold before me."
- "I have a deep well of resources within myself."
- "I trust myself to make the best decision for me."
- "I choose friends who love me and approve of me."
- "I surround myself with people who treat me well."

Rachel, married and in her mid-twenties, felt ugly and incompetent. Every day, she woke up to thoughts of "I'm not good enough," "I'm ugly," and "I'll never get it right." At the suggestion of a friend, she began writing affirmations on index cards, which she then taped to her bathroom mirror, a place she would see several times a day—most significantly, early in the morning and just before she retired for the evening.

A variety of affirmations came and went over time. Her abusive husband sometimes even threw them in the trash, but Rachel retrieved or rewrote them. Over time, her self-esteem improved and, with the help of her therapist, she ended the marriage and went on to live a healthier, happier life.

Self-Care

This is also the time to begin building a list of self-care activities, things clients can do for themselves. These activities are often as simple as lighting a candle, offering a prayer of thanksgiving, making a cup of tea, or walking out the door for a breath of fresh air and a new look at God's creation. Clients could phone a friend, write a love letter, reread a favorite book, or watch a favorite video. When learning new behavior or when under stress, sometimes the challenge is simply to remember what they *can* do, which is when a self-care list can come in handy. Encourage them to write down what they think they can do to help themselves feel better; they may add to this list over time. When they need a lift, they can refer to the list and pick something. Most rewarding self-care activities cost little, if anything. The options are endless. Here are a few suggestions for clients:

- "Surround yourself with colors and art and lush fabrics that you find comforting."[251]
- "Wear clothing and colors that make you feel good, on which you get compliments."
- "Go for a swing in the park. Take along the family dog and watch how he or she explores."
- "Spend time with, by, or in water. Take a fragrant, candlelit bath, or go to the beach and enjoy floating weightlessly."[252]
- "Lie on the ground and look up at blue sky through the green leaves. Look for shapes in clouds."
- "Cultivate the skill of using music as a mood maker and a mood breaker. Sometimes it is highly appropriate to indulge in a good cry. Once that's

finished, put on some music that is uplifting, perhaps tunes that make the feet want to start moving—and dance![253] Surrender to the sheer pleasure of movement simply because you want to. Sing. Shout!"

- "Take naps."

Visualizations

Teach clients about visualizing safe places. Encourage clients to visualize being in beautiful settings (in a cozy lodge when it is snowing outside, walking through the forest surrounded by birdsong and gentle breezes, sitting beside a babbling brook, etc.). It can be something real, like a room somewhere (parents' room, grandmother's room, bedroom, etc.), a retreat center, or a place where they vacationed. It could also be an imaginary place. My safe place is a beach I created in my imagination a long time ago in different exercises. It is a beach in the Mediterranean on a bright, sunny day, with no clouds in the sky and no bugs. I am the only one on the island; it is well stocked with food, and I am well taken care of. A client can visualize the ideal life, as he or she wants to live it, in a safe place surrounded by people who are learning who the client is and who care about him or her.

Accentuate the Positive

Always accentuate the positive. Encourage clients to consciously choose to think about the good things in, and about, life. For many, keeping a gratitude journal is an eye-opener. The practice is designed to slow people down long enough to take stock of what they have to be thankful for, like a sunny day or rain on the dry grass. For an asthmatic, air might go on the list; for an athlete, a body that performs well; for a scholar, an inquiring mind. Every day, clients can look for new and different positive things for which to be thankful.

Find a Task

It is helpful for clients to find tasks that let them see their progress. For instance, when doing laundry, one starts with a pile of dirty clothes. After washing, drying, and folding the laundry, the rewards include stacks of neatly folded, clean-smelling clothing. When clients paint something, the reward is likewise immediate.

Take Breaks

Clients should remember to take breaks. It is rarely necessary to work fourteen hours in a row. Even the government requires that workers be given a break every few hours! A client may try setting an alarm as a reminder to get up and stretch, find something to eat or drink, and look at different scenery. If clients are stuck in a cubicle at work, they can put up lovely pictures that speak to their soul. These pictures should allow clients to rest your eyes and get an internal lift—images that feed their soul, like a serene lake with mountains in the background, kittens or puppies at play, woodlands, or cityscapes. When working with one survivor, I recommended that she take a candlelit bath. The thirty-year-old woman had never done that before. She described the experience thus: "Amazing! I played a little music, locked the door, tuned out everything else. I stayed in there for thirty minutes—and I have done it three more times since then."

Volunteer

> Eva, a woman in her late fifties, suffered from depression, especially around the holiday season annually. Rather than rely solely on medication, her therapist told her to walk out the front door and find someone to help. From that year forward, she volunteered at various soup kitchens and other ministries that helped the homeless, which helped her get through the holidays. When she shifted to helping in some capacity all year round, the depression with which she had struggled was no longer an issue.
>
> When an elderly woman's depression did not yield to therapy and medication, the therapist asked if he could meet with her at her home. When he walked in the door, he discovered that every room in the house was graced with prize-winning African violets. Once she had mastered propagation, her collection grew. The therapist, who was also her minister, proposed an unorthodox course of treatment, to which she reluctantly agreed. She took on the responsibility for providing every shut-in, every church member in hospital, and every person on the prayer list with one of her African violets. To no one's surprise but her own, the depression lifted and she soon became an active, productive member of the community.

The HEART Model

Lower Self-Protective Walls

Self-protection is often viewed or described as building walls around the self in order to keep out the bad things as much as possible.[254] Unfortunately, those walls also keep out the good things. Worse yet, the antiquated structures, useful when they were erected, later tend to function like prison walls, keeping healthy self-expression walled in.[255] Part of improving one's self-image involves lowering the self-protective walls enough for God's love and light to penetrate, often in the form of unexpected kindness from friends or strangers. It also allows the space to step outside the old, familiar confines of secrecy, shame, and self-protection. At first, some people find they can take only short trips out into the sunlight of freedom and forgiveness, but those first few, halting, unfamiliar steps are a preamble to deeper healing. Creating a positive self-image has immediate rewards. For what may be the first time, it is the chance—the opportunity and the imperative—to live for oneself.[256]

When dealing with DID clients, the first five parts or stages of the process can take years, because it is a matter of going through things, working things out, negotiating, and gathering up the various pieces of self. The process can be long and tedious. For other clients, the same ground might be covered in a session or two. Up to this point, the goal has been to get to a place where there is nothing untoward—and, therefore, no conflict—going on between the adult and the child parts.

At this stage of forgiveness, I perform a ritual. I ask the child if he or she can forgive the adult, even for nothing more than waiting all this time to come around. Often, people will balk at the internal forgiveness ("I don't have anything to forgive"). Then I go the other way: "Can you forgive the child, even for just being in the situation?" If the answer is "yes," then that stage has been completed. If the answer is "no," then it means there is more conflict and more to work out. I ask what is in the way, or what is keeping the process from moving forward. At the point of forgiveness, the client accepts, "We really do not need to be separate from each other, because we *are* each other"; then, it is time to move on to Stage Six, bringing those split parts together.

Chapter Five Notes

CHAPTER SIX

Awareness of God and Processing Possible Distortions of God

Persons who have accepted Jesus as their Lord and Savior are regenerated in spirit (Titus 3:5; John 3:3, 3:7), yet they still experience carnal attachments in their souls (comprising the mind, will, and emotions) and bodies. Our souls must go through a continual and gradual process of salvation as we grow in Christ and continue in the word of God toward maturity. This is what the apostle Paul meant when he said, to "work out [our] own salvation" (Philippians 2:12 NKJV). The working out of our own salvation—the reordering of our disordered carnal desires, which are constantly pulling us away from God—is a process. Our regenerated spirit seeks to do good, the will of God, yet our flesh (the mind, will and emotions of our soul nature) wars against our spirit, as Paul so aptly described in Romans 7:22–23: "For I delight in the law of God according to the inward man. But I see another law in my members [my flesh, i.e., soul and body], warring against the law of my mind [spirit], and bringing me into captivity to the law of sin which is in my members" (NKJV).

SPIRIT, SOUL, AND BODY

So, although our spirit is saved through our belief, our soul undergoes a process of purification. (Some denominations will discuss this as "working out salvation"; it is my belief that salvation is a gift from God and does not need to be "worked out" to be effective, though we come to a place where we willfully want more of what God has for us and move ourselves more in line with God's truth). In other words, our spirit is saved, our soul is being saved, and our physical body will be saved. In the end, when we receive the glorified body promised to all believers, we come into the fullness of this concept (1 Corinthians 15: 35–44). Until then, our spirit is continually battling with our soul, even as we eagerly await the redemption of the body (Romans 8:23). True wholeness, then, is the combination of the spiritual, the psychological, and the physical and its completed healing.

Gall, Basque, Demasceno-Scott, and Vardy (2007) reviewed completed questionnaires from a sample of 101 men and women who were survivors of sexual abuse.[257] The instrument involved looking at the survivors' relationship with God. Results indicated that a relationship with a benevolent God is related to the experience of a less negative mood and a greater sense of personal growth and resolution of the impact of abuse. An additional benefit is that being in relationship with a benevolent God correlates with self-acceptance and hope. These findings are consistent and seem to indicate a progression in salvation.[258] True wholeness cannot come unless every part of our make-up is addressed. Just as the dissociative disordered client cannot be integrated unless each personality (alter) is addressed in some way, so it is with any of us: we cannot experience true fulfillment and completeness (wholeness) if the needs of our body *and* our soul are not met. Paul understood this when he wrote: "May your whole spirit, soul and body be kept blameless at the coming of our Lord Jesus Christ. The one who calls you is faithful, and he will do it" (1 Thessalonians 5:23b–24 NIV).

Though many try to separate the soul and mind from their spiritual needs, I believe it is a delusion to think that such separation can succeed. The spirit is the part of us that is most often neglected; this is why, I believe, many people attempt to fill the empty space in their beings with drugs, alcohol, sex, romance, money, fame, and countless other things, which can never quite fill the void. Only the spiritual can fill our spirits. Some might believe that they really do not need God—that all they need is good health, love from family and friends (to satisfy their emotional, or soulish, needs), financial security, accomplishment of their goals, and comforts (to satisfy their emotional and intellectual needs). They nourish their bodies and souls but neglect their spirits. The other extreme is to super-spiritualize everything without taking care of the needs of the body and soul. Either extreme is out of balance.

Just as one cannot truly separate the Trinity of God, one cannot truly separate the human body from the soul and spirit. If the mind or the heart is sick, it shows up in the body. Likewise, if the body is sick, it usually affects the emotions, mind (soul), and spirit. If one's spirit is oppressed daily, this tends to show up somewhere in the body or in one's mental well-being. The truth is that few of us put much thought into maintaining total health of the body, soul, and spirit.

Our souls must go through a continual and gradual process of spiritual maturing as we grow in Christ and continue in the word of God. I believe that God wants us to know how to minister effectively and operate in the threefold-ness of our nature. The proper balance of this threefold nature of body, soul, and spirit starts with becoming aware of God's presence, with us and around us, at all times. Many people give lip service to believing in God, but to truly have an awareness of God's ongoing presence can be a striking and startling change. This awareness is called contemplative prayer.

Contemplative prayer has been around for a long time.[259] Benedictine monks a couple hundred years after Christ started this technique in order to improve their awareness of God's presence and, eventually, to facilitate direct dialogue. That is, they expected to hear answers directly from God's voice—from thoughts entered into, or confirmation from others in addition to direct personal experiences, shortly after asking questions. It was certainly used in the Middle Ages by monks, priests, and religious leaders striving to experience a deeper walk with God.[260] Ambrose and Augustine, in the fourth century, spoke about talking with God and deepening the walk and relationship with the Spirit of God. Bonaventure, in the thirteenth century, focused on contemplative prayer, and in modern times, the Linn brothers spoke about the deeper walk by truly knowing God.[261]

The practice of contemplative prayer involves simply being aware of God's presence in your immediate consciousness and allowing yourself to do nothing—that is, no prayer, no pleadings, no well-crafted words, but simply experiencing God's presence for a period of time. This experience can be unnerving to some people, because many of us are churched to believe that our interaction with God is mostly one-way, person to God, and relies on one's intentions, thoughts, and statements.

> Ten years ago, I worked with Abby, who was a forty-two-year-old female dealing with issues of early childhood sexual abuse and adult prostitution. She was an avid church attendee (Baptist) who had great difficulties experiencing and expressing a personal connection to God. The abuse that she received in childhood was from a pastor in her Sunday school class, and she had always associated God with the abuse she suffered in the church.
>
> I introduced her to what I call "practicing the presence of God," that is, allowing oneself to sit and be in the presence of God without the need to do anything

outward. This type of prayer proved to be difficult for Abby, because she was so used to upward prayer and asking God for things needed in her life. During sessions, I reminded her that Scripture states, when two or more are gathered, God is in the midst (Matthew 18:20), and I asked her if we could agree that this was true. She replied that this was absolutely true, and went on to recall numerous times she had prayed with friends and others for a wide variety of situations and illnesses. I simply asked her to close her eyes and be aware of God's presence in the room with the two of us, and when she felt or sensed something, to describe it to me.

Abby started by telling me she felt a warmth in the room that was familiar and comfortable to her and that with her eyes closed, she could sense a light in the distance. I asked her if she could allow that light, warmth, and comfort to move close to her. When she told me that she could, I asked her to allow herself to sit there for a few moments in God's presence, sensing or feeling what God might have to say or emanate toward her. This simple exercise proved to be quite difficult in that she kept wanting to pray out loud, to which I responded by reminding her to sit and be still. Following this brief exercise, I asked her about her experience, to which she replied that "the most difficult part was remaining quiet." She felt she needed to explain to God all the things that were wrong and out of place, in an attempt to win favor.

The constraints of the exercise, and not being allowed to voice these concerns, forced her to experience God in a new and somewhat frightening way. She did not expect care, love, and warmth. She did not expect light; she expected darkness. It would take many more sessions for her to embrace fully the concept of God as warm and loving without her needing to perform or vocalize anything. Simply being in the presence of God, over time, allowed her to hear God's voice "speaking" to her.

The practice of being in God's presence allows for a unique inner experience and serves as an opportunity for God to speak to us directly if we allow it. Murray-Swank and Pargament have shown that clients searching after God can have that experience enhanced through spiritual interventions integrated with therapeutic content.[262]

AWARENESS OF THE PRESENCE OF GOD

Becoming aware of God's presence on a real, tangible level is something many Christians take for granted. I believe that people who are searching for God, or who have lost their faith and are trying to find their way back, often look everywhere to find what they do not have. This drive is sometimes spurred by spiritual curiosity or insight, but more often than not, it comes out of a place of need, hurt, and looking to God for completion. Sometimes, we as counselors see beyond the immediate surface to a deeper level of soul issues. However, only God can see the deepest, most buried emotions and issues and touch those hidden places to bring healing and restoration.

As a counselor, if you are hesitant to bring up spiritual issues, please note that many clients look for and desire therapists who demonstrate a knowledge of spiritual matters and who can weave spiritual and psychological issues together. Marsh and Low have made a case for the importance of working with religious material psychotherapeutically while at the same time being attentive to the pitfalls that may arise in doing so.[263] Often, clients themselves sense a need to address the spiritual side of things.[264] The Bible reminds us that everyone has a deeper knowledge of God, even though some "[do] not like to retain God in their knowledge" (Romans 1:28 KJV). Each of us is born with an innate awareness of God and the spiritual side of life.[265]

It is by going through the hurts, the issues, and the pain—not by going around them or walking the other way—that healing occurs. The Bible refers to memory over 250 times. *Memory* denotes whole actions: for instance, remembering the Sabbath Day and keeping it holy; and, remembering the Lord our God. Remembering the Sabbath Day, for most of us, is remembering to get up, get dressed, and go to church. For some, it may involve getting up earlier to attend a Sunday school class before the hour-and-a-half church service. Remembering the Sabbath day in biblical times was much different. It entailed cleaning the house thoroughly the day before so not even a crumb could be found. It meant cooking a meal the day before and having it set out already. It meant having clothes laid out the day before so that all attention could be on enjoying God and family. It was utilizing all five senses to experience the creation and all that God had given.

The same can be true for remembering the Lord our God. This is not just a remembrance of prayer, but of making time for God, seeing God in others, pondering the enormity of who God is, and trying to conceptualize our relationship with God. Remembrance takes in all of who God is, the totality of the whole.

DISTORTIONS OF GOD

The problem for many clients, however, is their negative image of God and particularly, their image of God the Father. This is an especially difficult issue with survivors of severe trauma and sexual abuse. Many clients falsely relate their traumatic experience with their concept of God. Reinert and Edwards have explored this dynamic by looking at attachment theory: the relationship of verbal, physical, and sexual mistreatment to attachments to God and to concepts of God.[266] They found that each form of mistreatment was related adversely to religious measures, but that attachment to parents mediated the relationship between maltreatment variables (verbal and physical mistreatment), attachment to God, and the concept of God as loving or distant. Attachment to parents, however, did not mediate the relationship between attachment to God and sexual abuse. Sexual abuse was strongly related to difficulties with attachment to God and one's concept of God, regardless of one's quality of attachment to one's parents.

Our view of God is often mediated by our personal experiences, particularly those in childhood. Allowing ourselves to be in God's presence can also bring up our negative feelings about God, our relationship with God, and our image of God. These factors will be addressed in the next section.

Luethje claims we have what may be called a sixth sense that allows us to intuit or discern a presence.[267] Have you ever walked into a room and started to feel uneasy, later to find out that there had been an argument or disruption of some sort in that space? In the same way, says Luethje, we can sense or know the presence of God: we feel, emote, and connect, and it goes beyond words. That connection often brings up distortions of the image of God. These distortions come into play and often create tremendous turmoil, confusion, and frustration.[268] They were created and continue to be perpetrated by unhealthy interpersonal relationships, especially those that occurred during the early developmental years of childhood and adolescence. It is here that we confuse or equate "my father who abused me" with "my God who allowed me to be abused," or worse yet, "God, who abused me."[269]

Again, until we have a mental picture of God, as we understand Him to be, as truly good, healing, and gracious, there can be no lasting victory in our lives.[270] Tragic experiences result in our projecting that others, ourselves, or God will do the same. Out of this, we often choose bitterness, resentment, and disobedience regarding the development of our higher or spiritual self. By confronting God Himself, and the distortions, we can correct the false premise and begin to allow God's Spirit (the Holy Spirit) to assume His biblical role of paraclete. *Paraclete*, literally translated, means "the one called to be alongside of";[271] in other words, the Holy Spirit is called to be alongside of us, as a helper (John 15:26 ESV). A literal translation of the Greek word for *help* (e.g., in Romans 8:26), is "to take hold of [with] on the other side."[272] When we put this together, we learn that the Holy Spirit is the one to walk alongside of us and help us carry our burden. This is why it is so important to move through this process with God: so that the work is complete.

Our failure to trust and love God stems from a picture or concept of God as unlovable or untrustworthy. Our anger, therefore, is not really at God, but at our wrong concept and perceptions of God. Our pictures or perceptions determine how we act. Yet, many of us have developed our concept, vision, or image of God out of Hollywood.[273]

For instance, my first exposure to God was a movie based on an Old Testament story about the hand of God moving and writing on a wall. It did a wonderful job depicting this huge hand that appears and, with a finger of fire, writes Hebrew on the wall. It scared the living heck out of me! I was impressed with the awesome being who could just appear like that. The second reinforcement of my concept of God came in the movie *The Ten Commandments*, in which Charlton Heston as Moses stands by the burning bush, yet nothing is consumed by the fire. Later on in the film, this fire—this power—comes down from heaven and carves out the stone tablets bearing the Ten Commandments.[274] It spoke to me of a God who is awesome and powerful and mighty. I figured God was watching everything I was doing and taking note of everything I was doing wrong. That was my childhood image of God.

At a certain stage in therapy, a client must address his or her distortions of God. Many people have barriers that prevent them from believing in God or even acknowledging spiritual things. Sometimes the barriers have risen through painful experiences, learned attitudes, or reactive feelings, which can create cognitive distortions of the truth. These distortions come into play and often create tremendous turmoil, confusion, and frustration.[275]

As mentioned above, those who have suffered abuse or other kinds of trauma are especially prone to having a distorted belief about God.[276] Clients have sometimes distorted "my father who abused me" into "God, the father who raped me." Or, "my friend [my brother, my mother, etc.] who died" gets distorted into "God, who killed or allowed my friend [my brother, my mother, etc.] to die." I agree with David Seamands when he emphatically states, "Until we have a mental picture of God as truly good, healing, and gracious, there can be no lasting spiritual victory in our lives." [277]

The Heart Model

There are many ways in which we distort the concept of God away from love, His true essence. These distortions were created, and continue to be perpetrated, by unhealthy interpersonal relationships, particularly those that occurred during the early developmental years of childhood and adolescence. The original outside influence becomes a life pattern that shapes the way we see others, ourselves, God, and life itself. Out of this, we often choose bitterness, resentment, and disobedience regarding the development of our relationship with God.

We will be considering different aspects of distortions of God, and our presuppositions about God; then, we will move into a way of having a relationship and connecting with Him. More importantly, we will consider how to help our clients into a relationship with God in such a way that they can start to build trust in God from a framework that is not just "pie in the sky when you die." Faith in God is not just theoretical, or just something learned or heard in church. It is directly connecting with the Holy Spirit in such a way as to allow the Spirit to begin functioning as *paraclete* by confronting distortions of God.

Seamands has shown that one's image of God, as either a controlling or non-controlling entity, moderates the affective response to thinking about God. In particular, people who had a highly controlling image of God had a negative affective reaction when thinking about God. As Seamands explains, some common distortions about God include:[278]

- *Demanding/Domineering God.* The underlying message is that God is untrustworthy and accepts me only when I measure up. Rather than a nurturing parent, God is seen as critical and unpleasant. God is viewed as a cruel task master with an iron rod.

- *Legal God.* This version is one who keeps a constant accounting of wrongs as a scorekeeper, as if on a ledger.

- *Gotcha God.* This God is always watching for failure. He is expecting us to fall down and not to follow through as we should. God is seen as an austere, legalistic parent ready to condemn whenever we do not do or act the way we believe God wants us to.

- *Sitting Bull God.* He is off on a cloud somewhere, not involved in human life or existence. God is a sugar-coated nice guy who would never hurt a fly, no matter what (making Him powerless and shaped to one's desires).

- *Philosopher God.* He has long hair and a white beard and is off in a study somewhere, with all knowledge at His disposal. God is believed to be too far away to access or too disinterested to care.
- *Pharaoh God.* An unpleasant taskmaster, this God. The message to us mere mortals is that we should measure up, or else we will suffer (even more) dire consequences. God is seen in light of parental figures who have abused us, and we believe that He will treat us in the same way (i.e., "God only wants to hurt me"; "God never lets me have anything I want, and whenever I get close to it, He takes it away!").

This is by no means an exhaustive list of distorted concepts; these are merely some of the most common distortions. A benevolent conceptualization of God has been found to create a sense of greater spiritual well-being, while acting independently from God relates directly to a decrease in our sense of spiritual well-being.[279] Most people are limited by how they view God in their heart. If they have experienced rigid religion based on roles, rules, and regulations rather than having an interactive relationship with God, they will likely have barriers to work through with God. If people have experienced some kind of abuse at the hands of a parent (especially a father, or father figure), their concept of God as Father is typically tainted by that experience. Many times, the mere thought of going to another father figure and making themselves vulnerable to Him is more than they can bear. Inwardly, they have not realized that their heavenly Father will not harm them the way their earthly father did or does. What we have experienced in earthly relationships, and at the hands of authority figures and institutions, often shadows our concept of God.

Many people set up barriers to access God because they are afraid of feeling guilty if they acknowledge Him. Some are angry and resentful toward God for allowing so many bad things to happen to them. Often, they blame God for everything that has gone wrong in their lives, as revealed in the question, "How could a loving God let that happen?" Other barriers to a belief in God are set up by a personal spirituality that includes negative aspects. Common negative aspects include the following:

- Feeling guilt about past actions
- Seeing God as judge or scorekeeper
- Being angry or resentful at God for what others have done

The HEART Model

- Holding a rigid sense of roles about religion
- Being unable to forgive (this might include self, others, or God Himself)
- Using spirituality only in emergencies
- Feeling unworthy
- Isolating oneself from others

There are some people who refuse to acknowledge God because they are clinging to bitterness and do not want to forgive those who have hurt them. Others feel unworthy to communicate with God or to connect with Him. Still others use spirituality for emergencies (as in "foxhole Christianity") because they think of Him as being too busy for perceived trivialities, or because they simply don't think of Him at any other time. Even those who claim to dismiss God or intellectually reason Him away are often simply avoiding emotional and intense realities. Theological doubts typically come from unhealed emotional hurts inside. It is often less painful to nurse the doubt than to face the pain of whatever traumatic event triggered the doubt. Those who have experienced trauma or abuse also tend to have a sense of alienation from God. These people experience distance from God and more frequent religious doubting.[280] Other people may strive to believe in God deep down, but they are also afraid to risk the pain of being disappointed. Being let down is often based on their previous experiences of having hopes and beliefs dashed or discounted by other authority figures, or by persons who have deep meaning in their lives.

> Sheryl is a thirty-two-year-old mother of three who grew up in an Assemblies of God church in the country of Nicaragua. Local culture strongly emphasized honoring your mother and father and seeing God as an extension of an earthly father. Sheryl's father had a considerable problem with alcohol and was subject to tyrannical rampages when inebriated. Nothing she ever did was right, nor could she please her father, especially when he was intoxicated.
>
> When she was asked in session to be aware of God's presence, she reported that He was extremely distant, though present, with considerable dark space between Him and her. Upon closer questioning and exploration, she explained that she had not prayed to God in quite some time and had a number of personal issues

> she had not quite reconciled. She believed that for her and God to be close, not only did these things need to be resolved, but also her spiritual life needed to be reignited and rekindled.
>
> When asked how she viewed God, she replied that she saw God as a supreme being who kept account of all things done wrong and that He could be pleased with her only if everything were perfect in her life. She recognized in the session how illogical perfection was, but explained that the only time her father would give her positive attention (especially when drunk) was when everything was in its place and the home looked "perfect." It took a number of sessions for Sheryl to realize that her image of God was based on her image of her earthly father and for her to begin to distinguish her image of God from the image of her father.

Cognitive distortions of God often take months, and sometimes years, to correct in the therapeutic process, and they have varying effects on outcomes. Cheston, Piedmont, Eanes, and Patrice have been able to show that counseled clients are able to see significant reduction in psychological symptoms over the course of treatment when they have a positive image of God.[281] Bringing ourselves into a right relationship with God often means confronting our distorted concepts of Him, and a right relationship with God means seeing Him as benevolent, with this conception being mediated through pathways of hope and self-acceptance.[282]

In fact, our earlier childhood images of God often dictate the way we will see Him as we get older. Kwon has argued that to understand one's images of God, one must consider the relationship between the mental images constructed prior to the acquisition of language, as well as the cultural constructs that are collectively represented, and symbolically embodied, through the use of language.[283] We may be taught that God is a God of love, tenderness, justice, and purity, but the inner wounds and misconceptions in our hearts may tell us something very different. If, for instance, someone had a father who wasn't ever happy with anything she did, no matter how hard she tried, she would either not bother to try at all or might endlessly try to please God, never feeling as though she had done enough for Him or had been good enough to receive His love and acceptance. Or, if someone's father was distant or preoccupied, she may begin to think of God in the same way. If her father never had the time of day for her, why should she think that God does? All of these scenarios can easily color a person's ability to confidently ask God for anything.

The HEART Model

I think it is important to realize that not everyone can trust in the same measure. We are all given, at birth, the same measure of faith to start with (Romans 12:3), but not everyone ends up in the same place of faith as adults. Our different experiences either encourage or prevent the ability to trust, and our different personalities respond in different ways to what happens in life.

Children begin with an innate ability to trust. This is natural for them, and apart from trauma, they would not form all the hindrances to faith that many people have as adults. Jesus said, in Matthew 18:3, that we need to become as little children in order to enter the kingdom of heaven. Children are natural believers. They often believe in their parents and believe that their parents will always be there for them. If the parents are religiously oriented, the children learn to believe in God as their creator. The hearts of little children are far less contaminated than the wounded, skeptical, overburdened hearts of adults.

Only when influences come into children's lives that block their ability to believe do they begin to distance themselves from anything spiritual and from God. If little children are continually betrayed by those in whom they put their trust, their heart will eventually form layer after layer of mistrust and doubt. The more someone is wounded and betrayed, the harder it becomes to trust.

> Eileen, a pastor's wife, had been married for fifteen years and had two children. Early in the therapy process, Eileen revealed that she had been raped by an uncle around the age of ten and sold into prostitution at age fifteen. This uncle was her father's brother and very involved in the family. When relating the story, she indicated that she had been sexually abused over a period of two to three years, as she was often with him.
>
> During the counseling session a year later, she experienced an abreaction (reliving the experience) during which she was able to visualize an incident in a garage near the family home when her uncle sexually penetrated her. She was able to visualize his face, what he was wearing, and the smells in the garage, but fixated on a gold cross he was wearing. In the midst of this abreaction, she suddenly sat up and opened her eyes, stating that it wasn't God at all but her uncle who had raped her.
>
> When I probed further, she indicated that she had always blamed God for the rape, especially because God never came and rescued her. She also blamed God for not rescuing her from her brief life in prostitution. She realized that it was her

> fixation on the cross her uncle had worn that led her to the conclusion God had raped her. That same fixation on the cross led her to hold onto the misguided notion that God had sold her into slavery. Several sessions later, Eileen was able to connect with God in a way that was neither punitive nor abusive, and a process began that led her to a deeper spiritual reality and closeness with God.

If a young girl was sexually abused by her father, she will often have difficulty getting close to God as her Father. Even if she shows through her words and through intention that she understands God won't abuse her this way, an invisible barrier of fear and mistrust often exists, which she will need to confront and work through if she is to have a close relationship to Father God. There may be times in counseling when it is appropriate to encourage doubting clients and to pray like the man in Mark 9:24 (NKJV), "Help my unbelief," because "by grace are ye saved through faith; and that not of yourselves: it is the gift of God" (Ephesians 2:8 KJV). In other words, God offers the gift of faith.

WAYS TO PROCESS DISTORTED VIEWS OF GOD

As therapists, we have to address distortions in clients' view of God. For 20 percent to 30 percent of my clients, the distortion is resolved when we started talking about what God actually promises. God does not promise to rescue us from earthly suffering (2 Corinthians 12:8–10).[284] What God promises is to be there with us during those times (Romans 5, 8; 1 Peter 3:13–15).[285] For some of the people I work with, that was a complete paradigm shift. Prior to that time, they had always believed it was God's responsibility to remove them from bad situations, as in, "If God is in our lives, why didn't He intervene?" But God does not get in the way of free will, which includes the free will of people who think and perpetrate evil, because His doing so would make us puppets.[286] It would take away our ability to make choices. He does not get in the way of our decision making. We make choices about who we are, who we become, and what we do. The more we align with God's principles, the more we become Spirit-led or Spirit-directed in the process.[287] For many of the women who had suffered trauma, coming into that awareness was huge. They got it; they were able to make the shift and change the paradigm.

Spiritual issues in the therapy process can and sometimes do trigger criticism and suspicion from members of the professional community. Nevertheless, clients are often receptive to spiritual interventions and relieved to speak openly to someone about their spiritual experiences. They may have been afraid to tell anyone else about the spiritual experiences they have been through, believing that they may sound crazy to those who deny the spiritual realm.[288]

A counselor or therapist is one who brings guidance. A competent counselor does not resort to manipulation, condescension, or coercion; a caring and effective counselor or therapist demonstrates wisdom and insight, which benefits the one he or she counsels.[289] Though counselors may have insight and wisdom for those they counsel, it is not counselors' place to force treatment strategies or decisions upon those they counsel.[290] Rather, approaches and perspectives should be offered as options. Moreover, it is critical for therapists to stay out of theology, doctrine, and denominationalism.[291]

God is described in Isaiah 9:6 as a counselor who does not manipulate or control us. He does not counsel us in order to feel knowledgeable, needed, or empowered, and He does not need to. God already knows who He is. God does not pressure or condemn us, but simply holds out His hand of love and invites us to take it and receive His healing touch. He is the wisest and most skillful of all counselors, because He knows the exact pace to follow: when to press the issues, when to wait, when to confront, and when to comfort.[292] He is an ever-present listener, and it is up to us to make the choices about what He has to offer. To be aware of God is to allow God, as the Supreme Counselor, to work with our clients' issues and to watch transformations that often extend beyond our own work. Counseling, in and of itself, can do much to expose deep wounds and to help clients see how these wounds have affected their lives. Counseling can focus on and address areas that need changing in order for people to function more effectively in their lives.[293] Unless the wounds are healed, however, they remain open and subject to more wounding. It is God who can offer the final healing.[294]

When counseling those who are not ready to trust God, it is important to assure them that God is not angry with them because they do not trust Him. He is a God of compassion and understanding, He knows all that they have suffered, and He has seen it all while understanding why they have a distorted picture of Him or of Christianity. Rather than rejecting the client because of his or her mistrust, God is saddened by the false picture of Him, which keeps the client from knowing who He truly is. Much like the cognitive distortions outlined earlier regarding internal conflict, the cognitive distortions between self and God must also be addressed. Enmity and barriers between the self and God must be explored and confronted, but more importantly, they must be overcome for the process of inner healing to be effective and long-lasting.

Cognitive-behavioral interventions often help to limit the cognitive distortions that occur when an ego weakens under stress.[295] Metaphors are useful, particularly with a biblical reference, in addressing cognitive distortions in a person's image of God.[296] Turell and Thomas have explored the misogynistic context of Christianity, the role of women's suffering, and the mandate to forgive, finding the need to reframe these in a way that produces healing.[297] It is incumbent on techniques like the use of metaphor, cognitive-behavioral counseling, and forgiveness to address the issues that separate us from God. Such methods begin to open other avenues to resolve the aforementioned enmity regarding our relationship with God.[298]

Specifically, clients must reframe their image of God and find a way to let Him off the hook for not coming to their rescue. In much the same way that we have to forgive ourselves, I believe we must forgive God. When Exline, Yali, and Lobel looked at the issue of forgiving God for the negative events that one has experienced in life, they found that those who are unable to forgive God have a higher incidence of anxious and depressed mood.[299] Two psychological factors emerged as central in explaining the link between difficulty in forgiving God and emotion: (1) an angry disposition and (2) feelings of alienation from God. They also found that those who currently believe in God and forgive Him for a specific powerful, injurious incident have lower levels of anxious and depressed mood. These findings suggest that an unforgiving attitude toward God serves as a potent predictor of negative emotion.

Cognitive distortions of God are therefore dealt with by confronting the underlying issues that set them up in the first place. Not surprisingly, an examination of etiology, or causes, will often bring back painful memories. Confrontation along with basic theological reframing can be very useful. The answer to the question, "Why didn't God rescue me in the situation?" is that God never promised to rescue us from anything. However, He did promise always to be with us. He was with the client in the past, and He is with him or her now. The answer does not justify anything, but it reframes and realigns thought and, hopefully, leads to spiritual growth. Use of metaphor, cognitive behavioral counseling, dealing with our negative thoughts and feelings regarding God, realigning our view of God with biblical truth, dealing with our personal experiences, and forgiving God are all therapeutic vehicles to reframing cognitive distortions of God.

The bottom line is that it is necessary to forgive God for not being who the client expected Him to be: the rescuer. Self-forgiveness is likewise necessary. People can find through experience that love and acceptance of, and from, God is (and always has been) there. This Spirit of God therefore bears witness to and within their spirit. Allowing a sense of love, freedom, and forgiveness from the Divine allows them to solidify their self-forgiveness and offers them hope and freedom in the future—freedom from their distortions and from a contorted belief system.

Chapter Six Notes

CHAPTER SEVEN

Receiving Forgiveness from God

The seventh stage, having to do with receiving forgiveness from God, builds off of what has been set up in the last two chapters. We have come to a place where clients have been able to forgive self and to reframe distortions about God—mainly, their views of God that did not match their expectations. It becomes important to have clarity about the nature of God and how God interacts with people on a personal level. One of the things that I expressed in an earlier chapter was that people need to forgive themselves for being a doorway through which pain entered their life. If they haven't truly let themselves off the hook, how can they believe God will forgive them? Self-forgiveness doesn't render the need for God moot at all: in fact, if anything, it further highlights our need for God.

God's Perspective of Us

When I reflect on some of the models of forgiveness, particularly the one Everett Worthington has offered, I do not think God necessarily follows his two-step outline.[300] Worthington believes that step one focuses on God's intention to forgive and then step two concentrates on our feelings catching up to the process of forgiveness.[301] I believe God's intention all along was to be in fellowship with us and for our relationship with Him to mirror a companion—that is, God walking alongside of us. According to Robert McGee's wonderful book, *The Search for Significance*, people's sense of self-esteem often rests in how well they have performed and what others have said about them. McGee says that "we can't believe this Satanic lie because it's important to believe who God said we are. As Christians we have to get ahold of that concept—of who God *truly* says we are."[302]

Jesus referred to us as brothers and sisters. He says we are "joint heirs" with Him (Romans 8:17 NKJV) and that we will do greater things than He did (John 14:12). I often confront clients, sometimes even colleagues, with the question, "Do you believe you, along with the Holy Spirit, can or are doing greater things than Christ did?" If we do not believe it, then we do not really believe what the Bible says or who He says we are. Do we truly believe a vision of God in a side-by-side relationship with us, which is clearly what the Bible describes? *Do we really believe what the Bible says to us about who we are as children of God?*

I can tell you that this concept has made a huge difference in my life, both personally and professionally. I did work for Robert McGee's organization (RAPHA, Inc.) for several years, and I started to see myself walking alongside of Jesus, understanding that the Holy Spirit was there to be a companion. I began having the insight that the work I was doing was not simply good work but was, in fact, building God's kingdom here on earth. How we deal with others, how we conduct ourselves, and how we conduct business has everything to do with understanding the nature of God and following His dictates.

I hear in my counseling office all the time, "How do I know what God wants from me?" I often smile, because I do not believe that is the paradigm. I truly believe God gets behind our choices and nudges us toward a path. God does not make the choices for us. It is not predestined. It has everything to do with choice. This certainly ties in well with the concept of free will. I have the choice to follow God or not. I have the choice to go toward righteousness, honesty, love, and trust—areas most of us feel are important in relationships and integrity.

Receiving God's forgiveness is opening our hearts to no longer carry the burden of what has happened in the past. The past is over; it is complete and finished. I would love to say that I get it all right, but I do not. There are times when I, like all of us, make mistakes and wrong choices. There are choices that will lead to nothing but pain, suffering, and hurt. But sometimes, I just want to take control and make decisions. I find that when I do that, to the exclusion of God and everyone else, is when I get into trouble. But interestingly, God even has an answer to that, because He has made a way to take care of and forgive even the sin we will do in the future. We just have to accept and appropriate God's forgiveness. When I appropriate it, I open my heart to the depths of where God may take me, and I open myself to the possibility that life does not have to be pain and suffering. It can be joyous and interactive with others. True love, trust, and care can exist. I open myself to the possibility that God can love and care for me, and that I can just accept it. I can be thankful for it, and receive it with awestruck humility, as I hold on to the realization that God wants nothing more than for me to be healed, whole, and restored.

I realize that for some, my discussion here is a bit existential and that it might not detail enough of a structure or process. The process is in learning to be open and to receive from God. The process is learning to hear His voice. The process is being accountable to what I know about God and to appropriate that in its fullness.

Dr. Brende's Program Model

The process of opening ourselves to God is ultimately personal, and no one person's experience will be exactly like anyone else's. Nonetheless, there are programs and structures that can help us find our way. A dear friend of mine, Dr. Joel Brende, is a retired psychiatrist who worked for many years with veterans, both at the VA and at a treatment program in Georgia for veterans with PTSD. Joel's program was modeled on Alcoholics Anonymous and twelve-step programs in general, but he took a different approach.[303] He arranged the twelve steps into three groups, the first having to do with issues around trust, the next with issues of memory, and the third with issues of commitment. His model showed God as the center of a person's life. The process was to reclaim the joyful child within and to experience and resolve what is real in life. I hope this sounds familiar and relevant to where we are at this juncture of the HEART Model.

Trust

At first, we must look at issues of power and the meaning of life. Learning to trust oneself and others, and ultimately learning to trust God, are at the core of the healing process. Trust requires vulnerability, which can feel extremely risky when one has previously experienced pain or trauma.

Memory

One of the scariest steps in recovery is taking a fearless inventory of one's own mistakes and sin. The lengthy and difficult moral inventory includes everything from significant occurrences like being harmed, hurt, abused, left alone, or cast aside, to minor annoyances. Taking accountability for our own actions can be quite scary. Anger is a powerful emotion, but so is fear—for when we are afraid or angry, we are at our greatest loss of control.

This step also encompasses dealing with guilt. I have learned that many Christians, particularly those in charismatic circles, often carry around huge burdens—feelings that they do not measure up to God's standards and ways of being. It is important to keep a biblical frame of mind regarding what Christ actually says: we are forgiven, and our sin is no longer remembered.

Commitment

The four areas we put under the overall heading of "commitment" are life, justice, finding purpose, and bringing love and relationships into our lives. In Dr. Brende's thinking, it is not only healing that is important, but also investing in life as it is today. This encompasses investing in justice, fair play, and right and wrong, as well as allowing oneself to have moral values and embrace virtues that represent Christ, Christianity, and spiritual growth in one's life. Knowing that things like prejudice and bias are wrong, and having the willingness and guts to do something about it, is indeed living a purposeful life in God's sight. Being confident that one's life is lived with integrity, that what one says accords with what one lives and does, brings a new level of peace and trust in oneself and in God.

Love

Among the aspects of commitment, love and relationships are especially critical for ongoing health. I have a dear friend who used to do workshops in the area of physical and emotional healing. In one of the teachings, she said that she believes life here on earth is a classroom. Our lesson or purpose of life, she submitted, is to discover all the different ways to love our neighbors, our friends, the world, our country, our children, our partners, and so on. The list could get quite long, but each time we come into contact with other people is an opportunity to connect with love. One of the many things I like about that teaching is that it describes a journey—a journey that goes to our very heart and soul, where we find Jesus.

The more we love, the more we grow.

The more we love, the more we learn.

The more we love, the greater the impact we make.

First Corinthians 12–13 talk about the gifts of the spirit. Though faith and hope are highlighted, there is a verse that says, "But the greatest of these is love" (1 Corinthians 13:13 NIV). The highest virtue is love. Opening ourselves to receive God's forgiveness is opening ourselves to the most vulnerable part of our soul. To open up to that place is, indeed, to have a change of heart, which is what *repent* means—to have a change of heart, or a change of wholeness (see the Introduction; also, see Luke 7:48–50 and Mark 1:4 NIV).

When we receive God's forgiveness into our lives, it blocks out all the sin in our life and all the wrong turns, choices, and ways we have taken. Forgiveness resets our life. It says, "Start from this point, with a clean slate and a clean heart." If we continue the journey, we continue to a deeper place of love and commitment—toward those around us, ourselves, God, and our vocation. Forgiveness takes us to a place where we connect to the kingdom of God. Sometimes it is a bumpy ride, but it will take us there.

I love the idea that the twelve steps are broken into the three categories of trust, memory, and commitment. These areas are legs of a journey that leads to healing from anger, fears, and guilt, and to commitment to life, justice, love, and relationships. God is at the center of all of that. His desire is to help people heal from their experiences at all different ages, from their experiences of Him, and from their pain at the hands of others, and to integrate all of it. Integration is to have the oneness and wholeness of the Spirit of God. This is where absolute healing resides.

Chapter Seven Notes

CHAPTER EIGHT

Merging the Split Parts

Psychological theories have been the underlying strength of counseling and therapy for almost 150 years. From the psychosexual model of Sigmund Freud to the existential awareness of ourselves as humans[304] to the spiritual overturns of transpersonal psychology,[305] we as persons have been trying to understand ourselves in order to heal from the pain and suffering we have experienced in our lives. These various theories have been the thread of our dealing with different parts of self from a psychological perspective.

Fritz Perls, the founder of Gestalt therapy, defines Gestalt as the parts that make up and complete the whole, with the whole being greater than the sum of the separate parts of self.[306] Self and heuristic psychology suggests that all the work we do is for the purpose of becoming our truest self—that is, our truest sense of ourselves. Another example of this comes from the transpersonal psychological model, which strives to connect to what is beyond the self and to experience the true self. The HEART Model draws out and combines aspects from several of these schools of psychology: it is a little bit Gestalt, has a major component of cognitive theory, and strives to deal with object relations and cognitive distortions. Its purpose is to focus on the healing of self and bring together parts of self that are wounded, suffering, and in need of healing.

The HEART model's origins begin with Fritz Perls and his thoughts of healing the different parts of the self in order to make a stronger person or stronger whole of self. In the 1980s, David Seamands wrote two powerful books: *Healing for Damaged Emotions* and *Healing of Memories*.[307] When I first read the books in 1985, I was enthralled with his work and began to systematize what he wrote about, including what he described as his own process in working with others. Despite not being a counselor at the time (although he later studied to become a counselor), he ended up being an excellent practitioner and saw many people healed in the process. Over the years, I have adjusted,

The HEART Model

rearranged, added to, deleted from, and conceptualized his system, with the result being what you see in this finished book. I even spent a weekend with Seamands to discuss how his material encouraged me and how his influence can be seen in the current product. Without me asking, he gave his blessing and was quite pleased with the additions and changes, particularly with the way in which his work was systemized and developed into a treatment model and focus. (See Chapter Eleven for further discussion of Seamands and his work.)

In modern times, the idea of parts coming together as one really took hold in the 1950s with the writings about Sybil[308] and the work of Cornelia Wilbur,[309] and the *Three Faces of Eve*,[310] discussing multiple personality disorder. Over the next thirty years, multiple personality disorder become a political issue in psychology and counseling despite its definition in the DSM. In fact, it was so misunderstood that the first comprehensive book dealing with its diagnosis and treatment was published by Frank Putnam in the late 1980s.[311] Particular attention was focused on the coming together of split parts of self. Putnam discussed much of what we now know about developmental psychopathological processes—that the early trauma suffered by these patients might have irreparably damaged them, so that a unified sense of self would be impossible to achieve in later life.[312] He went on to say that he had seen some patients undergo a transformation over a course of treatment so that the alter personalities lost their separateness and appeared to be absorbed into a more integrated sense of self.[313]

In the mid-1990s, multiple personality disorder was renamed *dissociative identity disorder*. The new term was informed by work and research showing that it was not separate entities within ourselves, but a single personality, that had fragmented. The new diagnosis was far more descriptive of the condition as well as its healing process, wherein those parts eventually combined and integrated into one personality. Later research described in journal articles discussed brain scans on some of the alter personalities, which found that the cognition of each alter personality was in different parts of the brain and that each alter showed up as such.[314] Putnam also observed that the hippocampal fluid volume (in the brain) decreases following significant trauma.[315] This significant discovery that the hippocampal volume returns after therapy was the first time in psychological research we had biological proof that therapy works!

THE FINAL STAGES

In the discussion of dissociative identity disorder clients in therapy, the majority of the work is complete when feelings have been processed, cognitive distortions have been neutralized, and significant issues between parts of selves have been reconciled. Harmony has been restored to a system that was in dissonance. The client has accepted the diagnosis. You have met and developed a trust relationship with each part of the personality system that exists, and the histories, functions, and other characteristics of all the alters are known. Internal communication and cooperation have been established among the various alters, and all the parts of self have reconciled and have ameliorated problems and issues. The process of therapy has increased unity of interests, purposes, and goals within the system. From the outside, you can see that the dissociative walls between the alters have begun to erode. At this point, you, as a counselor, are ready to move the client toward fusing and integrating the parts; the client, of course, is the one doing the work. All the preparatory work has come to this point of integration. The same is true for those who are non-dissociative. The dissonant parts of self are ready to merge into a unified whole.

Fusion and Integration

While the terms *fusion* and *integration* are often used interchangeably in parts therapy, for our purposes here they will be distinguished.

Fusion is what I consider the precursor to integration. Integration occurs when the divided identities of self are united into one whole. It involves the restructuring or synthesis of the fragmented personality system and generally takes many weeks or months to complete. In fact, integration occurs through the middle stages of therapy, in an ongoing process. It is not just a single, final event. When dealing with personality parts that are adult and child, that fusion/integration process may occur during stage 4, after the parts forgive each other and let each other off the hook, and when both, but especially the adult, want to take the child out of the emotionally tortured place they have been for years. Were the therapist to refuse to encourage integration at that point, it would do the client a disservice and set therapy back considerably.

Once again, I would like to remind readers that the HEART Model is a circular theory and not a linear theory. We may go back to previous stages periodically to process new emerging memories, forgive a different part of self, or revisit various historical pieces that surface throughout the counseling process. The long-term goal of any parts work, whether DID therapy or working from a HEART Model standpoint, is for the parts to come together as one and for the unified self, with all the parts contributing, to make day-to-day decisions, long-range plans, and all other choices together as a unified whole.

In essence, fusion is the beginning process of integration, and from here on out, I will use the words *fusion* and *integration* interchangeably. That said, integration is a more thorough process than fusion in that it is more pervasive. Fusion lays the groundwork for integration as it peels away the dissociative barriers and merges one or more parts that are ready to come together.

Signs That the Client Is Ready for Fusion

Before the therapist makes any attempts to bring about fusion, it is important that the parts be ready to fuse. The client usually knows when and if they are ready to fuse or integrate. Forced or premature fusions or integrations are usually short-lived, if they work at all. When certain parts show evidence of co-consciousness or simultaneous awareness of things, they are probably ready for fusion. They may acknowledge having the same memories or the same skills or the same knowledge of an event. Or, they may have blurred or experienced an overlapping sense of identity (an "identity crisis"). In some cases, the parts might even say they would like to fuse or are ready to fuse. Sometimes they prefer fusion over the discomfort they are experiencing with continued separateness.

Preparing the Client for Fusions

I recommend that you always consult the client's most recent personality system map, if available, before attempting fusion. Parts who are close to each other or share a common connection according to the system map usually fuse together more easily than those who are from separate groups or families. Fusions of those from divergent groups can take place later. Start with those most closely linked and then work at merging others with the resultant fusions (or larger blended parts). If there are still blank areas on the client's system map, it is best to explore these areas before continuing with a fusion attempt—especially if there is a blank area between two of the parts who wish to fuse.

Before beginning a fusion, the therapist should take some time to check for residual areas of conflict between the parts planning to fuse. Each part should be given the opportunity to talk about any areas that might signal hidden conflicts or issues not yet exposed. If problems surface through this search and discussion, they should be dealt with before a fusion is attempted. This can also be true of non-dissociative clients who, when working step 4, are working with a separated child and adult within a two-chair dialoging system. This two-chair model developed by Fritz Perls, Ralph Hefferline, and Paul Goodman,[316] and subsequently enhanced by John Bradshaw, allows for the dialoging process in step 4 to take place as if they truly were separate entities.[317] The fusion often produces emotional and physical effects similar to those reportedly experienced by dissociative clients.

Helping the Client Through the Process

Once it is clear that the parts have worked through their differences, you can proceed to the next step, which is to discuss the method the client is most comfortable with to bring about the integration. Some clients like to use visual images or metaphors to facilitate the integration process. They might, for instance, find it helpful to think of how water from two separate cups flows together to become one. Or, as the client prepares to merge two or more alters, you might suggest that they think of blending several ingredients together into a bowl to create one delicious cake with a uniform consistency. They might even imagine having been like a bunch of ingredients separated by dividers in a cake pan, and now it is time to remove some of the remaining dividers and allow the ingredients to blend together.

Yet another image might be the mixing together of different colors of paint. I often will suggest that the metaphor of color is like the color blue and the color yellow mixing together to make the new color of green. To have green, you must have all of the yellow and all of the blue so that nothing is lost and everything of the separate essence is included in the new product. Other ideas include the molding together of different kinds of clay, weaving different thread into one fabric, or bringing two separate substances, such as silver and gold, into a piece of jewelry.

One word of warning: the use of such imagery is not meant to take on power of its own. I like to clarify to the client that the pictures they have chosen to think of in their imagination are not real in and of themselves but are only intended to provide an analogy that helps to relieve the potential tension during the fusion process. And, since most dissociative clients are quite imaginative, they tend to find the images helpful in enabling them to move more easily into integration. In most cases, especially when the client knows the Lord and is receptive to inviting God into the integration process, I begin with prayer and encourage them to think of God bringing the alters together. (See Chapter Nine for further discussion of visualization or imagery as a technique.)

Whatever imagery or metaphor is used, it is best to discuss it with the alters and the client as a whole beforehand so as not to happen upon an image that may have unpleasant associations for any part of the personality system. You should also be careful to avoid images and metaphors that suggest elimination or banishment of the parts involved. The images need to allow for the preservation of all the elements involved in the blending process.

When the client is ready to begin a fusion, I usually start by having the alters involved "stand side by side." Then I encourage them to hold hands or link arms as they each close their eyes and prepare for integration. If they are open to allowing God to complete this process, I then encourage them to focus on the Lord and allow Him to bring about the integration. I then say a prayer to invite the Lord to do the work. And, as they go through the fusion process, I continue involving the Holy Spirit, praying with them through the process. The Lord created them to be one and, as their creator, knows exactly how to blend them together into a unified whole. I have discovered that those clients who pray through this process and seal each fusion and integration with the Lord's mending power have more stable fusions than those who do not. In fact, I have yet to see a case where the integration unraveled after having been sealed by the Lord through prayer.

The process I most prefer to use involves having the client visualize the two (or more) parts of themselves coming together as one. I will talk to them about how the Lord desires for them to be in a place of wholeness and completeness, not only in and of themselves, but in God. God was there when they were first formed; He was there during the trauma; He was there when the alters were created; He has been with them during the healing process; and He is here now to complete the process and make them whole. Accordingly, when we pray through the process of integration, I include the infilling of the Holy Spirit as part of that process. It is this infilling, I believe, that completes their integration.

I also like to have them talk aloud through the process, describing what is happening and the chain of events bringing about the fusion. This helps the experience to take on a greater reality and also keeps you informed about what is happening.

After clients allow the personalities, with their memories and experiences, to blend into one, and allow their spirit to connect fully to God's Spirit and become a whole, complete, and vital force, the next thing for them to do is share the experience. Sharing the experience is a way of validating and solidifying it. It is the same principle of confession used in the Scriptures: "...if you confess with your mouth the Lord Jesus and believe in your heart that God has raised Him from the dead, you will be saved. For with the heart one believes unto righteousness, and with the mouth confession is made unto salvation" (Romans 10:9–10 NKJV). There are a number of other Scripture references that remind us of the importance of speaking that which we believe. Something happens when we share aloud our testimony or speak out a scriptural truth.

Why the Lord attributes so much power to the spoken word I do not know. Perhaps it reflects how He first spoke the creation into existence. I am not suggesting that we have the same power to create with the spoken word as God does, but since we are created in His image, I cannot help but wonder if we have inherited some portion of this word power. After all, many scriptures confirm that our tongues do indeed have power. For example, "death and life are in the power of the tongue" (Proverbs 18:20 ESV). And, "with his mouth the godless man would destroy his neighbor" (Proverbs 11:9 ESV).

Though, again, I am not suggesting that speaking by itself has power of its own to transform, it is undeniable that something happens when clients share their integration experience aloud. It seems to cement the experience. On the one hand, it could be likened to describing a delicious meal after having eaten the food, which fosters the desire to return and taste it again. Sharing can also be a vehicle for reliving the experience, which can put clients in that wonderful place again. Therefore, I like to conclude the integration experience by talking about it and hearing from client what happened.

With God as the lead therapist in the partnership, allow the journey of inner healing to bring the client to a renewed place of wholeness.

Working Through Multiple Layers

Sometimes, DID clients will have layers of personalities, and as you work with them, you come upon a hole in the floor, so to speak. When you look through the hole, there is another room and there are more alters. It is not that the therapist has missed something; it is that the work has progressed further, so enough trust has been built up for the client to allow the therapist into deeper levels. While multiple layers are not common, it is not unheard of to encounter them. The percentage is not high, but it is definitely a possibility.

> The client I referred to earlier had been used for child pornography for about six years by her father, passed around to her father's friends, and pimped out by her father. The pictures were very explicit, and all of her experiences were verifiable. Her sister was used in the same way, and they corroborated each other's story. The client presented with about fifty well-defined alters; the rest were fragments, which integrated relatively quickly. Those fifty or so alters took a lot of work and a lot of blending over time. At some point, I had her do a mapping exercise. A sort of a whirlwind appeared in the rendering of the picture or map, which represented three distinct levels. Up to that point, we were only working on the first level. There were three alters at the second level, all of which were pervasive and characterized serious emotions of deep hurt, betrayal, and shame. Those emotions were certainly evident on the top layer, but they were pervasive underneath everything. There was only one alter at the third layer, that of deep melancholy, which also pervaded her whole experience.

Integration does not happen until the latter stages of Phase 2, which can be one-and-a-half to three years into therapy or more when dealing with dissociation. With non-dissociative clients, this process is sped considerably and may actually take a relatively short period of time. Psychiatrists have convoluted some of this, because many of them treat DID as schizophrenia. As a result, they prescribe a cornucopia of antipsychotic medications, which does not stop the voices. It just tamps them down a bit, suppressing them to a degree. With true DID, the voices should *not* be repressed. They must be able to communicate with each other. An antidepressant or anti-anxiety medication can be useful in some situations because of overwhelming stress or some level of debilitation due to depression, but in most cases, DID is not something that can be medicated.

We do the same thing with our veterans suffering from PTSD. Psychiatrists put them on all kinds of medication to try to regulate the symptoms—but they cannot be regulated! Here again, some of the symptoms can be tamped down; they become somewhat immobilized when clients take antipsychotic medications. I assert that when working with a traumatized population, they are in more danger with the antipsychotics than without. When prescribing a medication, the better choices would be either an antidepressant, an anti-anxiety drug, or a mood stabilization medication, the use of which is backed up by the literature.

DID and PTSD both have classic symptoms like flashbacks and memory avoidance. These symptoms are not used for the diagnosis, but they occur repeatedly in this population. Though I tell insurance companies that DID and PTSD are often comorbid, sometimes they will not pay for DID but will pay for PTSD. I am, however, telling them what the real problem is: trauma.

FINAL INTEGRATION

The principles and techniques used for fusions are basically the same as those used to blend all the alters, fused alters, and groups of alters together into one single identity. At the start of the process of integration, there might be several alters, or groups of alters. Gradually, a series of fusions between closely linked alters takes place, and then fusions of each fusion, which are often composites of the various groups of alters previously fused together, until you are finally left with only one or two remaining alters. Integration is completed when these remaining personalities merge into the final single identity desired. This process usually takes several years. For the non-dissociative client, this process is much faster and may happen in a single session. The single session should not be the goal, however; if it takes several weeks or months, so be it.

Spontaneous "Final" Integration

While spontaneous fusions do occasionally occur, it is rare for a final integration to take place away from the therapy setting. Usually, when a client claims to have made this final fusion into one single identity on their own, it is another example of resistance. Like "flight into health," in which the dissociative client claims not to have DID, claims of spontaneous final fusions are usually a means of escape or denial. This will sometimes happen when a client recognizes that the remaining course of treatment is expected to be long and painful. They want it to be over, so they pretend that it is.

When your client claims they have experienced a spontaneous final integration, it is best to express a sincere appreciation for their wish to be integrated while still remaining aware of the likelihood that it is not really happened. Let them know that even if the fusion is real, they are still going to need further therapy in order to function well in society as a single personality. Remind them that integration is not the end of therapy. It is just the end of one phase of treatment and the beginning of another.

When dealing with non-dissociative clients, spontaneous fusion is even more rare, because they do not experience themselves as fragmented. The issues can cause an experience of being fragmented, and thus they may have similar feelings and emotions as those who are dissociative. The same caveat about continuing therapy applies, however, as they may be frightened about what comes next, or may be concerned about long-term issues that may keep them in therapy for an extended period of time. It is always best to confront the fears and deal with the issues that arise.

Dealing with Relapses

In my experience, DID clients who allow the Holy Spirit to bring about their final integration rarely suffer relapses. It is possible, I suppose, for some Christian clients to unintentionally get ahead of God and convince both you and themselves that the process is complete when, in reality, it is not. They may want so badly to finish their course of treatment, or to please you or God, that they "talk themselves into it," so to speak, and actually believe it is done before it is begun. The truth of the matter is that the Holy Spirit knows a whole lot more than we do about what is really taking place and when the time is right to complete the integration process. If, for instance, there are still some hidden alters remaining at the time you and the client both feel it is right to integrate, God may hold off integration until these alters are uncovered and their issues addressed. Perhaps one of the remaining personality composites does not want to merge with the others. The point is, there could be any number of reasons why the Lord wants you to wait. Be open and patient for the Lord's perfect timing.

The unexpected emergence of an alter after integration signals either failed fusion or relapse. Or, in some instances, an alter or alters may make themselves known to the client, who then conceals this information from you, either because they do not want to disappoint you or because they do not want to go through any further abreactive or uncovering work. Some clients might also simply pretend to integrate to please you, to speed up the therapy process, or to secure some secondary gain.

Non-dissociative client may go through a similar process, as one part of self may want to act out or choose not to fuse, or have other reasons that have not been resolved yet that keep the integration process from happening. While sometimes when this happens, it is experienced as frustration, it is important to know that without the relapse occurring, the work itself would be incomplete. It is important that the work be as complete as possible in order to allow the client to move forward.

Indications That Integration Has Failed or Relapse Has Occurred

Sometimes, in cases of the secular approach to DID self-work, there can be an unraveling or a relapse. According to Ross, the most common reasons are:[318]

- Discovering a new layer of alters or fragments of personalities. This is not a true relapse. (I worked with a client who had about 250 splits. Not all of them were personalities, because some were just fragments, but there were two other layers of alters, including about fifty alters that were defined and clear; the map the client drew indicated three distinct layers.)

- Reemergence (separation) of previously fused alters. Alters that had integrated sometimes pop out for various reasons, usually when clients revert to old coping techniques or dissociations when under pressure.

- Creation of new personality states. I usually try to stop that in the first or second session by making an internal agreement for them to refrain from creating any new alters while they are in therapy. Some of it results when they get in a situation they cannot deal with. When an existing alter does not come out to take care of it, another one will be created to take care of the situation. They think, "I need somebody to take care of this. Since nobody is coming out, I will invent another one"—which is how they have coped for all the intervening years. It seems that the mere suggestion or mention of "no new alters" is usually enough to prevent new creation since they have adapted well to where they are at the time (although sometimes, a new alter will be created to deal with the therapist).

- Feigned integration (also not a true relapse), which is possibly done to try to please the therapist. It is a symptom of still "trying to do it right," to be the "good" patient, or to be perfect in order to achieve safety and acceptance. While the cooperation is positive in that it indicates a level of trust, there is a reason for the deception, and the client trusts the therapist enough to communicate that it did not really happen. The therapist should then facilitate looking at why it did not really happen, which is the important issue. At that point, the client is aware of his or her behavior and can choose to take responsibility. It moves you and the client to the next level of trust in the relationship.

The HEART Model

- Reoccurrence of dissociative symptoms or short emergence of a full alter personality, which needs to be dealt with on a short-term basis. The client has begun to dissociate again, or an alter has come out to deal with a stressful situation for a short duration.
- Further trauma.[319]

If you suspect that an integration has failed or that the client is experiencing a relapse, you may need to do some probing. This basically involves keeping an eye out for the same kinds of clues you looked for during the early stages of diagnosis, when you suspected DID in the first place. Some clues include:

- Evidence of amnesia
- Evidence of covert switching
- Self-destructive or suicidal affects
- Intense and inappropriate social behaviors
- The reappearance of psychosomatic symptoms or the reappearance of old somatic problems
- Chaos, disruptions, or impasses during therapy
- Transference or countertransference issues
- Emergence of obvious alters

Unexplained behaviors and incidents are often a sign of amnesia. Another possible sign of amnesia is the client appearing to forget something that just took place or asking the same question over and over during therapy. Or, the client might not remember certain significant details about their previous therapy session. They might get confused about changes in appointment scheduling or turn up at the wrong time.

If you notice sudden changes in facial expressions, voice, body language, or mannerisms, or other personality-type changes during sessions, this many indicate covert switching. Other signs might be unusual stress or anxiety, sudden onset of unexplained somatic symptoms like headache, dizziness, or digestive disturbances, or an inappropriate intensity in the client during sessions.

Another common signal of continued dividedness is depression, particularly if it comes on suddenly and without apparent reason. If the client begins to withdraw from social activities or involvement, they may very well be trying to conceal existent alters. If a normally sophisticated or "proper" kind of client suddenly starts to use foul or crude language or demonstrate inappropriate behavior, you are probably witnessing the emergence of an alter.

In other words, look for all the same clues you were watching for at the beginning of therapy. And, when alters are discovered, you will have to work with them just as you did the others until they are ready to integrate with the rest of the previously fused alters.

One way you can specifically probe for unsuspected alters is to ask the client to review all the events associated with the early creation of the alters. If all the alters have been fully integrated, the client should not have difficulty listing these events or recalling their life history. The integration likely would have resulted in the recovery of a fairly complete memory of the traumatic events of their life. The client may at this point be much less emotionally intense or disturbed in relaying the history of the traumatic events. It is a good sign if they describe the events in the past tense. They may, in fact, say something like, "Well, this happened to so-and-so, but now it's as if it happened to me." That is definitely a positive sign of integration.

If, on the other hand, they have not completely or properly integrated, they will likely have a problem relaying a coherent history without significant gaps. You might even see some of the hidden alters come out in response to the triggers of certain memories.

When fusions fail or relapses occur, it is usually because there has not been a complete resolution of traumatic events and emotional issues. However, some dissociative clients can purposely unravel the fusion shortly after integration in order to revert to dissociative methods of coping with current life issues or stressful situations. This is why it is so important for clients to stay in therapy after integration. They need to learn new ways of coping as a single personality.

What to Do When Fusions Fail

It can be disappointing to the client (e.g., the host or some of the remaining alters) when they realize that a fusion has not worked. Sometimes, this disappointment can turn into despair as they wonder if they will ever change. They might turn once again to thoughts of suicide and self-hate. They may be afraid you will reject or look down on them for not having "performed" well enough to keep or complete the integration. On the other hand, some of the remaining alters might gloat over the failed fusion, believing themselves to have succeeded in maintaining control over the client and the therapeutic process. So, there are a number of reactions that often take place after an incomplete integration.

One thing that will help avoid some of this profound despair and sense of failure afterward is proper preparation beforehand. If, for instance, you overstress (either overtly or unconsciously) the importance of integrating throughout therapy or near the end of this phase, you risk setting up the client (and yourself) for disappointment when the mutual expectation is not met. Even though integration is a major goal, you need to be careful not to place too much emphasis on this goal and make it seem like the most important part of therapy. *Every part* of therapy is important, not just the integrative phase. It is best if you try to keep things as even keel as possible throughout therapy.

What you tell clients at the point of their disappointment should be a *reinforcement* of what you have already been telling them all along. Let clients know over and over, throughout the whole therapy process, that *they* are more important than what they accomplish. God loves them whether they are divided or not. God loves every part of them and is concerned for their welfare. He has never rejected them and never will. He is most interested in the heart of who they are, whether integrated or not, and less interested in what they *achieve*. Yes, He wants them to be whole and is ready and able to help them become whole. But His love is not dependent upon that wholeness or on their failure or success in what they attempt to do.

In addition to assuring them of God's unconditional love and acceptance, assure them of yours. Let them know you are not going to reject them or ridicule them if they do not do things according to the ideal plan or hope. Even if you were to reject them—which you are not going to do, even if you part company or have a different opinion—or anyone else rejects them, it does *not* determine whether they are a failure or a success.

Remind them that you are just as human as they are and just as subject to making mistakes or missing the mark. But that does not make you a failure, because you know who you are in Christ Jesus. Christ is the victor over sin and death; if clients allow Jesus to live and work in them, He will bring them to the same victory. It does not depend on how much they achieve or how quickly they get to a goal. Achievements do not define how perfect they are, how good they are, or how accomplished they are. Christ's victory is all about heart attitude. God looks at heart, and that is where He finds His winners.

STAY POSITIVE—PRACTICE ENCOURAGEMENT

Encourage them as much as possible whenever they take a step in the right direction, no matter how small or big, and whenever they get past a hurdle or make a positive change of any magnitude. Do not wait until you see a big change or a whole goal achieved. Encourage them when they make the tiniest bit of progress, even if it does not seem like progress to them at the time. When a previously disruptive alter first abides by contract rules and keeps the peace, praise them. Encourage them when they start to communicate and cooperate with the others. Encourage them all along the way, at every possible turn.

When the client (or one of their alters) starts berating themselves for not "performing" well enough or getting "cured" fast enough, remind them that "there is therefore now no condemnation for those who are in Christ Jesus ... who walk not according to the flesh (but according to the Spirit)" (Romans 8:1 ESV). Ask God to help you love and accept the client as He does. If you demonstrate this kind of love and acceptance whether they are "good" or "bad" during therapy, you will reduce the risk of them falling into despair after failing to complete or keep a fusion.

It is important to encourage your client through the process and not expect too much from them, but you're likely to need some encouragement yourself. Working with DID can be grueling for therapists, too. It is not uncommon to pick up some of the same kinds of responses to therapy as your client has. For instance, many therapists find themselves feeling the same sense of hopelessness or frustration as their client when a fusion fails or when therapy takes an unexpected turn for the worse. When you start to feel negative reactions coming on, encourage yourself in the Lord, just as King David did in 1 Samuel 30:6. Negative words and thoughts are highly contagious, so be on guard against them before they have a chance to sink in and take root. And, if they have already taken root, crowd them out with positive words and thoughts.

Remind yourself that nothing is hopeless, because God is a God of hope. Release your tongue to speak positive, faith-filled, hope-charged words into the situation and into your own heart. Speak scriptures that plant hope into the situation. Praise and worship the Lord. If there is anything that helps pull us out of a dark pit of depression and despair, it is praising and worshiping God in spirit and in truth. You might not be able to do it with much gusto at first, but do it anyway and let the gusto follow afterward.

If you stay positive, merciful, and hopeful while ministering to your clients in therapy, they are going to notice, and it will eventually rub off on *them*! Moreover, remember that it is easier to resist negative thoughts before they take root than it is to try to shake them off once they have embedded themselves in your soul.

One word of caution: in your efforts to be positive, be careful not to tip into intensity. Do not let your positive attitude become flippant or insensitive to your client's pain and struggles. A truly positive attitude is not the sort of superficial baloney you see in people who say thoughtless things to hurting people, like, "Well, it could be worse!" or, "You need to stop feeling sorry for yourself and just trust God!" or, "Nothing is worth getting so depressed about! Think about all the good things in your life." You need to find the right balance in sharing your clients' pain without allowing it to drag you into a bottomless pit with them.

The Bible tells us to share one another's burdens (Galatians 6:2). Some burdens can be overwhelming to carry all alone, but a burden is much easier to manage when someone caring comes along to take one end and help you carry it. True encouragement or exhortation never lacks compassion, mercy, and sensitivity to a person's needs or struggles. Encouragement and exhortation see light at the end of the tunnel and then, gently and tenderly, help the person through the darkness to the light.

Dealing with Your Own Negative Reactions

When you find out that your client purposely deceived you about integrating, it can be hard not to get angry. Often, you feel humiliated for being so gullible and allowing them to fool you for so long. The resultant anger and shame can quickly turn into resentment, and the resentment can soon become outright rejection of the client. If you feel like you are too overcome with anger and other negative feelings toward the client, you should take a break from seeing them until you can sort things out. You might need to seek out another trusted therapist to work through your own emotions and countertransference issues before you can deal with the client again. Get in close with God, and allow Him to bathe you in His peace and refresh you.

Share Your Observations with the Client

If you start to see obvious signs that clients are not fully integrated, let them know. If they have been purposely hiding this fact from you, they might become defensive or argumentative about it. They might insist you give them "proof." Do not get trapped in an argument with them about the matter. Simply tell them as clearly and directly as possibly what you have seen that indicates their dividedness. Then, be prepared to work with them through the same kind of process you did in the earlier phases of denial, resistance, and working with the alters. If there are newly discovered alters to meet, get to know them as you did the others. Those alters who came unfused or pretended to fuse should be addressed and worked with, to resolve remaining issues.

Remember, a failed union is not a major setback. It does not mean you failed as a therapist, and it does not mean the client failed. It just means there are more issues and trauma to work through before you proceed to the next phase of integration. Usually, the time spent working with the unfused alters at this point is far less complicated, chaotic, and enduring than in the earlier phases. The alters who have failed to fuse or became unfused most likely only have residual issues to work through, rather than the whole gamut. And, when they re-fuse, they do so much more easily and neatly. In essence, it will not be as long a haul as before.

When a Client Refuses to Integrate

In some cases, dissociative clients prefer to remain dissociative rather than to integrate. This is, of course, their right. Nonetheless, it is usually not in their best interest. I know I cannot force a client to choose wholeness over fragmentation, but it still saddens me when it happens. Some therapists consider it just another alternative for the dissociative who chooses to remain divided, but I see more problems than benefits for clients when they do so.

There are a number of reasons why some clients choose to remain dissociative. Sometimes, it is advantageous for the client to display their fragmentation publicly. For instance, there are often certain alters who are exceptionally talented, skilled, knowledgeable, or adept in particular areas, and clients may like being seen as superhuman. It boosts their ego to demonstrate certain abilities that outshine regular "singles." Some alters, for example, speak one or more foreign languages fluently. Others may have exceptional physical strength, stamina, or abilities. And, still others may demonstrate special artistic gifts, extensive book knowledge, or high levels of profitable skills. In some instances, they have gained access and favor with certain people, groups, or positions specifically because of these exceptional abilities. Some dissociatives are afraid they will lose or, at best, water down these special abilities. The initial loss of such abilities that commonly occurs shortly after a first fusion can reinforce or trigger their fear. Another factor that can fuel clients' fears of "losing themselves" is the experience of post-fusion

The HEART Model

problems, limitations, and changes they are not equipped to deal with. In some cases, they actually may have come to enjoy the special attention and fascination they have elicited in exposing their fragmentation.

When dealing with a dissociative client who wants to remain dissociative (or one whom I *suspect* wants to), the first thing I usually do is try to find out why they desire this option. If their reasons are based in false assumptions or fears, I address this as directly and diplomatically as possible. If, for instance, they fear that they will lose the abilities and characteristics of their alters, I try to assure them that need not happen. I tell them that it most certainly can happen during the initial adjustment period after fusion or integration, but that this symptom should eventually even out. I tell them that we will be working together to stabilize the fusion and integration process and help them learn appropriate, non-dissociative ways of coping (including many that they already know after Phase 1). If fusion and integration are done properly and completely, they will not have to permanently lose parts of who they are, including special skills and abilities the alters demonstrate.

On the other hand, if clients want to remain dissociative because they like getting special attention, gratification, and privileges as such, I then attempt to lay out the consequences, some which may overshadow what they consider positive benefits. One thing you need to be on guard against, however, is attempts to pressure or manipulate your clients to make the decision you consider most appropriate. It can be very tempting to try to influence your client (subtly or not-so-subtly) to your way of thinking or progressing. While your methods of persuasion may be based upon good intentions and a desire for what you believe is truly best for the client, it is nonetheless inappropriate to resort to such tactics. The client has been through quite enough attempts at manipulation and control from past abusers; they do not need your contributions in this arena, however well intended.

It is right for you to present the potential consequences and drawbacks, to discuss their motivations, and to opt to work through some wrong assumptions they may have formed. Yet, once this is accomplished, you need to step back and allow clients to make the choice *they* prefer. Whether or not you agree with their decision, you need to remain available to walk them through the final stages of therapy if they desire this. For instance, perhaps they have chosen to remain fragmented, but want you to help them learn how best to function as a unit or "corporation." They might want to operate like a one-owner business rather than a conglomerate of mixed opinions. They will still need your assistance in helping them to resolve residual issues and replace maladaptive behaviors and responses with better coping tactics.

If your client remains fragmented at the conclusion of therapy, it is important that you do not take the blame or consider the case a therapeutic failure. As long as you have done your best and have informed them of the potential drawbacks, you have served them well. Be careful not to fall into the trap of over-responsibility. If, in fact, you have allowed the client to make their own decision in the end, you have done well. If a client has achieved a significant improvement in his or her ability to function effectively in society and in relationships, the therapy has been a success.

POST-INTEGRATION THERAPY—ISSUES TO DEAL WITH AFTER INTEGRATION

It is very important to continue therapy after the client has fully integrated. After having operated as a multiple for so long, clients need to learn new ways of coping with the world as a single personality. They need time to get used to being one identity rather than many, and they need to adjust to responding to stress or crises in non-dissociative ways. If they do not, they are likely to resort to their old dissociative coping mechanisms and suffer relapse. If you send them off to work on their own immediately after integration, they are bound to suffer much more than they could imagine. The post-integration part of therapy usually takes several months to a year, and sometimes more.

Adapting in Relationships

One important area in which clients often have conflict is being in relationships, particularly romantic and other close relationships in their lives. Often, significant others in their lives are not excited about their integration. Spouses, children, families of origin, friends, and other loved ones often prefer to have them the way they were before. Since many multiples get involved in relationships that are unhealthy to begin with, when *they* get healthy, others in their life are still stuck in unhealthy patterns. Sometimes, such people will try to pull the integrated client back into being fragmented, because they "want the old person back"—that is, they want back the part of the client's self that presented to deal with them. When clients are fragmented, they have a distinct advantage to be whomever and whatever their significant others want them to be. Now that they have learned healthier ways of relating, others around them are often not impressed and, in fact, do not know how to handle the "new person." This can result in lots of stress in relationships. In most instances, clients automatically assume *they* are the one at fault and believe *they* are the one who needs to change to please others.

Clients need a lot of extra support and reassurance during this phase of therapy. It is important for them to recognize when someone in their life is using inappropriate or manipulative tactics. Likewise, it is important for them to recognize the difference between reasonable and unreasonable or unhealthy demands on them. So, it becomes a priority to work through those kinds of things with them.

Learning Non-dissociative Coping Strategies

Many newly integrated clients experience substantial difficulties in adjusting to life afterward. Whereas they used to split up responsibilities among many different "selves," they must now learn to handle these things as a unified whole. This is not without significant challenges. When they were fragmented, some of the alters were excused from participating in many important responsibilities. Some of the alters were either too young, too fragile, too ill, or too inexperienced to handle responsibilities. Once clients have integrated, however, they face many new challenges.

They have learned all their life to use dissociation to handle whatever stresses and difficulties came their way, but now, if they are not successful in using new methods to cope with stress, they can easily become overwrought with all the stressors and revert to old coping strategies. Stress is often an unwelcomed guest who does not have the decency to leave after overstaying its visit. When more stressors are added, it increases the possibility of incapacitation and the use of old coping skills. If clients have limited or no resources to fall back on, the initial joy of becoming whole can quickly disintegrate into depression. It is therefore absolutely vital to work with clients through this difficult adjustment period after integration.

Often, the now-unified client must come to terms with problems previously avoided by dissociating or being amnestic. At this point, many integrated clients realize what a mess their life has been. It is as though they have woken up from a drunken stupor only to find scattered evidence of what they did while "under the influence." Various people might start coming out of the woodwork, looking for their previous attachment to one of the client's previous alters. Many of these old relationships may indeed be unwholesome and troublesome. Married clients might have to face up to the affairs some of their alters got them into, and will now have to sort things out with their spouse face to face. In other words, consequences of the previous fragmentation must now be dealt with, without resorting to dissociation or other forms of evasion or denial.

It may be important for clients to accept responsibility for the pain and suffering they themselves caused. This can be a new and intimidating experience for them, especially for those parts of themselves that used to be weak or child alters who were never given responsibility, or for those who constantly passed it on to another alter. It is important to help the client understand that while they do need to accept responsibility for their actions (or inactions), even those that resulted in someone else's pain and suffering, they also need to recognize that they acted out of their own pain and distorted perceptions. As they face this new and painful challenge and attempt to make things right, they will need a great deal of prayer, encouragement, support, and guidance.

Even though the client has worked through past traumas during much of the therapy prior to integration, it is still important that they come to a new place of acceptance and understanding of these traumas as a whole person. It is also important for them to view these traumas and other past experiences as a continuous whole rather than as fragments and flashbacks. At first, it can be overwhelming for clients to realize how much has happened to them and just how horrible it all was. They will need your support as they work through their feelings in this area. Keep in mind that the client, when fragmented, compartmentalized many contradictory feelings and views about the abuse and the abusers. Now, as an integrated whole, the client will have to face and resolve these different feelings and perceptions. You will need to help them assimilate their past experiences into one continuous memory, while helping them keep intact their sense of oneness as they work through these past events. Do not be surprised if more abreactions occur as this stage of therapy; it is not uncommon. The difference in abreactions at this point, however, is that they are not likely to be personified by alters.

Learning to Deal with New and Mixed Feelings

The newly integrated client must now learn how to identify, express, and appropriately respond to feelings. Strong and intense feelings can frighten the client who has not had to experience such feelings as a unified whole before. You may need to explain where some of these feelings are coming from, assuring them this is normal and that it is okay for them to feel these things. However, they often will need further guidance in learning to manage these feelings in appropriate, non-dissociative, non-destructive ways.

Most non-fragmented clients are used to having mixed feelings on occasion. Dissociative clients, on the other hand, handled any mixed feelings by simply switching between or among parts of themselves, each of whom personified one of the particular feelings.

In this way, the multiple did not have to deal with simultaneous and contradictory feelings. They basically divided the emotions out among the parts. It can therefore be rather stressful for the newly integrated client to tolerate mixed feelings without wanting to dissociate.

Allowing the Client to Grieve Their Losses

There are a number of things integrated clients will need to grieve. They may need to grieve the loss of normal childhood, the loss of an idealized view of their parents or abusers, the loss of the alters as they were, and the loss of what they could have done or might have become had they not been fragmented. Many fragmented persons create internal worlds where they can escape from trauma. These internal worlds are often a place of refuge—an idealistic place of peace and beauty and sweetness. In times of loneliness, the fragmented client might look to this internal world and keep company with the different parts of self. In this way, they did not need to feel so alone anymore, even if they were isolated from other people. If they felt misunderstood by others, they could turn inward and find parts of themselves who would understand and offer them comfort.

Now that clients have integrated into one unified whole, they can no longer turn to this internal world of parts. This can make clients feel terribly lonely, and they need time to grieve these losses. Help them to identify the source of their loneliness and other mixed feelings, and encourage them to allow themselves to mourn.

Often, fragmented clients have unrealistic expectations about what it will be like as a single personality. When the initial euphoria of integration wears off, and the reality hits them that life as a "single" is not always a bed of roses, it can be almost devastating. They may need to grieve the loss of their idealized dream of being a single personality. As they let go of the way things were and accept the way things are now, complete with all the problems of living in the world as a "single," they should know that it is okay to feel and express their disappointments. When they do so, however, try to help them move on to the good aspects of being integrated so that they do not get stuck too long in a deep, dark pit. Help them to see and discover the many benefits, joys, and rewards of being whole. Once the client works through some of these initial adjustments to being integrated, they will soon find life less complicated and frustrating, and much more enjoyable, than before.

WHEN TO END THERAPY—RELEASING THE CLIENT INTO INDEPENDENCE

It becomes important to empower your client toward independence from therapy. You do not want them to be solely dependent on you alone, even to get them through the difficult time of adjusting to life as a single. One way to do this is to encourage the client to develop other supportive relationships outside of therapy. Encourage them to connect with problem-solving groups, such as classes or support groups on parenting, dealing with stress, or assertiveness training, which will help them adapt to the various struggles they face. They might even make some good friends in such groups. If they can expand their social network and find friends who are supportive, they will move faster in their journey toward true wholeness. If they are Christian, encourage them to get involved in church activities or church support groups. Clients of other faiths should be encouraged to attend places of worship and spiritual exploration. Many churches have groups specially aimed at helping people work through personal problems. There are recovery groups, single-parent groups, divorce recovery groups, groups that help members work through marriage and family problems, and many others. If clients attend a church that does not offer these kinds of groups, you can point them toward groups like this in other areas of the local community.

Follow-Up

After therapy has officially concluded, it is a good idea to suggest one or two follow-up appointments with the client, scheduled a month or so after the last session. Follow-up appointments provide the opportunity to see how well the client is adjusting. You may want to do a little systematic probing at the first follow-up appointment to see if any relapses have occurred. Look for anything that signals dissociative methods at work. How have they adapted to old relationships? Have they developed new ones? If so, are they healthy attachments? Are they communicating clearly? Are they more confident than before? Can they identify and express appropriate feelings without becoming agitated at the process? Are they comfortable being a single personality, or do they still miss multiplicity? Do they still need to work through certain issues?

Essentially, you want to find out four main things during follow-ups:

1. Have they remained together without major setbacks?
2. Are they adjusting adequately to being integrated?

3. Do they still require therapy to work through new or residual issues? And if so, to what extent?

4. Are they happy to be integrated? Or, do they demonstrate evidence of longing to go back to the way they were?

As long as they are progressing well enough on their own and feel comfortable with their integrated self, they will probably be fine without further therapy. They might need an occasional appointment every now and again over the next year or so. Accordingly, I always assure them that they can feel free to call for an appointment if they think it is appropriate. If you have done a good job of encouraging them toward independence, your job then becomes walking alongside them and being a support, should they ever need your assistance.

Chapter Eight Notes

CHAPTER NINE

Infilling of God

Most counseling and psychotherapeutic techniques lead to awareness of self and an attempt to gain freedom from emotional blindness.[320] Positive change, therefore, may be the result of connecting to disconnected or dissociated parts of self, re-embraced to bring about a sense of wholeness. Becoming aware of our ego states, or parts of self, becomes essentially the first job in therapy. When we reclaim these discordant parts of self, we tend to fuse or integrate them into ourselves within the framework of wholeness.[321] This is the concept postulated first by Fritz Perls in the 1960s,[322] followed by Irving and Mariam Polster,[323] in Gestalt therapy.[324]

The basic premise of Gestalt therapy is to look at discordant splits of self and to reintegrate those parts using various techniques (i.e., empty chair, projective identification, visualization, etc.). The term *Gestalt* itself means "completing the whole."[325] The writings and videotape work of John Bradshaw[326] championed an inner healing process he called *homecoming*.[327] This process used visualization to reclaim discordant parts of the childhood self, in order to heal from the hurts and shames of early childhood. The process of HEART is similar, in that it entails reclaiming discordant parts of oneself, but also reclaiming and resolving discordant parts of one's belief system about the nature of God. And so, in this ninth stage, we seek not only to integrate disconnected and discordant parts of self, but also to integrate the presence of God into our very being.

VISUALIZATION AND INTEGRATION

Once it becomes clear that the client has worked through cognitive distortions of self and God, the integration phase can begin. Visual imagery or metaphor can facilitate this process (see discussion in the previous chapter). As a person going through this process prepares to merge two or more parts of self, all issues have been fully discussed, all affect has been processed, and the need for separation no longer exists. The person is aware of God's presence, and in fact, God *is* present in the moment of the integration or union.

While I know that I have used the terms *visualization* and *imagery* quite a bit as therapeutic techniques, I realize that some in the Christian community have a difficult time with these techniques.[328] I can understand the concern, since many people do abuse visualization and use it in ungodly or spiritually damaging ways. I do not believe, however, that the use of visualization and imagery is inherently wrong; in fact I maintain that it can be a powerful and effective tool, which God can use for His purposes. In his book on imagery, H. Norman Wright reminds us that we all use imagery.[329] Basketball players use imagery when they shoot hoops; they visualize the plays and the moves, replaying them over and over in the mind's eye. Architects also have some type of imagery in their heads as they design beautiful cathedrals.[330] Musicians, especially vocalists, "hear" the sounds in their heads before they produce the notes. The examples are endless. Even the prophets of the Bible used visual aids to help the people understand their message. Jesus constantly used pictures and imagery to communicate. His parables were vivid and effective. We, too, can use visualization and imagery in a godly way that promotes true healing.

God and Integration

When the client is ready to integrate ego states or parts of self, I would encourage that individual to visualize the separate parts and to be aware of God's presence, both in the moment of the imagery and in the room where we are sitting to do the visualization. I encourage both the child of then and the adult of now to focus on the presence of God and allow Him to bring about the integration. I might say a prayer and invite the Lord to do the work. The Lord God created us to be *one* with Him, and as our creator, He knows exactly how to blend discordant parts into a unified whole. I have discovered that those who pray through this process and seal the integration with the Lord's mending power often complete this process and have a true, loving, and healing completion.

Sandy had been in therapy for two years and had been struggling with all the issues of dissociative identity disorder. She had integrated many parts over her time in therapy and seemed to be at a place where a final integration could occur. There were three alters left: herself; a child alter around the age of seven; and a protective alter who had been instrumental in getting Sandy to therapy in the first place, awakening her to her deep spiritual commitment to God.

I asked her to visualize the three of them in her safe place, in the internal world of her mind. I asked if there were any other issues for any of them to work out or to discuss and received an answer of no from each alter. I asked if she could visualize the three of them locked arm in arm, each wanting to be connected and no longer separated from each other. When she responded in the affirmative, I asked that all alters be aware of God's presence and when that awareness came to them, to tell me how it was experienced. Sandy replied that there was warmth about them and a bright light surrounding the place where they were. I simply asked if she could visualize the three alters moving toward the center in a group hug and that as this happened, each alter would blend and merge into each other until she could see only one image.

When Sandy told me that she could see the one image, I asked if she could allow the bright light and warmth that she experienced from God's presence to surround her completely. I also asked if she could find a way to allow the light and the warmth to come into her so that God's presence radiated from the outside to the inside and from the inside to the outside, completely surrounding, filling, and embracing her. Sandy replied that she could feel God's warmth and presence all around her. When I asked her to open her eyes and become aware of the room, she reported that all alters had integrated and that God's presence was in the center of her being. Time would show that the experience remained permanent. Sandy has now been integrated for over twenty-six years.

God was there when we were first formed (Genesis 2). He was and is with us in our lives, including during any trauma we may experience (Psalm 139). He is with us during the healing process and in the moment (Deuteronomy 31:8). He is with us to bring us to a place of wholeness and completeness (Philippians 1:6). When we pray through the process of integration together, I ask the Holy Spirit to be present as a part of that process. It is this infilling, I believe, that completes the integration procedure. I simply ask the parts of the self to come together until clients can see one image in the visualization. I also ask that they allow God to be a part of that process so that the Spirit of God fuses with the discordant parts of the self and one image is seen. I ask that they

The HEART Model

be aware of God's presence and to visualize God surrounding them, coming inside of them so that His presence radiates from the outside to the inside and from the inside to the outside. When the process is complete, with the discordant parts of self and the infilling of the Holy Spirit merged into one image, the only step left is to return with new insight.

> Elise, a thirty-two-year-old newlywed who was particularly distraught over several life issues, described her feelings as being "spiritually constipated," as if her prayers were reaching no higher than the ceiling. In other words, she felt disconnected from the Holy Spirit. She had been a Christian for as long as she could remember and believed in the Lord, but did not have a sense of His presence when she craved His comfort and enlightenment. She was at the end of her rope, having tried everything she could think of to resolve the upsetting situations, all to no avail. At the end of her rope, she finally called her father, who was a minister and therapist. He listened intently and then asked what she wanted him to do.
>
> "I want you to tell me what to do now. I've tried everything I know to do and I'm not making any headway, and my prayers aren't making any difference. I don't think God even hears me."
>
> "Okay," he said, "but you're probably not going to like what I have to say."
>
> "So please, tell me what to do," she pleaded.
>
> "First of all, remember that God is the constant here. If anyone or anything has changed, it's you, not Him."
>
> "Okay, but that still doesn't help me much. Now what?"
>
> "My best advice is for you to do three things: Sit down, shut up, and pay attention." Then he hung up the phone.
>
> She sat there for a few minutes, crying in frustration. She finally raised her hands upward and said, "I give up." Then the kitten in her lap stopped playing and went to sleep. The automobile noise outside stopped, and the garbage truck left the neighborhood. Elise prayed a prayer of thanksgiving for all the blessings in her life and surrendered to the Lord's will. Then she made herself still, her hands resting on the sleeping fur-ball in her lap.

> She became aware of the gentle presence of the Holy Spirit in and around her, comforting and loving. The tears changed from sadness and frustration to tears of joy. When she breathed in, it was as if she were breathing in the peace and love promised in the Bible.
>
> After a time, the kitten woke up, the neighbors offloaded several children, and the bulldozer at a nearby construction site started up again. But she was no longer upset, nor did she feel that was she alone.
>
> Elise experienced being in the presence of God, in the form of the Holy Spirit.

As Jesus said, "Behold, I stand at the door and knock" (Revelation 3:20 ESV). That persistent availability is God's gift to us. The next part of that same verse demonstrates that each one of us has the option to open the door, in order to receive what God is offering as an expression of His constant love.

Chapter Nine Notes

CHAPTER TEN

Refocusing and Returning to Life with New Insight, Purpose, and Hope

Not surprisingly, for many DID clients, the first year following full integration is the most challenging. The reasoning is not difficult or convoluted. If nothing else, what is required is breaking old habits, which were survival tactics and had become the norm for most of their lifetime. In place of the unhealthy, discordant familiar part, they must learn a whole new way of being, an entirely different method of handling life's challenges. The same is true for those who are not dissociative but are split, in the sense of their parts of self—the child of "then" and the adult of now. The technique of merging discordant parts of self, whether it be the alters of DID or split parts of self in non-DID clients, is very much the same.

Consider amputees, who typically experience the phantom limb for a minimum of about twenty-one days. In *Psycho-Cybernetics*, Maxwell Maltz states that following facial surgery, his patients required about twenty-one days to get used to seeing their new faces.[331] Fr. Richard Rohr, Franciscan priest and author, has asserted that it takes about sixty days to establish new habits.[332] Others in the field say the time frame can range between two and eight months. Remember that those habits are generally thought of as relating to lifestyle changes, such as remembering to exercise, getting up on time, eating healthful foods at reasonable intervals, etc. A reintegrated DID person is faced with getting used to *being* an entirely new way—a new being, fresh and unskilled at operating from a single, integrated personality. It is also true that those who are not DID are learning to operate from a place where the reconnected or restored parts of self, the child of then and the adult of now, also create a new being, unskilled at operating from an integrated personality.

> Lorraine is the mother of a daughter who was diagnosed with bi-polar disorder in her teens. The daughter, who was also plagued with dyslexia and attention deficit disorder, remembers feelings resembling depression as early as age three. When the daughter finally agreed to begin taking medication, she was in her forties. According to Lorraine, it was like having a brand-new person born into the family. The daughter heard, for the first time, things that her family had been saying for decades. Her stock in trade was to deliver a scathing diatribe and then leave. The next day, to her, it was as if nothing had ever happened, while the rest of the family wandered around like walking wounded, shell-shocked.
>
> There were great gaps in the daughter's memory, but after starting the medications and therapy, she began recognizing some of the emotional damage she had caused with her words and actions. Prior to that point, the daughter was completely unaware of the pain and suffering she had caused; then, she was plagued with guilt over having hurt people she loved. Once she had distinguished how her behavior affected others, she set about, with the help of a skilled therapist, working to develop ways of responding (verbally and behaviorally) that would not inflict damage. The phenomenon of becoming aware of a possible new way of living, one that did not hurt others who were important to her, was in itself cause for great joy. Her new favorite Bible verse became: "Create in me a clean heart, O God, and renew a right spirit within me" (Psalm 51:10 ESV).

When the merging takes place, it is a brand-new place to stand. Clients have a whole, healed heart, and new eyes with which to view the world. This is the actual merging of the split parts, whether conflicted parts of self or full alters, that lies at the HEART of the healing. A fresh perspective and healing occur even in healthy people when they take the time to look at a piece of themselves not ordinarily or previously examined, discovering all kinds of attendant feelings or emotions. The reclaiming, or taking yourself back, is an act of creation—of making something new, not just changing or fixing something.

The post-integration process focuses on the individual in areas of education and support and includes large segments of strategizing and problem solving. In other words, that new entity has to handle things in an entirely different manner. When dealing with the final integration of someone who has DID, that person is for the first time—often in twenty to fifty years—living life as a single personality, which entails a radically different focus and orientation to the world. DID clients then must grapple with what Carol Parker calls "single personality disorder."[333] Once integration has occurred, it is necessary for clients to reorient to everything. They can no longer dissociate to make it through the day. No longer can one personality check out and let another part handle the difficult situations. Therapy issues are often broader and more general. Clients must deal with unfamiliar territory in the realms of:

- Sexuality
- Religion and spirituality
- Work and other external responsibilities
- Social relationships
- Close and familial relationships (children, partners, etc.)
- Common, day-to-day problems

> Early in my career of working in trauma, I met Sandy, who came to my office looking to heal after having seen a variety of therapists regarding early childhood sexual trauma. Sandy had been seen many years earlier by one of my supervisors. At that time, Sandy was working with marital issues, so her necessary individual work had not been done, although she had been diagnosed with DID. For many years after that, she had worked as a teacher overseas doing workshops around the technique of hypnosis, of which she had become a practitioner. Sandy came to therapy highly motivated and purposely scheduled up to three sessions a week in hopes of moving her therapy process along.
>
> For close to two years, she worked on resolving and healing difficult traumas from the past. Her father was both a perpetrator and a purveyor of pornography, in which Sandy was displayed predominately. She worked through the emotions of hurt, betrayal, love, and "exoneration of the perpetrator," one of the most difficult areas, where the internal battle of love and hate is often waged at the price of rationalizations and excuses for the perpetrating behavior. "I love him because he saw me as special and did good things for me. I hate him because he harmed me and made me have sex with him and his friends." That internal war took quite a while to resolve. The resolution of those issues rekindled the desire for closeness in a relationship and dealing with sexuality, which she had stopped completely for years. The resolution also brought up new issues around spirituality and who she

THE HEART MODEL

> was as a spiritual person, particularly in light of things she had previously seen as shameful and for which she blamed herself.
>
> The simple understanding that she had been groomed and set up as a child took quite a while to settle in. This understanding, though, gave her the freedom to leave it behind. I wish I could tell you that resolving these difficult issues was quick and easy, but alas, most of us are just not built that way. I find it amazing that sexuality can be seen in the form of early childhood abuse, including pornography and filmed sexual encounters with her father's friends, and yet when resolved can be something beautiful, in a committed relationship that ultimately leads to marriage. I do know that she was able to recapture a sense of herself, including her ability to be in relationship, but it took a while to get there.

The merging of parts is a fusion of thoughts, ideas, abilities, and emotions. Nothing is lost. Sometimes, clients will need to grieve losing the familiar experience of separateness. They may also need to grieve any loss of connection, childhood, innocence, and so forth. They often must work out how to connect to the emotions they have kept at bay for so long. Wholeness, for most, is a reclaiming of self. For DID clients, it is even more critical, because they are now an integrated whole for the first time since the original trauma. In Western culture, 97 percent of the clients who present with DID have the condition as a result of early childhood sexual trauma.[334]

AUDITING AND DESENSITIZATION

Some soldiers are taught to dissociate before going into battle, which can become a form of DID. In Scientology, the technique is based on 1950s Korean brainwashing methods. What Scientologists do is, literally, cause the client to dissociate. They put the subject in a situation where he or she becomes his or her own "higher self," which amounts to doing away with all emotional reaction to any situation or anything that has happened earlier in life. Then they retrain the person to dissociate himself or herself into the Scientologist mindset, using the process they call auditing. Converts go into counsel with someone with whom they talk about a situation that happened in their lives. If there is any emotional attachment at all, converts talk about it and revisit it, over and over, until their response is neutral and flat. That procedure is repeated for anything that has happened in life, good or bad, to which there is an associated emotional charge. As a result, the past becomes basically flat and numb, and the present, including the spiritual classes, get the attention. In this way, converts learn to split. It is an example of total desensitization.

Bostonian Stephen Hassen works with clients and relatives of people who have been influenced by cults. He himself was a Moonie, and he has written at least three books on destructive cults and what he describes as mind control used to recruit and retain members.[335] Cult awareness therapists do the work to help converts reintegrate (family, church, and clients' historical environment) by distinguishing what is cultish and what is not, and then to help them reconnect to their backgrounds. It is a different methodology from working with trafficked clients.

DIFFERENCES OF PTSD AND DID

Following such tragedies as the 9/11 attack, shootings, and bombings, survivors do not usually split or create alters, unless they were already dissociative and had created one or more personalities to deal with earlier trauma. Instead, the literature shows that adults tend to develop post-traumatic stress disorder (PTSD).[336] Typically, those survivors are haunted by the memories (of buildings collapsing, people dying, etc.). I have worked with several trauma teams connected to universities where I have taught. The first one was at Regent University in Virginia Beach, Virginia, where the team responded twice to the earthquake in Haiti in 2010. We found that people were disturbed by memory intrusion from seeing people's bodies in the streets, buildings burning, and people dying. The team also responded to the hurricane and flooding in New Jersey from Hurricane Sandy in 2012. The memory intrusion was regarding rising water lines and personal fears about drowning; near the water line, only tops of houses could be seen as the initial waters swelled to between seven and nine feet high.

My second and current team is at Divine Mercy University in Sterling, Virginia, where the team responding to California and Oregon wildfires dealt with people who had made narrow escapes from fire that completely surrounded them. Memories of entire buildings going up in flames, driving through walls of fire in hopes of escape, and for some, watching loved ones succumb and die from smoke inhalation. This same team responded to the domestic terrorism in Charlottesville, Virginia, in 2017, during which neo-Nazi groups formed an armed demonstration regarding the removal of a statue of Confederate Major General Robert E. Lee slated to go to a museum in Richmond, Virginia. Interviewing the residents of Charlottesville two days later while doing field

The Heart Model

trauma work, members of this team were told stories of the armed group holding people hostage in churches and synagogues, threatening to kill anyone who walked out of the buildings, and also talking—loudly enough for the people to hear—about burning down the buildings with the people inside. We also were told stories about the death of Heather Heyer, who was killed by a neo-Nazi member when the latter drove his car into a group of protestors, as well as memories of ambulances, police, and total chaos.

Most who directly experience this sort of trauma tend not to dissociate as a defense mechanism, but instead form a reaction that leads to the symptoms of post-traumatic stress. These symptoms, if left unchecked, may well develop into post-traumatic stress disorder (PTSD). In all of the instances listed above, memory intrusion was often the culprit. Traumatic memories started to weigh heavy on emotions for those who were coping and had a significant reaction to what they had experienced or heard. Basic symptoms of post-traumatic stress disorder include the following:[337]

1. Exposure to actual or threatened death, serious injury, or sexual violence, in any of the following contexts: (a) direct experience, (b) first-person witnessing of trauma to another person, (c) learning that the traumatic event happened to a close family member or friend, (d) if the trauma was experienced repeatedly, or (e) extreme exposure of details to the traumatic event(s). In cases of actual or threatened death of a family member or friend, the death must have been accidental or violent.[338]

2. Reactions to triggers—that is, things that remind the person of the traumatic event. This can be anything from sights, smells, and sounds to internal cues of feelings, thoughts, or emotional reactions, to name but a few possibilities.

3. Avoidance of anything that reminds the person of the trauma; this can also include avoidance of people and withdrawing from normal activities.

4. Hyper-arousal, or waiting for the next shoe to fall—guarding oneself against any kind of potential confrontation, stress, or trauma. The person is constantly searching for safety.

5. Irritable mood.

It should be noted that intrusive memories can take the form of recurrent thoughts you cannot seem to shake out of your mind, flashbacks, bad dreams or nightmares, or dissociative reactions that return the person (in thought) to the original trauma.

These symptoms can be quite broad, and can include problems with sleep, exaggerated startle response, reckless or self-destructive behavior, angry outbursts, negative beliefs about oneself, and dissociation.[339]

> On one of the trauma team trips, during my time working with the second team, we had the opportunity to work with clinicians from Syria. An organization called Witness as Ministry (WAM) organized a series of trainings in Beirut, Lebanon, to give Syrian clinicians the opportunity to learn techniques that would help survivors of the recent war to process memories and begin the healing process from PTSD. The leader of the group came to me very distraught and upset because his administrative assistant had been involved in a recent situation where an eleven-year-old boy had died, and she was blaming herself for his death. It turned out that she was a part-time tutor who was mentoring this boy and was running fifteen minutes late for her appointment. She called the boy and stressed that he must not go outside because of the danger and that she would be there in the next 15 mins. Of course, eleven-year-olds being quite curious, he did not follow instructions and went outside to play. At that very moment, ISIS insurgents in the city of Aleppo released a volley of bombs, one of which landed next to the boy, who immediately died.
>
> When Cora (not her real name) arrived for her appointment, she was horrified and became emotionally uncontrollable. For the two weeks prior to the workshop, she had not been able to work much, despite coming to the office, and was often seen crying uncontrollably. The director asked me if I would work with her using a technique we were teaching—eye movement desensitization reprocessing (EMDR), a rapid technique for processing memory related to traumatic events.
>
> That evening, I met with Cora and she told me that she blamed herself because this was the first time she had ever been late, and that she should have known better—that he would go out and play rather than follow directions. Maybe it was in the form of her directions or the tone of her voice, or maybe she should have arrived earlier. She was having ongoing memory intrusions and could not shake the thought of seeing that boy dead in front of her; she could not get the sound of the bombs out of her mind. I spoke for about thirty minutes with Cora, getting necessary information and her version of the story. I came to realize that at the

> moment of the trauma, when she came upon the body of her student torn apart from the bomb, she literally dissociated and disconnected a part of herself.
>
> For another hour and a half, I used various techniques, predominately EMDR. At the end of that time, she was able to reconnect with her younger self, who she felt was irresponsible, uncaring, and distant. Through the process of therapy, she was able to see the reality that the boy was a victim of war and not a victim of her irresponsibility. She was able to see that she was responsible for calling him and instructing him properly, and that while it was a tragic event and she will miss him greatly, this was not something that she did. In the process of that hour and a half, she was able to reclaim her rational mind and bring that rationality to her emotional self. She still felt the loss of her student but no longer held on to the blame for what had happened.
>
> Six weeks after the workshop, I received an email from the director of the program in Syria, letting me know that his administrative assistant returned back to work, fully capable and reconnected to herself. In fact, he said that she laughed often and was back to being a support not only to the ministerial outreach but also to her family.

During the process of healing, it may be necessary to grieve the loss of separateness that has lasted through a great portion of the client's lifetime. Some may need to grieve the unfamiliarity of connectedness and the loss of any connection, childhood, and innocence. They may also need to work out the connection to, and experience, the emotions they have kept at bay for so long. The post-merge/integration process focuses on the individual in areas of education and support, with much strategizing and problem solving. Keep in mind that DID and PTSD are often listed as comorbid. For many DID clients, the first year following full integration is the hardest. At this point, DID clients must deal with "single personality disorder," to use Parker's term again.[340] They can no longer check out and let another part handle the difficult situations. Therapy issues are broad and general after overcoming the following basics: sexuality, religion and spirituality, work, relationships, and the myriad challenges of daily life.

A New Orientation to Life

Overall, the new entity must deal with things entirely differently. For the first time in decades, the person is living life as a single personality which is, at its core, a different orientation to the entire world. The individual is required to get responsible for his or her whole self. Wholeness, for most, is a reclaiming of self. For DID clients, it is much more, because they become an integrated whole for the first time since the original trauma.

Many of us would not want to go back in time to reexperience the angst of adolescence. The DID client who is working to heal has been reliving the trauma over and over, often for decades. Part of healing requires looking those horrors squarely in the eye and choosing to view them differently. The mere act of choosing to face them yet again, and then to interrupt old patterns in favor of unfamiliar ones, takes courage and strength. Making that choice begins building the muscles of wholeness. What is at stake is the entirety, the wholeness, of the self. Growth will already have occurred throughout the healing process, and greater strength is then brought to the challenges. It takes practice and regular work to settle into the new way of living.

Just as working out builds physical muscles, the ongoing, continual choice to live a new way, in the present as a whole heart, builds emotional muscles; but, it takes time to break old habits and form new ones. During that time, with constant, consistent choice-making, brand-new neural pathways are being built in the brain. Scientists tell us that "what fires together wires together." A catchy phrase, and it does describe the function of retraining the brain, which is part and parcel of developing mastery over the new life.

The good news is that every choice to live as a whole self, in one's entirety, and to do so in the present, serves to add to the early, tentative steps when strength and hope first began to make themselves known. The process has been described as breaking in a new pair of shoes. They are the right size when you buy them, but it takes a while for the feet to make the shoes adapt or mold themselves to the proper, comfortable shape.

Achieving and Maintaining Balance

Finding and keeping a balanced lifestyle can be tricky for any of us who live in this chaotic, rushed world that has so many ups and downs. It can be that much harder for clients who have recently experienced a healing process. Often, they are learning to come to terms with new ways of coping, thinking, functioning, and relating to others as well as themselves. How are they to balance the onslaught of activities and demands on their time, especially if they are expected to handle twelve or thirteen things at once? How are they to balance domestic responsibilities with relationships, work, ministry, errands, and a thousand other disruptions in our schedules? It is not easy for any of us to handle all these things at once, but for those who have learned to cope by dissociating, this can all be overwhelming. Those who dissociate learn to deal with everything by dividing functions and activities among parts of themselves. It would be tempting, even after healing, to revert to previous strategies, so learning and exercising new ways of functioning becomes essential.

As therapists, we try to steer clients away from dissociative coping strategies, which have consequences such as poor health, irritability, and strained relationships. If we want balance and wholeness in our lives, I believe the best way to start is by allowing the presence of God into our lives and by allowing Him to balance us out. When we talk about coming to a new way of looking at life, we come into a relationship with a vibrant, living God. When we worship, meditate, bask in His presence, walk with Him, talk with Him, and choose to live His way, we find ourselves on a solid spiritual path. The Bible says, "The fear of the LORD is the beginning of knowledge" (Proverbs 1:7 NIV). I believe "fear," or respectful acknowledgment, of God is also the beginning of wholeness and balance.

This is where I direct my clients when they are feeling overwhelmed. Jesus Christ really is the solution to all the new problems they will face. When they struggle and think about falling back into old patterns, His presence can help them focus.

THE FATHERHOOD OF GOD

As discussed in a previous chapter, clients who have experienced sexual trauma often struggle with the issue of God as Father. Often, they see God the Father as restrictive and punishing. This is often a borrowed view from their experience with their own fathers or stepfathers. I frequently steer them into a deeper relationship with Jesus or the Holy Spirit before expecting them to feel comfortable with the Fatherhood of God. If they have been receptive to Jesus for most of their therapy and seem ready at the time of integration for a relationship with the Father, that usually means they have progressed through the memories, and their healing progresses well.

It is wonderful for clients to get to a place where they know they can embrace God when they need comfort. Seeing God as their Father is like coming into a new and deeper place with Him. The idea of God as Father presents many new images and concepts: Father God is our provider. He is the one who designed us in the womb. He is the one who takes care of all our needs; this includes good gifts. I love to give my kids good things—not just what they absolutely need to survive, but extra things as well. God is the same way with us. He loves to bless us. As a good Father, He also knows what is best for us. Trusting God as Father is a big step for trauma survivors. When they get to this point, it is incredibly healing. Clients who are ready to see God as Father are clients who talk with God, walk with God, and know Him intimately.

It is important that we, as therapists, do not push clients in any way. Their relationship with God must be their own. That relationship is formed in talking to God and being in God's presence. The "Christian overlay" in the HEART model means coming to know God in a personal way.

UNITY WITHIN SELF

While it is true that we are made up of body, soul, and spirit, the Lord sees us as one person, one whole being, not a division of parts. We cannot affect one part of who we are without affecting the rest of who we are. We are not designed to be divided; we are designed to be whole and complete in Christ Jesus. Division is Satan's idea, while unity is God's. Jesus said, "If a house is divided against itself, that house cannot stand" (Mark 3:25 NIV). Division creates heartache, chaos, and all kinds of trouble, not just for an individual, but also for humankind. That is why God urges us in His word to be of the same mind, to work together in unity as the church, the body of Christ. Likewise, if the church is to have victory in these last days, or in any spiritual battle, we need to learn to work together. Satan knows if he can keep the members of the body of Christ preoccupied in fighting against each other, he will gain more ground for himself.

There is strength and power in unity. When people with the same goal join forces to accomplish a purpose, whether good or evil, it can have a great impact. Consider the beauty in the perfect synchronization of choreographed dancing or skating; consider also the destruction of mobs and gangs. It is disturbing to see so many Christians spending so much time disagreeing over the tiniest issues, while other groups unite to create havoc in the world. When the body of Christ is divided against itself—when there are Christians who think they can be rid of those in the body of Christ who do not think or act as they do, without jeopardizing themselves—we need to focus again on Christ's prayer that we "may be one, as You, Father, are in Me, and I in You; that they also may be one in Us" (John 17:21 NKJV).

Division or conflict within oneself is a prime illustration of the chaos, confusion, and impediments that division causes. The fight between the adult and the child self in therapy exemplifies that well. When one part of the self attacks another, people sometimes do not realize how much damage they are doing to themselves. This is a great deception for those who deal with dissociative identity disorder (DID). People need to work together in unity, whether it be within themselves, within the body of Christ, or in the union between themselves and God. To be in continual disagreement and division is to pave the way to our destruction, at best. When we hurt others, particularly in the body of Christ, we also hurt ourselves.

Jesus, as the head of the body, takes it personally when any part of the body is hurt. When the Lord confronted Saul of Tarsus on the road to Damascus, He said, "Why are you persecuting me?" (Acts 9:4 ESV). He did not say, "Why are you persecuting these Christians?" He considered their persecution to be His.

Experiencing Jesus in Integration

When I see the wonderful way in which Jesus brings about the completion of the integration process through the Holy Spirit, and brings healing in those who have been divided into selves due to dissociation, I am always impressed at those individuals' ability to survive. On the other hand, when I see clients who do not want to involve God in their healing and integration process return to separateness and struggle, my heart is grieved. I do not take it as a personal failure when this happens, because I know I cannot force a person's will. Clients are ultimately free to choose the path they wish to take. I can encourage them in a particular direction, and I can present the issues and options; but, the final decision, along with its consequences, is always theirs.

There is a difference, however, between the concepts of "believing in God" and "knowing" God. In my experience, many people who call themselves Christians talk about their great depths of belief in God. They talk about the various concepts of Christianity and about doing good works. Fundamentally, understanding a concept like faith is far different from knowing the still, small voice within, and feeling the movement of the Holy Spirit as He goes about healing the hurts and providing access to joy and peace. Experiencing God is far different from *describing* that experience. It is something like the difference between reading the menu at a fancy restaurant and savoring the explosion of flavors as you eat what may have been described, however, elegantly, on the menu.

Again, my experience is that the merging or integration does not unravel when God is part of the process. I think God seals the deal—that His presence brings the parts together in a way that is binding and finishes the job. However, within a secular framework, that piece is missing.

The merging of parts is a fusion of thought, ideas, abilities, and emotions. After the discordant parts of self, memories, experiences, and situations have all blended into one, and the Holy Spirit has been allowed to connect fully and become a part of the whole self, the creation becomes complete, a vital force. It becomes important, then, to share the experience as a way of validating, solidifying, and keeping the experience alive in the present, in the here and now (see Chapter Eight).

Talking about the experience is only one way to keep it alive and to share it with others. Another way to keep the experience alive is to go to God in prayer. That does not necessarily mean standing on a corner and carrying a banner, or praying out loud in a group or church setting. The private return engagement with God is available at any moment. Some call it prayer; others call it meditation. Many people experience moments of connection when surrounded by the majesty of nature, whether taking in magnificent vistas or marveling at a lady bug's spots or a butterfly's delicate wings. It is experiencing the connection with God, being present in the moment and *knowing* that the Lord is available when snuggling with a beloved pet, or being thankful for having loved ones in one's life.

New behavioral and mental, emotional, and spiritual habits, such as the habit of gratitude or thankfulness, can with cultivation become deeply ingrained. Corrie ten Boom was from a family of Dutch Christians who were instrumental in helping many Jews escape the Nazis during World War II.[341] After she and her family were caught and sent to a Nazi concentration camp, she was released mere days after her sister's death there. She authored a number of books and is quoted as saying, "You can never learn that Christ is all you need, until Christ is all you have." For those who have experienced the horrors of trafficking or complex trauma, when they reach rock bottom, God is there, waiting with open arms to heal and soothe. Corrie ten Boom's book, *The Hiding Place*, derives its title from the scripture, "You are my hiding place and my shield; I hope in your word" (Psalm 119:114 ESV).[342] She consciously cultivated the practice, or habit, of deliberately placing herself in the presence and awareness of God. In fact, if spiritual refuge is available in the physical immediate moment, we do not go there, we miss out on the experience of "the peace of God, which transcends all understanding, [which] will guard your hearts and your minds in Christ Jesus" (Philippians 4:7 NIV).

When survivors stand at the beginning of a new phase of life, they are in a brand-new place that they could not even imagine previously, though they hoped and wished desperately for a break from their pain and the suffering of being so disjointed. Corrie ten Boom asserted, "Some knowledge is too heavy ... you cannot bear it ... [but] your Father will carry it until you are able."[343]

Healing one's spirituality is the opposite of alienation. It is a passion for life and a feeling with connection, of being a part of life. There is a part of everything living that wants to become itself—the tadpole turning into a frog, the chrysalis into a butterfly, or a damaged human into a whole one.[344] Spirituality is not only our connection to God but also the choice to heal, to be healthy, and to be fully alive. It is becoming your whole and true self. A reformed life with new insight involves having clarity and staying centered, to see and know what is essential and let other things fall away.

Spirituality and the following of that inner voice of God's Holy Spirit is a connection to the deepest source of love. With that love comes a sense of belonging, a sense of safety, and a deeper experience of faith in the capacity to heal. Having a relationship with God is not a shortcut through the process of healing or a way out of dealing with situations, feelings, or loss. God's presence enhances our ability to heal and is a constant source to draw comfort and ongoing inspiration. With God as the lead therapist, in partnership, we can support those with whom we work in their journey of inner healing and find that they are brought to a place of integration, awareness, and wholeness.

Chapter Ten Notes

CHAPTER ELEVEN

Trauma and HEART Model Research

When we talk about trauma, we are talking about catastrophic events that may have a significant emotional impact resulting in difficulty with daily life.[345] Dealing with these emotions may disrupt relationships, cause severe family problems, or cause work situations to implode. While anyone can be subject to trauma, there are some factors that put people at greater risk of experiencing trauma:[346]

- High-crime and chaotic neighborhoods
- Severe marital discord
- Low socio-economic status
- Overcrowding
- Father engaged in criminality
- Mother with a psychiatric disorder
- Parents with an authoritarian perspective
- Maternal figure with high anxiety
- Father with low employability
- Transient parenting or caregiving
- Poor quality of mother–child interactions
- Admitting child to care of authorities [347]

The Heart Model

Traumatic events that occur before the age of eleven result in three times greater risk of a traumatic stress reaction in adolescence. When four or more risk factors are present, the chance of permanent problems increases tenfold.[348] Many families fall into these risk factors. You can see that the problems generated in these circumstances are likely to be perpetuated for a long time.

Some resiliency factors do help offset the impact:[349]

- Children with high verbal abilities who have learned how to navigate an adult world verbally
- One caring or parental figure in the immediate surroundings (and that could be you!)
- Capacity for goal-oriented behavior
- Open, supportive educational climate
- Early identification and intervention
- Trauma that is not of human design and was not within the family, such as natural disasters, allows faster recovery, since it is not so personal

When trauma occurs, it is like putting a mask over someone's face. The person sees everything through this mask: work, family, friends, school, religion, and so on. Trauma then becomes the filter through which everything is seen from that point on, until the trauma is resolved.[350]

Trauma can also interrupt the narrative memory.[351] When a trauma occurs that is overwhelming and overpowering, the feelings are stored in the implicit memory. The younger the victim is, the more likely this is to occur. The person suffering trauma never wants to feel or experience this overwhelming set of emotions, so the body naturally tries to forget it.

Survivors of human trafficking often have not worked out the trauma connected to their traumatic situations. Elements of the trauma show themselves in repeated patterns of behavior that attempt to work out resolutions but often spin into cycles of defeat. This frequently creates situations in which memory fragments of feelings and sensations find their way into conscious memory, having been released from the implicit memory as a reaction to a trigger. The work of the therapist, therefore, is to attempt to allow the client to connect the narrative memory and the implicit memory in order to complete the full narrative. The trauma can then be integrated into the person's life, because the story and the associated feelings are all present. Consider this quote by Judith Herrmann:[352]

> Repeated trauma in the adult life erodes the structure of the personality already formed, but repeated trauma in childhood forms and deforms the personality. The child trapped in an abusive environment is faced with the formidable task of adaptation. She must find a way to preserve a sense of trust in people who are untrustworthy, safety in a situation that is unsafe, control in a situation that is terrifyingly unpredictable, power in a situation of helplessness. Unable to care for or protect herself, she must compensate for the failures of adult care and protection with the only means at her disposal, an immature system of psychological defenses.

The above description encapsulates what children go through in order to cope with difficult traumatic situations that create an emotional overload to their systems. Situations that can cause this type of disruption, which we consider trauma, include the following:[353]

- Physical, emotional, or sexual abuse
- Crime victimization
- Death of a loved one
- Divorce
- Car accidents
- Military combat/war
- Natural disasters
- Difficult surgery
- Overwhelming shame

> When I was in China, I encountered a woman whom I interviewed in a hospital in Shanghai. Our treatment team was looking at differences between dissociation and schizophrenia. She talked to us for two separate hours over two days about being fifteen years old and waiting for her parents to pick her up to bring her home. On the third day, I had the wherewithal to take her to a restroom where

The HEART Model

> there was a mirror and I asked her to describe herself. She said, "There is an old woman there with bad makeup."
>
> Most of you, reading this, may have chuckled a bit or laughed, as did most of the Chinese psychiatrists in the study. However, by the time she got through describing herself, she was back to her true age of forty-two and had no recollection of talking to us for two hours over the last couple of days as a fifteen-year-old. In fact, she thought we were absolutely crazy. It took the doctors a few hours to convince her this had happened.
>
> What we found out later that evening, after checking her history in her chart, was that she had failed a test at fifteen years old—by one point. This was the test in China that determined if she would go on to college or become a factory worker. She believed that it brought so much shame to her family, she literally split in her psyche and compartmentalized her parts. Her diagnosis was clearly dissociative identity disorder. It was the shame that caused the compartmentalization and the split.

Sometimes lesser-scale situations that can cause disruption are:

- Perceived hurts
- Slights
- Guilt
- Shame[354]

Results of Unprocessed Trauma

Traumatic events of this nature can cause a wide range of symptoms in the victim, including PTSD, borderline personality disorder (BPD), and even dissociation. When we talk about the symptoms of PTSD, we are talking about reexperiencing the event in the form of abreactions, flashbacks, dreams, and memory intrusion. This causes intense psychological distress at exposure to reminders. A common effect of PTSD is survivors persistently avoiding people or events that remind them of the trauma. The individuals often become hypervigilant regarding safety and conditions that are present in their environment. These symptoms are often accompanied by irritability and unstable moods.[355]

Those with borderline personality disorder experience some of the following symptoms:

- Frantic efforts to avoid real or imagined abandonment
- Unstable, intense relationships that start out connected and blow up in a relatively short amount of time
- Relationships that alternate between idealization and devaluation[356]

Other behaviors that frequently show up are:

- Identity issues, or unstable self-image
- Impulsivity (spending, sex, drugs, alcohol, shoplifting, binge eating, reckless driving, etc.)
- Recurrent suicidal behavior, gestures, threats, or self-mutilating behavior
- Affect instability
    - Dysphoria, or a mix of depression, anxiety, rage, and despair
    - Irritability
    - Anxiety
- Feelings of emptiness
- Inappropriate, intense anger or lack of controlling anger (temper, fights, etc.)
- Transient, stress-related, paranoid ideation (jealousy)
- Dissociative symptoms
- Addiction
- Triangulation, or a form of manipulating and controlling communication and relationships[357]

At the further end of the dissociative continuum are other dissociative disorders.

The HEART Model

Dissociative phenomena include:

- Trance or autohypnosis
- Personality splitting or compartmentalization
- Automatic behaviors, or automatisms
- Derealization and depersonalization
- Amnesia (total, selective, or partial)
- Fugue states, or having no memory of how you got somewhere
- Somnambulism, or sleepwalking
- Regression, or behaving and thinking as you did at an earlier time in your life, usually childhood
- Time distortion
- Dissociative identity disorder
- Anesthesia or analgesia, or feeling numb
- Sensory delusion or hallucination[358]

THE DISSOCIATIVE STRUCTURAL MODEL

The current theory with which many therapists are working is called the dissociative structural model.[359] The dissociative structural model looks at the structure of dissociation rather than at the separate parts of self. Dissociation itself happens on a continuum, where mild or minimum levels of dissociation may occur in adjustment-type situations, whereas significant dissociation may happen when a person's reactions and feelings are so overwhelmed that the person becomes dysfunctional. The dissociated person experiences an intrusion and then immediately takes actions designed to withdraw from the intrusions or their aftereffects. This happens in a variety of disorders across dissociative categories.

People dealing with post-traumatic stress disorder illustrate this point when they experience flashbacks of something that happened in the past, yet experience it in the present time. In fact, there is a history of intrusion and withdrawal that occurs in a wide variety of disorders; for example, obsessive-compulsive disorder is marked by the intrusion of the compulsion, followed by the withdrawal of whatever coping mechanism is employed to deal with the intrusion.[360] PTSD deals with the intrusion of the flashback and the withdrawal of emotions and sensations. The personification of the modules—that is, the separate parts, ego states, alter states, or compartmentalized parts of self, such as happens with DID—is secondary to the intrusion and withdrawal. In fact, all of the following involve some form of intrusion and withdrawal:

- Post-traumatic stress disorder
- Dissociative identity disorder
- Obsessive-compulsive disorder
- Borderline personality disorder
- Impulse control disorder
- Dissociative schizophrenia
- Somatization disorder[361]

The above discussion leaves us, as therapists, with the puzzle of how best to help victims of trauma process the experience and heal. The HEART Model can be used to help those who have suffered early childhood trauma, complex trauma, or the use of dissociative mechanisms to deal with difficult things in life. It is an overlay that does not dictate particular styles of counseling, meaning you could use any theory of counseling with clients: cognitive-behavioral, Gestalt, existential, person-centered, or psychodynamic. The HEART Model is a process that could be employed and used with every client in the treatment centers. It is circular, or non-linear, in nature. The HEART Model has the capacity to heal the symptoms of dissociation and PTSD, and also to promote increased resilience by empowering individual autonomy and providing a positive experience with an interactive faith and belief in a power (God) greater than the self.[362]

HEART MODEL RESEARCH

The history of the HEART Model dates back to the mid-1980s, when I had the opportunity to read two books that greatly impressed me. Both books are by David Seamands, who had been a missionary. In the mission field, he was confronted with a wide variety of counseling situations and did not know what to do. He had only one counseling text with him, a thick volume on how to apply Jungian theory[363] to individual, child, adolescent, and family therapy. Seamands dissected each page of the book until he understood both its concepts and its application in working with others. I was impressed by the story and by his treatise, written in 1983, titled *Healing for Damaged Emotions*.[364] This book was followed quickly by a 1985 book, *Healing the Memories*, in which he outlines a step-by-step process for healing childhood trauma and children who have been in adult situations.[365] As I mentioned in Chapter Eight, I was so impressed that I sat down and sketched out this model.

For the next twenty years, I worked on developing this model, holding workshops around steps I found necessary in the healing process. In 2006, I began doing HEART Model workshops after being challenged by a local ministry—Restoration Ministries in Washington, DC—to address how one might work with survivors of human trafficking. The founder of Restoration Ministries, Candace Walker, was looking to hold a conference regarding survivors of human trafficking, and she invited me to participate. Six months later, we put on that conference, and I have been actively developing the model ever since. Shortly after my experience with Candace, I was introduced to the director of a program in Baltimore, called The Samaritan Women, for survivors of sex trafficking. Through those connections, I was introduced to an organization called Abolition International Shelter Association (AISA), now known as Hope for Justice, which was developed and run for shelter programs across the United States that worked with victims of trafficking.

Human trafficking happens in two forms: it sometimes happens to enslave people for labor, but the predominance of trafficking is for various kinds of sex work, which affects both men and women. In the United States alone, 100,000 adolescents are trafficked every year.[366] It is estimated that 3.4 million people are trafficked globally each year.[367] Traffickers often look for disenfranchised youth and adolescents starting at the ages of twelve to fifteen. They may begin a set of grooming behaviors that ensnare youth into a myriad of conflicting feelings, as the pimps often set themselves up as the victims' boyfriend. The perpetrators isolate the victims from friends and family who love them, and manipulate them into a life of prostitution, addiction, and torture.[368] (See Chapter Twelve for more in-depth discussion of human trafficking, its victims, and its survivors.)

As the HEART Model was becoming a viable format for working with this population, I wanted to see if this format would produce results. And, if I was right in what this model could do, I wanted to be able to establish it as an accepted treatment model and be able to do the research necessary to establish it as one of the first, if not *the* first, faith-based trauma treatment model to be considered a best practice for trauma. I wanted to establish an alternative to a strictly secular model of treatment, but one that would not conflict with the secular models, since the goal was to establish it within a community of mental health professionals. Often, professionals disregard spiritual formats. This is due to the fact that many such models are not subjected to the rigor of research and are considered anecdotal in their reports of applying spiritual disciplines, integrated formats of programming, or direct treatment to effect healing and significant changes.

Major concern exists among providers and researchers regarding the treatment effectiveness of phase-based interventions in the treatment of complex trauma and survivors of sex trafficking. Research must aim to illuminate the experiences and the conditions that influence successful negative-symptom reduction for persons exposed to and suffering complex trauma. The purpose of our overall study was to determine the effectiveness of the HEART Model in reducing depression, anxiety, hopelessness, and the other traumatic symptoms of sex trafficking victims, which included the five major symptoms of PTSD (intrusion, reaction to triggers, isolation or avoidance, hypervigilance, and affect irritability), along with depression, anxiety, and dissociative symptoms. Accordingly, I set out to fully research the efficacy of this alternative method.

My colleagues and I intended to do a three-year study, which became a seven-year study as we sought enough subjects to make the study viable. We continued collecting information, added two programs part-way through, and added data until our funding (initially from AISA) ran out and we could no longer sustain the ongoing collection of data.

A number of dissertations came out of the research. The first was by Megan Jones: "Leaving 'the Life': The Recovery Journey of Sex Trafficking Survivors Using the HEART Model of Intervention."[369] Postulating that the decision to leave the life of trafficking was an important one in the life of a survivor, she used qualitative research to determine which needs and experiences had to be quantified for further research. This particular study addressed the gap in the literature by investigating the experiences of the survivors themselves, with the HEART Model as their form of intervention. The qualitative approach, a phenomenological research design, was chosen because it was important to understand the shared experiences of the survivors. At the time, we used it as a pilot study, because the model was so new to the literature and there were only eight to ten participants total. All the participants were women in one of the Hope for Justice residences in a southeastern state; they were between the ages of eighteen and seventy

The HEART Model

years old, had histories of complex trauma, and were survivors of sex trafficking. Anyone who was actively psychotic, suicidal, or homicidal was screened out of the study.

Essentially, we wanted to answer some questions: What is essential for the lived experience of the recovery journey of the sex-trafficked survivor? What are the lived experiences of sex-trafficked survivors living in a residential treatment facility? What are the lived experiences of sex-trafficked survivors participating in the HEART Model as an intervention modality? And what aspects of living in a residential treatment facility are the most helpful in reducing the effects of trauma, according to the survivor?

The HEART Model is based on a three-phase model, but it uses seven to ten stages. The three-phase model was developed by Judith Herman in 1992 in her book, *Trauma and Recovery*.[370] The seven stages are represented as standardized treatment within the structure of a secular program, while the ten stages allow for a spiritual, faith-based overlay to be added to that secular model.

Phase 1 in that three-phase model deals with rapport building, safety issues, crisis stabilization, orientation to the therapeutic process, boundary issues, dissociative mapping of the internal system, and introducing coping skills to help the individual regulate emotions.

Phase 2 deals with everything pertaining to uncovering memory, processing feelings and affect, cognitive restructuring of twisted ways of thinking, fusion, and some integration. This is usually the longest period of treatment.

Phase 3 deals with final integrations, learning to live as a single personality, relational and sexual issues, spiritual issues, closure and termination of therapy, and ultimately, learning to live independently as a fully integrated human being.

The seven stages of the secular portion of the HEART Model deal with creating the safe environments, connecting and anchoring to the memory, processing emotions, and negotiating between the adult and the inner child. This section is largely based on John Bradshaw's work on connecting to disconnected parts of childhood.[371] It focuses on bringing the adult of now and the child of then into a present space of integration and congruence. The individual deals with the issue of forgiving oneself for being harmed, for being in that situation, and for whatever self-blame is present from being a victim of trauma, particularly sexual trauma. The rest of the model is focused on bringing the separated parts back together. As these parts come back together, they return with a new perspective on living and life itself.

When we add the spiritual overlay, those seven stages increase to ten. The first five stages are the same for both the secular and Christian models. We then add a stage regarding the awareness of God. Just as we have distortions of self, we often have spiritual distortions that twist how we see God (as discussed in Chapter Six). This stage also focuses on finding a way to accept God's forgiveness of us, a way to forgive God for not being what we wanted Him to be, and a way to let God off the hook.

Once that work has been completed, the merging of split parts takes on a whole different context, because not only do the parts merge, but also the spirit of God is at the center of that process and merges *with* us in order to be at the very center of who we are.

In the final stage, the individual returns with a whole new perspective, a new way of looking at the world and self. The timeline of this process varies for each individual. If the person encountered a single traumatic event, the process may take as little as one session. For others, this process can take months or even years.

As the research progressed and expanded, we worked with Wellspring in Atlanta, Georgia; Courage Worldwide in Rocklin, California; The Samaritan Women in Baltimore, Maryland; Redeemed Ministries in Houston, Texas; and Freedom Place, also in Houston. We added Grace Haven Home in Ohio after the initial three years, and Leticia's House in Williamsburg, Virginia. We also worked for a brief time with Phoenix House until they closed their program, but were unable to get any research findings from them. We strategically chose programs that represented all regions of the United States, to make sure we didn't overgeneralize based on findings from one portion of the country.

My colleagues and I went into treatment centers and safe homes for trafficking victims, both adolescent and adult. Survivors lived in a family-style atmosphere with four to eight others, which provided a place of safety to work through the model. We went in and trained all clinical staff and line staff, along with administrative staff, in the HEART Model, so that everyone understood what we were doing within the therapeutic process. With clinical staff, we would go much deeper and actually teach the skills and techniques. Over the seven years we did this study, we trained clinicians in administering the research tools we used to assess changes in the survivors' trauma symptoms, PTSD, anxiety, depression, attachment, spiritual well-being, resiliency factors, and God image. Initially, we gave the assessments at intervals starting with intake, four months, eight months, twelve months, sixteen months, twenty months, and twenty-four months. However, that was changed to every six months, because the frequency proved too hard to maintain, both for the agencies and for the researchers.

The assessments we used were:

Adults

- Beck depression inventory (BDI)
- Beck anxiety inventory (BAI)
- Trauma symptom inventory (TSI)
- Ego resiliency scale (ERS)
- Cognitive distortions scale (CDS)
- Multi-scale dissociation inventory (MDI)
- Spiritual well-being scale (SWB)
- Heartland forgiveness scale (HFS)
- God image inventory (GII)
- The Dissociative Experiences Scale (DES)

Adolescents

- Beck depression inventory (BDI)
- Revised children's manifest anxiety scale (RCMAS)
- Child PTSD symptom scale (CPSS)
- Ego resiliency scale (ERS)
- Spiritual well-being scale (SWB)
- Heartland forgiveness scale (HFS)
- God image inventory (GII)
- The Dissociative Experiences Scale -Adololescent (DES-A)

We looked at nine variables, all analyzed using basic statistical analysis, to measure the current trends of the effects of the HEART Model on each construct. We devised tables that showed the effectiveness of treatment. Regarding depression and anxiety symptoms in adult women, measured in the BDI and BAI, the mean depressive symptoms decreased from 94.67 at intake to a 70.67 at a six-month repeated measure. T scores for anxiety decreased from 84.33 at intake to 74 at three months and leveled out at 74.33

at the six-month re-measure. Our scales indicated significant decrease in both depression and anxiety symptoms.

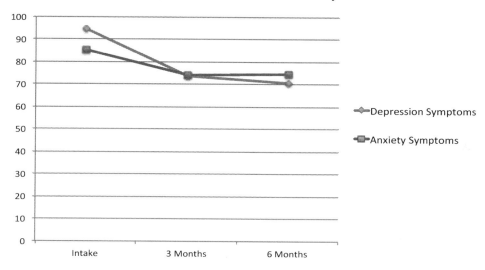

Figure 6: HEART Depression and Anxiety Trends (Adult Women)

There was a positive shift in symptoms, particularly when we looked at the subscales of trauma symptom inventory.

The HEART Model

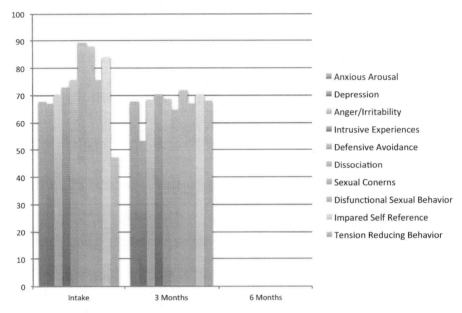

Figure 7: Trauma Symptom Trends (Adult)[372]

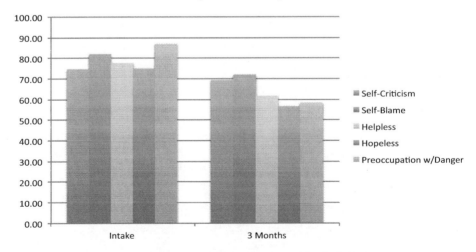

Figure 8: Cognitive Distortions Trends (Adults)[373]

The trending results over a three-month period showed a decrease in all trauma symptom subscales, except for tension-reducing behavior. When we looked at this particular area measured in adolescents, we found that there was only a slight rise in tension-reducing behavior. We supposed that it took extra time to adjust to the environment they were in, because they caught up to the adults at the six-month measure.

The scales showed effectiveness across the board in reducing symptoms, anxious arousal, depression, anger, intrusive experiences, defensiveness, avoidance, dissociative symptoms, sexual concerns, dysfunctional sexual behavior, and impaired self-esteem. There was a positive shift also in cognitive distortions. The CDS looked at self-criticism, self-balance, helplessness, hopelessness, and preoccupation with danger. The adult cognitive distortion trends we measured reflected a decrease in T score means in all of the subscales.

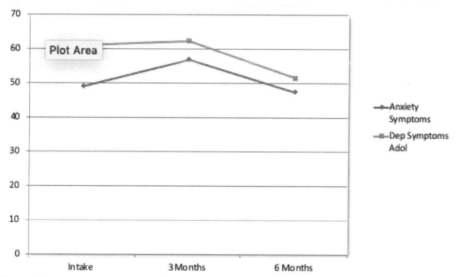

Figure 9: Mean Statistics: Adolescents Anxiety (RCMAS) & Depression (BDI)[374]

Adolescent anxiety and depression showed that they caught up to the adults at the six-month mark and continued to go down afterward. Where they had an increase of anxiety and depression at the three-month mark, we again postulate it had to do with adjustment to the environment. Whereas adults have adjusted to various environments,

The HEART Model

and often come into treatment motivated to begin work right away, adolescents are typically placed in the treatment center by courts or placement agencies, such as the FBI or the county sheriff, as alternatives to juvenile jail. As a result, these adolescents are often defensive to begin with, and sometimes less motivated.

In the area of forgiveness, we looked at three constructs: forgiveness of self, forgiveness of others, and forgiveness of the situation. Adult forgiveness trends were measured by the HFS. For the overall forgiveness construct, T score increased at three months and decreased at six months. The subscale of forgiveness of self increased slightly over repeated measures, with a decrease in the forgiveness of others. There was significant increase trend regarding forgiveness of the situation.

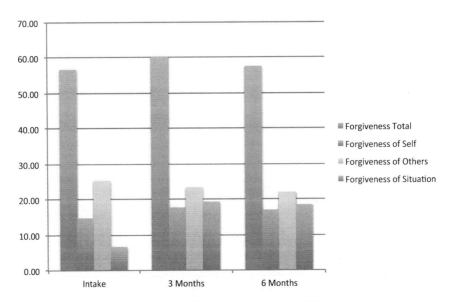

Figure 10: Forgiveness Scales[375]

When measuring spiritual well-being, we looked at three constructs: spiritual well-being, religious well-being, and existential well-being. Adults as well as adolescents showed an increase at both three- and six-month measures. In other words, it was working!

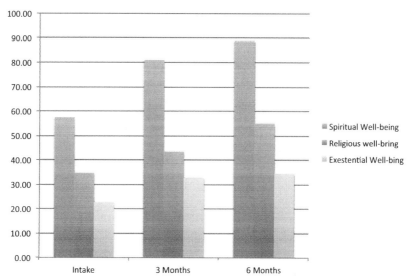
Figure 11: Spiritual Well-Being (Adults)[376]

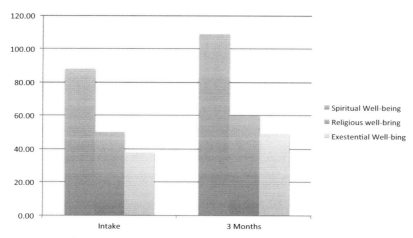
Figure 12: Spiritual Well-Being (Adolescents)[377]

In another study regarding the effects of trauma-informed services using quantitative research, looking at sex trafficking in aftercare residential facilities, our objective was to measure the differences in levels of trauma-informed care. We took a quantitative, statistical analysis-based look at whether professionals' education in trauma-informed care affected their coping strategies, compassion satisfaction, secondary trauma, compassion fatigue, and burnout. We felt that trauma-informed care and education helped to prevent the negative biopsychosocial effects of working with complex trauma survivors of sex trafficking.

The study was performed to identify the levels of trauma-informed training for the providers working with survivors of commercial sex trafficking within these residential facilities. We looked at staff members, coaches, and volunteers. We were also able to determine the effects of levels of trauma-informed care and knowledge on coping strategies, compassion fatigue, secondary traumatic stress, burnout and compassion satisfaction of those providers. The instruments we used for this were a demographic information questionnaire, a trauma-informed organizational self-assessment in trafficking, a coping strategy inventory short form, a secondary traumatic stress scale, and a professional quality of life scale. All of these are public domain. At the end of the seven years, we terminated the study, feeling like we had enough subjects to publish and put this information into circulation. Unfortunately, this was just before the COVID-19 pandemic, which delayed us in doing anything with our findings. Now, we feel we must get this information out.

In sum, our research regarding the effectiveness of the HEART Model showed that use of the model resulted in a decrease in dissociative and PTSD symptoms for trauma survivors. There was a clear indicator of an increase of a positive God image and an embrace of a positive spirituality. There were also clear signs of enhanced functioning, a decrease in negative behaviors, an increase in self-esteem, and an increase in emotional well-being. In short, after treatment with the HEART Model, survivors showed a solid increase in personal resilience.

We will be writing up the research project and publishing it with statistical analysis of all the results. Our purpose is to show the research and establish the HEART Model as a viable best-practice model. I am in significant debt to those survivors who participated in the study, both adults and adolescents. They have been a vital part of contributing research and literature on this area of treatment. I also want to thank co-researchers Dr. Vanessa Snyder, Dr. Lee Underwood, Dr. Frances Daily, and Dr. Teri Hourihan. Our hope is that our efforts lead to more residential facilities and beds available for those who are coming out of slavery.

We are also hoping that those who have read the preceding chapters of the HEART Model will see that there is life and hope in treating survivors of trafficking and other complex trauma. Whether you are a survivor, a clinician, or just someone who cares for the life and suffering of someone coming out of complex trauma, please use this information however you can. The purpose of writing this book is not to develop an empire of training or other books, or to create a tiered system of training, but to give the information away to those who will use it effectively. I hope you will join me in getting the word out. God bless you, and thank you!

Chapter Eleven Notes

CHAPTER TWELVE

Human Trafficking

Human trafficking for purposes of prostitution occurs on a global scale, and it affects almost every country in the world.[378] Victims are often from economically challenged backgrounds, are underemployed or unemployed, and lack social and safety networks within their home countries. Already compromised, victims are targeted because they are easy to recruit. Upon arrival in the promised land, instead of finding the jobs and opportunities they had been led to expect, these victims, mostly women and children, are forced into abusive conditions in a slavery-like atmosphere. From that point forward, they exist as sexual objects for the well-heeled, the sex industry, or pornography, or as menial labor. Physical, emotional, and sexual abuse is the norm for these victims. Once the survivors are freed, the road to recovery is fraught with struggle, pain, and even more wounds.

In his book, *A Call to Action: Women, Religion, Violence, and Power,* President Jimmy Carter states, "The most serious and unaddressed worldwide challenge is the deprivation and abuse of women and girls, largely caused by a false interpretation of carefully selected religious texts and growing tolerance of violence and warfare."[379] The International Labor Organization estimates that there are over 4.8 million people enslaved in sex trafficking each year.[380] The majority of victims—and thus, of survivors—are women and children.[381]

Human trafficking is defined to encompass all acts involved in the transport, harboring, or sale of persons within national or across international borders using coercion, force, kidnapping, deception, or fraud for the purpose for placing those persons in situations of forced labor or service, such as forced prostitution, domestic servitude, debt bondage, or other slavery-like practices.[382] This description was developed by the U. S. Congress in 2001, which means this country has been addressing the problem of

THE HEART MODEL

trafficking for only twenty years. I find it sad that the federal government has only been funding programs or otherwise making attempts to deal with this subject for about two decades.

Trafficking victims are often deceived into believing false promises of good jobs, economic stability, and expansive opportunities if they agree to travel to the United States or affluent countries in Europe. Women and children are usually trafficked from less-developed countries to nations with higher standards of living. Victims tend to be from regions such as Asia, Latin America, Eastern Europe, and Africa, which have high rates of poverty, violence, and corruption.[383] Most of the time, when those who have been trafficked arrive at the intended location, they find that the promises were empty; there are none of the expected opportunities. Instead, they are forced to endure horrendous human rights abuses such as forced prostitution, slavery-like conditions, rape, beatings, and starvation.[384] These sorts of conditions often produce severe physical, psychological, and emotional consequences, up to and including death.

Human trafficking now ranks as the world's fastest-growing criminal enterprise.[385] Its profits are so large as to rival the illegal drugs and arms trades. Depending on which report one consults, profits from illegal trafficking of persons are estimated to be $150 billion per year.[386] Two-thirds of that ($99 billion) comes from commercial sex trafficking, and $51 billion from forced labor. In revenue terms, human trafficking is comparable to the combined annual revenue of Starbucks, Nike, Facebook, and Disney.[387]

I have personally observed trafficking-related situations in a number of countries. In Kenya, representatives of the trafficking group would approach a father who was having a hard time making ends meet and would offer his daughters attractive sums of money to go overseas to work for wealthy families or to work in restaurants. They would readily take girls as young as twelve years old, but they would usually look for a sweet spot between thirteen and seventeen. They would offer money, food, clothes, school fees, or other incentives.[388]

The unsuspecting victims are often taken to areas where demand is highest and most consistent, such as large cities, vacation and tourist areas, or military bases. Because of the higher standard of living, the United States is a popular, and lucrative, destination country for the practice of human trafficking. Essentially, we Americans have the money that supports and undergirds the industry. Many trafficking victims are transported to the U. S. illegally by plane, boat, car, and train; some are even forced to travel on foot. Sometimes, traffickers are able to deceive immigration officials by providing victims with educational visas or tourist visas, or by creating false entry papers for women and children.

In many cases, the traffickers charge unknowing victims a huge smuggling or employment fee that can range from hundreds to thousands of dollars. As anticipated, when victims cannot pay the fee, the trafficker locks them in a vicious cycle of debt bondage or indentured servitude that effectively prevents the victims from being able to pay off the original fee.[389] Traffickers attempt to control their victims and break their will. Beyond holding victims captive and forcing them to engage in sexual acts in slavery-like conditions, such control is achieved using indebtedness, isolation, and the combined use of threats, intimidation, and violence.[390]

Due to advancements in technology, prostitution no longer looks simply like a girl or woman walking the streets. A lot of the transactions happen behind computer and phone screens, making prostitution much harder to identify. The sex industry consists of street prostitution, pornography, sales of individuals through online platforms, escort services, strip clubs, brothels, and businesses that are operating sex services behind the scenes (typically, massage businesses, nail salons, and other body treatment establishments). The expansion of the sex industry and the associated technology have made it much more difficult for law enforcement to track down the victims.

Penalties levied by the court system for trafficking are low when compared to those for dealing in drugs or illegal arms. For example, the statutory maximum for sale into involuntary servitude cannot exceed twenty years per count,[391] whereas the statutory maximum for dealing LSD or distributing a kilo of heroin is life in prison,[392] thus reflecting the low value placed on women and children. The sentences and the atmosphere of passive consent make it easy for traffickers to flourish here in the United States.

Faith-based organizations have attempted to interrupt the process, predominantly by relocating trafficked survivors to appropriate shelters. In particular, two groups have been extremely active since the late 1970s and early 1980s: these are the United States Conference of Catholic Bishops and the Lutheran Immigration and Refugee Service.[393] Other faith-based organizations have attempted to offer counseling services and support services such as food and clothing. They also offer legal services in cooperation with those organizations that are offering shelter. Over the past twenty years, other groups, such as the Salvation Army, are beginning to offer social services, drug and alcohol treatment, counseling services, employment services, legal support, and social support groups.

The need for such services is extensive throughout the United States. The bulk of an entire book could be devoted to the political and legal climate regarding trafficked survivors. However, the focus of this writing is on treatment and a methodology useful in working toward the healing of those who have experienced the horrific conditions of being trafficked for sexual purposes.

The trafficking in Romania used to be as brutal as in the U. S. They would beat, rape, and otherwise hurt women and girls, to force them to engage in sexual activities. That is not happening much anymore. The traffickers are now offering the women and girls top-line clothing, accommodations, and food.[394] The women are living a lavish and expensive lifestyle in exchange for sex. If they want to leave, they are welcome to leave, but traffickers know that they will be back, because they cannot sustain a lifestyle that provides them the perks that the trafficker offers. The traffickers even allow the girl or woman to keep some of the money, which does not happen in most other places. These "perks" come with a high price: usually, the victim is forced to have sex with somewhere between six and ten men per night. But in Romania, as in many parts of the world, parents would agree to this; the women or girls would also agree to this. And as in many other nations, the average target age for a victim is fourteen years old.

The largest regional purveyor of sexual slaves is the Middle East, particularly Saudi Arabia. Instead of opportunity, victims encounter beatings, rape, bondage, and other abusive conditions. In many countries, physical or sexual control tactics are used that produce both fear and dependency in victims' emotions. This dependency leads victims to crave attention and caring, so a mixture of sex and attention from the trafficker can be followed by a slap, punch, or kick, thus producing both emotional dependency and fear.

While victims can experience some differences depending on which country they are trafficked to and from, all traffickers will capitalize on the victim's vulnerability, whether that is poverty, previous abuse, lack of a support system, lack of education, their desire for a new reality, or lavish promises of education, employment, and wealth. All victims end up suffering severe physical, psychological, and spiritual effects, including:

- Addiction to drugs and alcohol
- Little to no medical or dental care (ongoing untreated medical concerns)
- Sexually transmitted infections (STIs)
- Ongoing safety concerns once leaving the life

Once a victim of trafficking has gotten free of the trafficker and is pursuing a different lifestyle, they will need significant assistance in the following areas:

- Crisis intervention
- Ongoing mental health treatment
- Medical and dental care
- Housing
- Job skills/education
- Support systems

WHAT YOU CAN DO

Within your own community, you can do a lot of things to bring awareness and services to those in need. Often, we are witnessing children and women caught in this trap right in front of our eyes, yet we are completely unaware of the endangerment and need in front of us. Becoming aware of the signs is extremely important. Some of those signs include:

- Not being allowed to speak up for themselves (someone else talking for them)
- Being controlled by another person
- Someone else controlling their money
- Minors consistently not being in school during school hours
- Fear of law enforcement or authorities
- Few to no personal belongings *or* a sudden increase in belongings
- Carrying more than one cell phone
- Working excessively long or unusual hours
- Having moved often from city to city
- Not sure of what city they are in

- Lack of a consistent address
- Changing phone numbers frequently
- Loss of sense of time
- Inconsistency with their story or activities
- Running away from home
- Changes in dress
- Changes in peer relationships
- Major changes in eating or sleeping habits
- Identification tattoos
- Signs of gang affiliation
- Sudden onset of drug and alcohol use

As you learn to identify potential victims, take the step to report. There are hotlines in every state, as well as a national hotline (888-373-7888). We can also find ways to educate ourselves on the issue. Some suggestions are:

Books

- *Renting Lacy: A Story of America's Prostituted Children,* by Linda Smith and Cindy Coloma
- *Made in the USA: The Sex Trafficking of America's Children,* by Alisa Jordheim
- *Inside the Devil's Bedroom,* by J. P. Storm
- *White Umbrella:* Mary Frances Bowley
- *Scars and Stilettos: The Transformation of an Exotic Dancer,* by Harmony Dust

Movies/Documentaries

- *Born into Brothels* (2004), directed by Zana Briski and Ross Kauffman
- *Nefarious* (2011), directed by Benjamin Nolot
- *The Pink Room* (2011), directed by Joel Sandvos
- *Sex and Money* (2011), directed by Joel Angyal
- *In Plain Sight* (2017), directed by Skye Borgman
- *Walking the Halls* (2013), directed by Doug Campbell

Community Organizations and Coalitions

- Local advocacy organizations
- Local task forces
- Local shelters and homes
- Local churches

International Organizations

- International Justice Mission (IJM)
- Shared Home International
- Courage Worldwide
- Uncaged
- Polaris Project

What the HEART Model Can Do

The journey toward health and wholeness is long, as every part of self (spirit, mind, emotions, body), along with every fractured part of self, must be given proper attention and be nurtured. Every part of self and every fractured part of self must also be challenged to face the reality of pain, along with the distortions of self, others, and God. The

The HEART Model

HEART Model, used by caring practitioners, has the ability to make the difference.

I will continue to pursue research, and encourage others to do the same, so that the HEART Model can become a recognized best-practice model and serve those who have suffered such immense trauma.

I pray you will become a part of this journey.

Chapter Twelve Notes

Afterword

We have attempted in this book to offer a comprehensive model for working with survivors with complex trauma and dissociation, which includes survivors of human trafficking. This model also addresses the trauma continuum targeted at survivors dealing with post-traumatic stress disorder, borderline personality disorder, adjustment disorders, and other related disorders that have co-morbidity with trauma. We decided to highlight human trafficking because of the severity of sexual and physical trauma and because the results of the seven-year study show significant improvement in functioning, resiliency, and spiritual growth in survivors treated according to the HEART Model. I think it can be extrapolated that if those with the severest of traumas can recover, so can others.

I have always believed that the intimate sharing of suffering, pain, and the affective symptoms of sexual and physical trauma are spiritual places in which counselors are invited to participate to effect healing. My personal walk with God taught me to question my faith and everything about God and religious values. That questioning led me to trust and value my experiences with God and brought me from a Judaic background into a personal relationship with the living God. To be able to share that experience with others on their journey of healing has been a great honor.

I owe much to the clients with whom I have been blessed to work, as they have taught me to be effective and to reach into the hidden places with the care that only skill, confidence, and time produce. Without their teaching and support, I am but an educated fool. I truly believe that Carl Rogers was right when he said, "93% of all counseling rests in the relationship between the client and the counselor, and the other 7% is attributed to theory and technique."[395] I would also be remiss in not thanking my co-researchers, Dr. Lee Underwood and Dr. Vanessa Snyder, and my editorial support, Melissa Herrmann. Without their help, this book would not have been possible.

In graduate school, my psychopathology instructor for my master's program entreated all of us, regarding counseling, "There are two types of counselors: the technicians who know the form and function of therapy and the artists who know how to create out of that form and function." For those of you who are counselors, I leave you with his exhortation: "Be the artist!"

Acknowledgments

The clients I have seen over the years have taught me many lessons. They have taught me to hear with my heart to see what's beyond in front of me and to care with passion and compassion. I will always owe them a debt I can never repay.

I deeply thank Melissa Herrmann, whose wisdom and insight guided the formation of the book both in concept and content. Her editing was a tremendous effort and help.

My professional readers and part of my inner circle were Dr. Harvey Payne, Dr. Kathie Erwin, and Dr. Kim Harris, all of whom gave so much excellent advice, additions, and other points of view. They also gave ample ideas in the building of support material.

I would be remiss not to acknowledge Dr. David Seamands posthumously. His amazing book *Healing of Memories* (1985) jumpstarted this part of the journey for me. I again mention Dr. Colin Ross, whose friendship and expertise have been such blessings in my life and in the making of this book. He wisely asked me to step away from the first version of this book several years ago and start again. Despite the disappointment, he was right! I am so grateful for his wisdom and direction.

Lastly, I thank my wife Kim, who has been my companion, lover, spirited and parenting guide, with a wonderful sense of humor and grounded common sense.

Thank you all for helping me get this book out.

I want to also thank the people at 'Speak It To Book' including Maria Floros, Joy Schneider, whose help on editing and clarification made this volume stronger, and Caleb Breakey (founder) who made this opportunity possible along with Mary Webber of Reknown Books who will be helping with marketing. I also know that there are many behind-the-scenes working with these wonderful, dedicated people to make this book possible. My second editor, Anne Needham, took much time to make sure the references were correctly positioned and has been a strong support with this and other projects. Thank you for having the skills to make me sound coherent and focused.

About the Author

Benjamin B. Keyes |
PhD, EdD, NCC, CCMHC, LPC, MCT |
Professor/ Director of Training and Internship for
Masters of Mental Health Counseling Program |
Divine Mercy University

DR. BENJAMIN KEYES's specialties include dissociative disorders, domestic violence, child abuse, addictions, mood and anxiety disorders, human trafficking, and work with refugees. Dr. Keyes received his doctorate in rehabilitation counseling in 1985 from International College and his doctorate in counseling psychology from the University of Sarasota in 2003. He also has doctoral degrees in theology, divinity, and ministry.

Over the years, Dr. Keyes has worked extensively with hospitalization programs and in private practice, establishing himself as one of the leading program innovators for partial hospitalization programs. He has been in private practice for over forty years and has been a researcher in trauma and dissociation for the last twenty-six years. Dr. Keyes and his colleagues have received the Richard A. Kluft Research Award for work and research in the People's Republic of China from the *Journal of Trauma and Dissociation* and the International Society for the Study of Trauma and Dissociation. His work dispelled the cultural model of dissociation and has resulted in dissociative disorders being treated throughout mental health facilities in China. Dr. Keyes has also received the Hope Award from Restoration Ministries for his work in establishing, the HEART Model, a faith-based trauma model for working with trafficked survivors and complex trauma.

Over the last six years, Dr. Keyes has been a professor and director for the Center for Trauma and Resiliency Studies at Divine Mercy University in Sterling, Virginia. As head of the Center for Trauma and Resiliency Studies, Dr. Keyes supervised the development and training of graduate students in first response and chronic trauma. Dr. Keyes also serves the university as a professor in the Clinical Mental Health Program. The Center's Trauma Team will deploy to traumatic events worldwide as needed, train professionals and paraprofessionals, and do research on the HEART Model and its efficacy with trafficking survivors. Dr. Keyes is also the executive director of the Green Cross Academy for Traumatology.

The book *The HEART Model* is a twenty-year project coming to fruition, following a seven-year study showing its efficacy.

Dr. Keyes is happily married to Kim and has two adult children, Shawn and Jasmin, as well as a newly adopted eight-year-old, Garite. Dr. Keyes and his wife also have three beautiful granddaughters—Violet, Amber, and Arella—and a grandson, Xander.

About Renown Publishing

Renown Publishing was founded with one mission in mind: to make your great idea famous. At Renown Publishing, we don't just publish. We work hard to pair strategy with innovative marketing techniques so that your book launch is the start of something bigger. Learn more at <u>RenownPublishing.com</u>.

REFERENCES

Notes

1. Seamands, David A. *Healing of Memories.* Victor Books, 1985.

2. Ross, Colin A. *Multiple Personality Disorder: Diagnosis, Clinical Features, and Treatment.* John Wiley and Sons, 1989.

3. Ross, *Multiple Personality Disorder.*

4. Bass, Ellen, and Laura Davis. *The Courage to Heal.* Harper and Row, 1988. (A revised edition was published by William Morrow in 2008.)

5. Keyes, Benjamin B. "The HEART Model Training." (workshop). Divine Mercy University. 2021.

6. International Society for the Study of Trauma and Dissociation (ISSTD). 2011. https://www.isst-d.org/.

7. Descartes, René. *Discourse on the Method and Meditations.* Penguin Books, 1968. First published in 1637.

8. Ross, Colin A., Benjamin B. Keyes, Heqin Yan, Zhen Wang, Zheng Zou, Yong Xu, Jue Chen, Haiyin Zhang, and Zeping Xiao. "A Cross-cultural Test of the Trauma Model of Dissociation." *Journal of Trauma and Dissociation* 9, no. 1 (2008): 35–49. doi: 10.1080/15299730802073635.

9. Descartes, René. *Meditations on First Philosophy: With Selections from the Objections and Replies.* Translated by John Cottingham. University of Reading, 1996.

10. Blue Letter Bible, "Strong's G3340 – *metanoeō*." https://www.blueletterbible.org/lexicon/g3340/kjv/tr/0-1/.

11. Seamands, *Healing of Memories.*

12. Seamands, *Healing of Memories.*

13. See, for instance, 1 Corinthians 13:11 (ESV): "When I was a child, I spoke like a child, I reasoned like a child. When I became a man, I gave up childish ways."

14. Seamands, *Healing of Memories.*

15. Watkins, Helen Huth, and John G. Watkins. *Ego States: Theory and Therapy.* G. F. Books, 1997.

16. Watkins and Watkins, *Ego States.*

17. Bradshaw, John. *Homecoming: Reclaiming and Championing Your Inner Child.* Bantam, 1990.

18. Ross, *Multiple Personality Disorder.*

Putnam, Frank W. "Pierre Janet and Modern Views of Dissociation." *Journal of Traumatic Stress* 2, no. 4 (1989): 413–429. https://doi.org/10.1002/jts.2490020406.

Krakauer, Sarah Y. *Treating Dissociative Identity Disorder: The Power of the Collective Heart.* Brunner-Routledge, 2001.

19. Grove, David J., and B. I. Panzer. *Resolving Traumatic Memories: Metaphors and Symbols in Psychotherapy.* Irvington Publishers, 1991. First published in 1989 by Ardent Media.

20. Rank, Michael Garnet. Personal communication. Department of Traumatic Stress Studies. School of Social Work. University of South Florida. April 2006.

21. Seamands, *Healing of Memories.*

22. Ross, Keyes, Yan, Wang, Zou, Xu, Chen, Zhang, and Xiao, "A Cross-cultural Test of the Trauma Model of Dissociation."

23. Carich, Mark S., and Karen Spilman. "Basic Principles of Intervention." *The Family Journal* 12, no. 4 (2004): 405–410. https://doi.org/10.1177/1066480704267320.

24. Sue, Derald Wing, and David Sue. *Counseling the Culturally Diverse: Theory and Practice.* 6th edition. John Wiley and Sons, 2013.

25. Gingrich, Heather Davediuk. *Restoring the Shattered Self: A Christian Counselor's Guide to Complex Trauma.* InterVarsity Press Academic, 2013.

26. Gelso, C. J., and J. A. Carter. "Components of the Psychotherapy Relationship: Their Interaction and Unfolding During Treatment." *Journal of Counseling and Psychology* 41, no. 3 (1994): 297. https://doi.org/10.1037/0022-0167.41.3.296.

27. Rogers, Carl R. "The Necessary and Sufficient Components of Therapeutic Personality Change." *Journal of Consulting Psychology* 21, no. 2 (1957): 95–103. https://doi.org/10.1037/h0045357.

28. Glaser, Danya. "Child Abuse and Neglect and the Brain—a Review." *The Journal of Child Psychology and Psychiatry* 41, no. 1 (2000): 97–116. https://doi.org/10.1111/1469-7610.00551.

29. Minuchin, Salvador. *Families and Family Therapy.* Harvard University Press, 1974.

30. Ivey, Allen E., Carlos P. Zalaquett, and Mary Bradford Ivey. *Intentional Interviewing and Counseling: Facilitating Client Development in a Multicultural Society.* 8th edition. Brooks/Cole Cengage Learning, 2014.

31. Rogers, "The Necessary and Sufficient Components of Therapeutic Personality Change."

32. Ivey, Zalaquett, and Ivey, *Intentional Interviewing and Counseling.*

33. Rogers, "The Necessary and Sufficient Components of Therapeutic Personality Change."

34. Ivey, Zalaquett, and Ivey, *Intentional Interviewing and Counseling.*

35. Smith, L., and Coloma, C. *Renting Lacy: A Story of America's Prostituted Children*. Shared Hope International, 2009.

36. Keyes, Benjamin B., Lee A. Underwood, Vanessa Snyder, Frances L. L. Dailey, and Teri Hourihan. "Healing Emotional Affective Responses to Trauma (HEART): A Christian Model of Working with Trauma." *Frontiers in the Psychotherapy of Trauma and Dissociation* 1, no. 2 (2018): 212–243. https://actheals.org/wp-content/uploads/2021/06/Keyes_Ben-The-Heart-Model-Session-Handout.pdf.

37. Vereen, Linwood G., Nicole R. Hill, Gloria Aquina Sosa, and Victoria Kress. "The Synonymic Nature of Professional Counseling and Humanism: Presuppotions That Guide Our Identities." *The Journal of Humanistic Counseling* 53, no. 3 (2014): 191–202. https://doi.org/10.1002/j.2161-1939.2014.00056.x.

38. Gingrich, *Restoring the Shattered Self*.

39. Vereen, Hill, Sosa, and Kress, "The Synonymic Nature of Professional Counseling and Humanism."

40. Vereen, Hill, Sosa, and Kress, "The Synonymic Nature of Professional Counseling and Humanism."

Hawkins, Ronald E., Gary A. Sibcy, Anita M. Knight Kuhnley, Steve E. Warren, Richard Justin Silvey. *Research Based Counseling Skills: The Art and Science of Therapeutic Empathy*. Kendall Hunt, 2018.

41. Vereen, Hill, Sosa, and Kress, "The Synonymic Nature of Professional Counseling and Humanism."

42. Vereen, Hill, Sosa, and Kress, "The Synonymic Nature of Professional Counseling and Humanism."

43. Vereen, Hill, Sosa, and Kress, "The Synonymic Nature of Professional Counseling and Humanism."

44. Vereen, Hill, Sosa, and Kress, "The Synonymic Nature of Professional Counseling and Humanism."

45. Danylchuk, Lynette S., and Kevin J. Connors. *Treating Complex Trauma and Dissociation: A Practical Guide to Navigating Therapeutic Challenges*. Routledge, 2016.

46. Vereen, Hill, Sosa, and Kress, "The Synonymic Nature of Professional Counseling and Humanism."

47. Grahe, Jon E., and Frank J. Bernieri. "The Importance of Nonverbal Cues in Judging Rapport." *Journal of Nonverbal Behavior* 23, no. 4 (1999): 253–269. https://doi.org/10.1023/A:1021698725361.

48. Grahe, Jon E., and Ryne A. Sherman. "An Ecological Examination of Rapport Using a Dyadic Puzzle Task." *The Journal of Social Psychology* 147, no. 5 (2007): 453–475. https://doi.org/10.3200/SOCP.147.5.453-476.

49. Vereen, Hill, Sosa, and Kress, "The Synonymic Nature of Professional Counseling and Humanism."

Ross, Keyes, Yan, Wang, Zou, Xu, Chen, Zhang, and Xiao, "A Cross-Cultural Test of the Trauma Model of Dissociation."

Sue and Sue, *Counseling the Culturally Diverse*.

50. Sue and Sue, *Counseling the Culturally Diverse*.

51. Vereen, Hill, Sosa, and Kress, "The Synonymic Nature of Professional Counseling and Humanism."

52. Sue and Sue, *Counseling the Culturally Diverse.*

53. Smith and Coloma, *Renting Lacy.*

54. Herrmann, M. M. Personal communication "An Introduction to Human Trafficking for Potential Staff in Recovery Programs" (workshop). Courage Worldwide, Stockton, California. April, 2019.

55. Substance Abuse and Mental Health Services Administration. *Trauma-Informed Care in Behavioral Health Services.* No. 57 of *Treatment Improvement Protocol (TIP).* HHS Publication No. (SMA) 13-4801, 2014.

56. De Jong, Peter, and Insoo Kim Berg. *Interviewing for Solutions.* 4th edition. Brooks/Cole, 2013.

57. Smith and Coloma, *Renting Lacy.*

58. Danylchuk and Connors, *Treating Complex Trauma and Dissociation.*

59. Gingrich, *Restoring the Shattered Self.*

60. Vereen, Hill, Sosa, and Kress, "The Synonymic Nature of Professional Counseling and Humanism."

61. Vereen, Hill, Sosa, and Kress, "The Synonymic Nature of Professional Counseling and Humanism."

62. Gingrich, *Restoring the Shattered Self.*

63. Danylchuk and Connors, *Treating Complex Trauma and Dissociation.*

64. McLaughlin, Darlene Magito, and Edward G. Carr. "Quality of Rapport as a Setting Event for Problem Behavior: Assessment and Intervention." *Journal of Positive Behavior Interventions* 7, no. 2 (2005): 68–91. doi:10.1177/10983007050070020401.

Gurland, Suzanne T., and Wendy S. Grolnick. "Building Rapport with Children: Effects of Adults' Expected, Actual, and Perceived Behavior." *Journal of Social and Clinical Psychology* 27, no. 3 (2008): 226–253. https://doi.org/10.1521/jscp.2008.27.3.226.

65. Gingrich, *Restoring the Shattered Self.*

66. Herrmann, "An Introduction to Human Trafficking."

67. Danylchuk and Connors, *Treating Complex Trauma and Dissociation.*

68. Danylchuk and Connors, *Treating Complex Trauma and Dissociation.*

69. Danylchuk and Connors, *Treating Complex Trauma and Dissociation.*

70. Gingrich, *Restoring the Shattered Self.*

71. Gingrich, *Restoring the Shattered Self.*

72. Gingrich, *Restoring the Shattered Self.*

73. Sue and Sue, *Counseling the Culturally Diverse.*

74. Gingrich, *Restoring the Shattered Self.*

75. Hawkins, Thomas R., and Diane W. Hawkins. *Restoring Shattered Lives.* Restoration in Christ

Ministries, 2006.

76. van der Kolk, Bessel. *The Body Keeps the Score: Brain, Mind and Body in the Healing of Trauma.* Penguin, 2014.

77. Hawkins and Hawkins, *Restoring Shattered Lives.*

78. Hawkins and Hawkins, *Restoring Shattered Lives.*

79. Hawkins and Hawkins, *Restoring Shattered Lives.*

80. Keyes, B. B. The HEART Model: Healing Complex Trauma and Human Trafficking. Workshop offered annually at Divine Mercy University, Sterling, Virginia, by the Center for Trauma and Resiliency Studies, as part of the certification through Green Cross Academy of Traumatology (GCAT), Certified Clinical Traumatologist. December 1–2, 2022.

81. Hawkins and Hawkins, *Restoring Shattered Lives.*

82. van der Kolk, *The Body Keeps the Score.*

83. Keyes, Benjamin B. Presentation on the HEART Model. Regent University, 2018.

84. Keyes, presentation on the HEART Model.

85. Hawkins and Hawkins, *Restoring Shattered Lives.*

86. Hawkins and Hawkins, *Restoring Shattered Lives.*

87. van der Kolk, *The Body Keeps the Score.*

88. Hawkins and Hawkins, *Restoring Shattered Lives.*

89. Rank, Michael Garnet. "Child and Adolescent Trauma" (workshop). Green Cross Academy of Traumatology, 2008. Used with permission.

90. Hawkins and Hawkins, *Restoring Shattered Lives.*

91. van der Kolk, *The Body Keeps the Score.*

92. van der Kolk, *The Body Keeps the Score.*

93. van der Kolk, *The Body Keeps the Score.*

94. Keyes, presentation on the HEART Model.

95. Keyes, Benjamin B., and Sandy Sela-Smith. *E Pluribus Unum: Out of Many... One.* Manitou Communications, 1999.

96. Keyes and Sela-Smith, *E Pluribus Unum.*

97. Hawkins and Hawkins, *Restoring Shattered Lives.*

98. Hawkins and Hawkins, *Restoring Shattered Lives.*

99. Hawkins and Hawkins, *Restoring Shattered Lives.*

100. Hawkins and Hawkins, *Restoring Shattered Lives.*

101. Dirix, C. E. H., J. G. Nijhuis, H. W. Jongsma, and G. Hornstra. (2009). Aspects of Fetal Learning and Memory. *Child Development* 80, no. 4. (2009): 1251–1258. https://doi.org/10.1111/j.1467-8624.2009.01329.x.

102. Shu, Jennifer. "When Can an Unborn Baby Hear Me? I'd Love to Be Able to Read and Sing to Them." HealthyChildren.org. American Academy of Pediatrics. April 20, 2021. https://www.healthychildren.org/English/tips-tools/ask-the-pediatrician/Pages/I%E2%80%99m-pregnant-and-would-like-to-sing-to-my-unborn-baby.aspx#:~:text=At%20around%2018%20weeks%20of,same%20level%20as%20an%20adult.

103. Hawkins and Hawkins, *Restoring Shattered Lives.*

104. Bradshaw, *Homecoming.*

Whitfield, Charles L. *Healing the Child Within: Discovery and Recovery for Adult Children of Dysfunctional Families.* Health Communications, 1987.

105. Ábrahám, Hajnalka, Ándras Vincze, Ilja Jewgenow, Béla Veszprémi, Ándras Kravják, Éva Gömöri, and László Seress. "Myelination in the Human Hippocampal Formation from Midgesstation to Adulthood." *International Journal of Developmental Neuroscience* 28, no. 5 (2010): 401–410.

Hawkins and Hawkins, *Restoring Shattered Lives.*

106. van der Kolk, *The Body Keeps the Score.*

107. Janet, Pierre. 1889.

108. Van der Hart, Onno, and Rutger Horst. "The Dissociation Theory of Pierre Janet." *Journal of Traumatic Stress* 2, no. 4 (1989): 397–412.

109. van der Kolk, *The Body Keeps the Score.*

110. van der Kolk, *The Body Keeps the Score.*

111. van der Kolk, *The Body Keeps the Score.*

112. van der Kolk, *The Body Keeps the Score.*

113. Hawkins and Hawkins, *Restoring Shattered Lives.*

114. van der Kolk, *The Body Keeps the Score.*

115. Hawkins and Hawkins, *Restoring Shattered Lives.*

116. Ross, *Multiple Personality Disorder.*

117. Landsman, Murray. Personal communication. 1979.

118. Braun, Bennett G. "Issues in the Treatment of Multiple Personality Disorder." In *Treatment of Multiple Personality Disorder*, edited by Bennett G. Braun. American Psychiatric Press, 1986.

119. Braun, "Issues in the Treatment of Multiple Personality Disorder."

120. Watkins and Watkins, *Ego States.*

121. Watkins and Watkins, *Ego States*.

122. Grove and Panzer. *Resolving Traumatic Memories*.

123. Gingrich, *Restoring the Shattered Self*.

124. Gingrich, *Restoring the Shattered Self*.

125. Bass and Davis, *The Courage to Heal*.

126. Yapko, Michael D. *Suggestions of Abuse: True and False Memories of Childhood Sexual Trauma*. Simon and Schuster, 1994.

127. Bass and Davis, *The Courage to Heal*.

128. American Psychiatric Association. *Diagnostic and Statistical Manual of Mental Disorders: DSM-5*. American Psychiatric Association, 2013.

129. Briere, John N., and Catherine Scott. *Principles of Trauma Therapy*. 2nd edition. SAGE Publications, 2014. First published in 2006.

Krakauer, *Treating Dissociative Identity Disorder*.

Ross, *Multiple Personality Disorder*.

130. Ross, *Multiple Personality Disorder*.

van der Kolk, *The Body Keeps the Score*.

131. Grove and Panzer, *Resolving Traumatic Memories*.

132. Grove and Panzer, *Resolving Traumatic Memories*.

133. Gingrich, *Restoring the Shattered Self*.

134. Hawkins and Hawkins, *Restoring Shattered Lives*.

135. Keyes, Underwood, Snyder, Dailey, and Hourihan, "Healing Emotional Affective Responses to Trauma (HEART)."

Seamands, *Healing of Memories*.

136. Seamands, *Healing of Memories*.

137. Danylchuk and Connors, *Treating Complex Trauma and Dissociation*.

138. Danylchuk and Connors, *Treating Complex Trauma and Dissociation*.

139. Seamands, *Healing of Memories*.

140. Wang, Qi. "Emotion Knowledge and Autobiographical Memory Across the Preschool Years: A Cross-cultural Longitudinal Study." *Cognition* 108, no. 1 (2008): 117–135. http://dx.doi.org/10.9707/2307-0919.1047.

141. Ross, Michael, and Qi Wang. "Why We Remember and What We Remember: Culture and Autobiographical Memory." *Perspectives on Psychological Science* 5, no. 4 (2010): 401–409.

142. Wang, "Emotion Knowledge and Autobiographical Memory Across the Preschool Years."

143. Swanson, H. Lee, Xinhua Zheng, and Olga Jerman. "Working Memory, Short-term Memory, and Reading Disabilities: A Selective Meta-analysis of the Literature." *Journal of Learning Disabilities* 42, no. 3 (2009): 260–287.

144. American Psychiatric Association, *Diagnostic and Statistical Manual of Mental Disorders: DSM-5.*

145. Laird, Donald A. "What Can You Do with Your Nose?" *Scientific Monthly* 41, no. 2 (1935):126–130.

146. Chu, Simon, and John J. Downes. "Odour-evoked Autobiographical Memories: Psychological Investigations of Proustian Phenomena." *Chemical Senses* 25, no. 1 (2000): 111–116. https://doi.org/10.1093/chemse/25.1.111.

147. Martin, G. Neil. "Olfactory Remediation: Current Evidence and Possible Applications." *Social Science and Medicine* 4, no. 1 (1996): 63–70. https://doi.org/10.1016/0277-9536(95)00334-7.

148. Chu and Downes, "Odour-evoked Autobiographical Memories."

149. Annett, Judith M., and Julian C. Leslie. "Effects of Visual and Verbal Interference Tasks on Olfactory Memory: The Role of Task Complexity." *British Journal of Psychology* 87, no. 3 (1996): 447–460. https://doi.org/10.1111/j.2044-8295.1996.tb02601.x.

150. Capacchione, Lucia. *The Power of Your Other Hand.* New Page Books, 2001. First published in 1988 by Newcastle Publishing Company.

151. Hawkins and Hawkins, *Restoring Shattered Lives.*

152. Hawkins and Hawkins, *Restoring Shattered Lives.*

153. Keyes, presentation on the HEART Model.

154. Keyes, presentation on the HEART Model.

155. Danylchuk and Connors, *Treating Complex Trauma and Dissociation.*

156. Ross, *Multiple Personality Disorder.*

157. Seamands, *Healing of Memories.*

158. Danylchuk and Connors, *Treating Complex Trauma and Dissociation.*

159. Danylchuk and Connors, *Treating Complex Trauma and Dissociation.*

160. Kalat, James W. *Introduction to Psychology.* 12th edition. Cengage, 2021. First published in 1986.

161. Kalat, *Introduction to Psychology.*

162. Kalat, *Introduction to Psychology.*

163. Danylchuk and Connors, *Treating Complex Trauma and Dissociation.*

164. Hawkins and Hawkins, *Restoring Shattered Lives.*

Corsini, Raymond J., and Danny Wedding. *Current Psychotherapies*. 11th edition. Cengage, 2019. First published in 1973.

165. Berntsen, Dorthe, and David C. Rubin. "When a Trauma Becomes a Key to Identity: Enhanced Integration of Trauma Memories Predicts Posttraumatic Stress Disorder Symptoms." *Applied Cognitive Psychology* 21, no. 4 (2007): 417–431. https://doi.org/10.1002/acp.1290.

166. Danylchuk and Connors, *Treating Complex Trauma and Dissociation*.

167. Seamands, *Healing of Memories*.

168. Friedberg, Robert D., and Jessica M. McCure. *Clinical Practice of Cognitive Therapy with Children and Adolescents: The Nuts and Bolts*. Guilford, 2015.

Gingrich, *Restoring the Shattered Self*.

169. Vygotsky, Lev S. *Mind in Society: The Development of Higher Psychological Processes*. Edited by Michael Cole. Harvard University Press, 1978.

170. Burchinal, Margaret R., Andrea Follmer, and Donna M. Bryant. "The Relations of Maternal Social Support and Family Structure with Maternal Responsiveness and Child Outcomes Among African American Families." *Developmental Psychology* 32, no. 6 (1996): 1,073–1,083. https://psycnet.apa.org/doi/10.1037/0012-1649.32.6.1073

171. Courtois, Christine A. *Adult Survivors of Childhood Sexual Abuse*. Workshop Models for Family Life Education, 1993.

172. Hawkins and Hawkins, *Restoring Shattered Lives*.

173. Hawkins and Hawkins, *Restoring Shattered Lives*.

174. Seamands, *Healing of Memories*.

175. Whitfield, Charles L. *Healing the Child Within: Discovery and Recovery for Adult Children of Dysfunctional Families*. Health Communications, 1987.

176. Keyes, presentation on the HEART Model.

177. Whitfield, *Healing the Child Within*.

Danylchuk and Connors, *Treating Complex Trauma and Dissociation*.

Vereen, Hill, Sosa, and Kress, "The Synonymic Nature of Professional Counseling and Humanism."

178. Felmingham, Kim, Andrew Haddon Kemp, Leanne M. Williams, Erin Falconer, G. Olivieri, A. Peduto, and Richard Bryant. "Dissociative Responses to Conscious and Non-conscious Fear Impact Underlying Brain Function in Post-Traumatic Stress Disorder." *Psychological Medicine* 38, no. 12 (2008): 1,771–1,780. https://doi.org/10.1017/s0033291708002742.

179. Danylchuk and Connors, *Treating Complex Trauma and Dissociation*.

180. Danylchuk and Connors, *Treating Complex Trauma and Dissociation*.

181. Potter-Efron, Ronald, and Patricia Potter-Efron. *Letting Go of Shame: Understanding How Shame*

Affects Your Life. Simon and Schuster, 2009. First published in 1989 by Hazelden Foundation.

182. Carver, Charles S., and Eddie Harmon-Jones. "Anger Is an Approach-related Effect: Evidence and Implications." *Psychological Bulletin* 135, no. 2 (2009): 183–204.

183. Hawkins and Hawkins, *Restoring Shattered Lives*.

184. Whitfield, *Healing the Child Within*.

185. Gingrich, *Restoring the Shattered Self*.

186. Gingrich, *Restoring the Shattered Self*.

Courtois, *Adult Survivors of Childhood Sexual Abuse*.

187. Gingrich, *Restoring the Shattered Self*.

188. Watkins and Watkins, *Ego States*.

189. Danylchuk and Connors, *Treating Complex Trauma and Dissociation*.

190. Danylchuk and Connors, *Treating Complex Trauma and Dissociation*.

191. Carver and Harmon-Jones, "Anger Is an Approach-related Effect."

192. Epstude, Kai, and Thomas Mussweiler. "What You Feel Is How You Compare: How Comparisons Influence the Social Induction of Affect." *Emotion* 9, no. 1 (2009): 1–14. https://doi.org/10.1037/a0014148.

193. Droz, R. Personal communication. Medfield Hospital, Largo, Florida. October 2006.

194. Gingrich, *Restoring the Shattered Self*.

195. Bass and Davis, *The Courage to Heal*. 87.

196. Bass and Davis, *The Courage to Heal*.

197. Benner, David G., ed. *Baker Encyclopedia of Psychology*. 2nd edition. Baker, 1985, 356.

198. Danylchuk and Connors, *Treating Complex Trauma and Dissociation*.

Gingrich, *Restoring the Shattered Self*.

Hawkins and Hawkins, *Restoring Shattered Lives*.

199. Courtois, *Adult Survivors of Childhood Sexual Abuse*.

200. van der Kolk, *The Body Keeps the Score*.

201. Domestic Violence Community Project. "Duluth Model: Domestic Violence Training" (workshop). Duluth, Minnesota. October, 2017.

202. Whitfield, *Healing the Child Within*.

203. Quote Investigator. "Sometimes I Sits and Thinks, and Sometimes I Just Sits." https://quoteinvestigator.com/2018/08/29/sit/#:~:text=the%20following%20saying%3A-,Sometimes%20I%20sits%20and%20thinks%2C%20and%20sometimes%20I%20just%20sits,prominent%

20baseball%20player%2C%20Satchel%20Paige.

204. Gingrich, *Restoring the Shattered Self*.

Greenberg, Leslie S. "Resolving Splits: Use of the Two-Chair Technique." *Psychotherapy: Theory, Research and Practice* 16, no. 3 (1979): 316–324. https://psycnet.apa.org/doi/10.1037/h0085895.

205. Greenberg, "Resolving Splits."

206. Gingrich, *Restoring the Shattered Self*.

207. Watkins and Watkins, *Ego States*.

208. Bass and Davis, *The Courage to Heal*.

209. Bass and Davis, *The Courage to Heal*.

210. Bass and Davis, *The Courage to Heal*.

211. Bass and Davis, *The Courage to Heal*.

212. Watkins and Watkins, *Ego States*.

213. Greenberg, "Resolving Splits."

214. Paivio, Sandra C., and Leslie S. Greenberg. "Resolving 'Unfinished Business': Efficacy of Experiential Therapy Using Empty-Chair Dialogue." *Journal of Consulting and Clinical Psychology* 63, no. 3 (1995): 419–425. https://doi.org/10.1037//0022-006x.63.3.419.

Wagner-Moore, Laura E. "Gestalt Therapy: Past, Present, Theory, and Research." *Psychotherapy: Theory, Research, Practice, Training* 41, no. 2 (2004): 180–189.

215. Peterson, Lorrie, and Robert Melcher. "To Change, Be Yourself: An Illustration of Paradox in Gestalt Therapy." *Journal of Counseling and Development* 60, no. 2 (1981): 101–103. https://doi.org/10.1002/j.2164-4918.1981.tb00651.x

216. Ross, Colin A. *Dissociative Identity Disorder: Diagnosis, Clinical Features, and Treatment of Multiple Personality*. Vol. 12 of *Wiley Series in General and Clinical Psychiatry*. 2nd edition. Wiley, 1997. First published in 1989.

217. Keyes, presentation on the HEART Model.

218. Parker, Carol. Personal communication. 2016.

219. Gingrich, *Restoring the Shattered Self*.

220. Herman, Judith. *Trauma and Recovery: The Aftermath of Violence—from Domestic Abuse to Political Terror*. Basic Books, 1997.

221. Bass and Davis, *The Courage to Heal*.

222. Go Ask Alice! "Rubber Bands—an Alternative to Self-injury?" June 18, 2021. First published November 2, 2007. www.goaskalice.columbia.edu/answered-questions/rubber-bands-alternative-to-self-injury.

223. Bass and Davis, *The Courage to Heal*.

224. Bass and Davis, *The Courage to Heal*.

225. Bass and Davis, *The Courage to Heal*.

226. Bass and Davis, *The Courage to Heal*.

227. Bass and Davis, *The Courage to Heal*, 60.

228. Bass and Davis, *The Courage to Heal*, 70.

229. Bass and Davis, *The Courage to Heal*.

230. McLeod, Saul. "The Preoperational Stage of Cognitive Development." Simply Psychology. 2018. https://www.simplypsychology.org/preoperational.html.

231. Bass and Davis, *The Courage to Heal*.

232. Bass and Davis, *The Courage to Heal*.

233. Seamands, *Healing of Memories*.

234. Keyes, presentation on the HEART Model.

235. Figley, Charles R., ed. *Encyclopedia of Trauma: An Interdisciplinary Guide*. SAGE, 2012.

Gingrich, Heather Davediuk, and Fred C. Gingrich, eds. *Treating Trauma in Christian Counseling*. InterVarsity Press, 2017, 246.

Hall, Melissa, and Joshua Hall. "The Long-term Effects of Childhood Sexual Abuse: Counseling Implications." (2011). Retrieved from http://counselingoutfitters.com/vistas/vistas11/Article_19.pdf.

RAINN. "Adult Survivors of Child Abuse." https://www.rainn.org/articles/adult-survivors-child-sexual-abuse.

Ullman, Sarah E., Liana C. Peter-Hagene, and Mark Relyea. "Coping, Emotion Regulation, and Self-Blame as Mediators of Sexual Abuse and Psychological Symptoms in Adult Sexual Assault." *Journal of Child Sexual Abuse* 23, no. 1 (2014): 74–93. https://doi.org/10.1080/10538712.2014.864747.

236. Bass and Davis, *The Courage to Heal*.

Pendergrast, Mark. *Victims of Memory*. Upper Access Books, 1995.

237. Keyes, presentation on the HEART Model.

238. Bass and Davis, *The Courage to Heal*, 149, 154.

239. Bass and Davis, *The Courage to Heal*.

Mccullough, Michael E., and Everett L. Worthington, Jr. "Encouraging Clients to Forgive People Who Have Hurt Them: Review, Critique, and Research Prospectus." *Journal of Psychology and Theology* 22, no. 1 (1994): 3–20. https://doi.org/10.1177/009164719402200101.

Tracy, Steven. "Sexual Abuse and Forgiveness." *Journal of Psychology and Theology* 27, no. 3 (1999): 219–

229. https://doi.org/10.1177/009164719902700302.

Walton, Elaine. "Therapeutic Forgiveness: Developing a Model for Empowering Victims of Sexual Abuse." *Clinical Social Work Journal* 33 (2005): 193–207. https://doi.org/10.1007/s10615-005-3532-1.

Weir, Kirsten. "Forgiveness Can Improve Mental and Physical Health." *Monitor on Psychology* 48, no. 1 (2017): 30. https://www.apa.org/monitor/2017/01/ce-corner.

240. Worthington, Everett L. *Steps to REACH Forgiveness and to Reconcile.* Pearson Learning Solutions, 2008.

241. Worthington, *Steps to REACH Forgiveness and to Reconcile.*

242. Bass and Davis, *The Courage to Heal.*

243. Ferguson, Bill. *Heal the Hurt That Sabotages Your Life.* Return to the Heart, 2004.

Menahem, Sam, and Melanie Love. "Forgiveness in Psychotherapy: The Key to Healing." *Journal of Clinical Psychology* 69, no. 8 (2013): 829–835. doi:10.1002/jclp.22018.

244. Ferguson, *Heal the Hurt That Sabotages Your Life.*

245. Matsakis, Aphrodite. *I Can't Get Over It: A Handbook for Trauma Survivors.* New Harbinger, 1992.

246. McGee, Robert S. *The Search for Significance.* Revised edition. Rapha, 1988. First published in 1984.

247. Bass and Davis, *The Courage to Heal*, 151.

248. Bass and Davis, *The Courage to Heal*, 154.

249. Nelson, Portia. "Autobiography in Five Short Chapters." In *There's a Hole in My Sidewalk: The Romance of Self-Discovery.* Popular Library, 1977.

250. Pearson, David G., and Tony Craig. "The Great Outdoors? Exploring the Mental Health Benefits of Natural Environments." *Frontiers in Psychology* 5 (2014): 1,178. https://doi.org/10.3389/fpsyg.2014.01178.

251. Curran, Linda A. *101 Trauma-Informed Interventions: Activities, Exercises and Assignments to Move the Client and Therapy Forward.* PESI, 2013.

252. Mathieu, Françoise. "Transforming Compassion Fatigue into Compassion Satisfaction: Top 12 Self-care Tips for Helpers." Workshops for the Helping Professions. 2007. https://compassionfatigue.org/pages/Top12SelfCareTips.pdf.

253. Stuckey, Heather L., and Jeremy Nobel. "The Connection Between Art, Healing, and Public Health: A Review of Current Literature." *American Journal of Public Health* 100, no. 2 (2010): 254–263. https://doi.org/10.2105%2FAJPH.2008.156497.

Stevens, John O. *Awareness: Exploring, Experimenting, Experiencing.* Real People Press, 1971.

254. Gingrich and Gingrich, *Treating Trauma in Christian Counseling.*

255. Gingrich and Gingrich, *Treating Trauma in Christian Counseling.*

256. Heller, Laurence, and Aline LaPierre. *Healing Developmental Trauma.* North Atlantic Books, 2012.

257. Gall, Terry, Viola Basque, Marizete Damasceno-Scott, and Gerard Vardy. "Spirituality and the Current Adjustment of Adult Survivors of Childhood Sexual Abuse." *Journal for the Scientific Study of Religion* 46, no. 1 (2007): 101–117. https://doi.org/10.1111/j.1468-5906.2007.00343.x.

258. Keyes, presentation on the HEART Model.

259. Fox, Jesse, Daniel Gutierrez, Jesssica Haas, Dinesh J. Braganza, and Christine A. Berger. "Phenomenological Investigation of Centering Prayer Using Conventional Content Analysis." *Pastoral Psychology* 64, no. 10 (2015).

260. Luethje, Kathy, ed. *Healing with Art and Soul: Engaging One's Self Through Art Modalities.* Cambridge Scholars Publishing, 2008.

Pennington, Basil. *Centered Living: The Way of Centering Prayer.* Image Book edition. Doubleday, 1988. First published in 1986.

Linn, Dennis, Matthew Linn, and Sheila Fabricant. *Praying with Another for Healing.* Paulist Press, 1984.

261. Linn, Linn, and Fabricant, *Praying with Another for Healing.*

262. Murray-Swank, Nicole A., and Kenneth I. Pargament. "Seeking the Sacred: The Assessment of Spirituality in the Therapy Process." In Jamie D. Aten, Mark R. McMinn, and Everett L. Worthington, Jr., *Spiritually Oriented Interventions for Counseling and Psychotherapy.* American Psychological Association, 2011. 107–135. https://doi.org/10.1037/12313-005.

263. Marsh, Robert, and James Low. "God as Other, God as Self, God as Beyond: A Cognitive Analytic Perspective on the Relationship with God." *Psychology and Psychotherapy* 79, no. 2 (2006): 237–255. https://doi.org/10.1348/147608305X52748.

264. Van Hook, Mary Patricia. "Spirituality as a Potential Resource for Coping." *Social Work and Christianity* 43, no. 1 (2016): 7–25. https://www.nacsw.org/Publications/SWC/SWC43_3Sample.pdf.

265. Coolman, Boyd Taylor. *Knowing God by Experience: The Spiritual Senses in the Theology of William of Auxerre.* The Catholic University of America Press, 2004.

266. Reinert, Duane F., and Christine E. Edwards. "Attachment Theory, Childhood Mistreatment, and Religiosity." *Psychology of Religion and Spirituality* 1, no. 1 (2009): 25–34. https://psycnet.apa.org/doi/10.1037/a0014894.

267. Luethje, *Healing with Art and Soul*, 306.

268. Luethje, *Healing with Art and Soul*, 306.

269. Luethje, *Healing with Art and Soul*, 306.

270. Seamands, *Healing of the Memories.*

271. Seamands, *Healing of the Memories.*

272. Seamands, *Healing of the Memories.*

273. Mazur, Eric Michael. Quoted in Mark Kellner, "When Hollywood Puts God on Screen." Deseret News. September 19, 2016. https://www. deseret.com/2016/9/19/20596523/when-hollywood-puts-god-on-screen#this-image-released-by-20th-century-fox-shows-christian-bale-left-and-ben-kingsley-in-a-scene-from-exodus-gods-and-kings.

274. DeMille, Cecil B., dir. *The Ten Commandments*. Paramount. 1956.

275. Luethje, *Healing with Art and Soul*.

Ross, Colin A. "Talking About God with Trauma Survivors." *American Journal of Psychotherapy* 70, no. 4 (2016): 429–437. https://doi.org/10.1176/appi.psychotherapy.2016.70.4.429.

276. Counted, Victor. "Understanding God Images and God Concepts: Towards a Pastoral Hermeneutics of the God Attachment Experience." *Verbum Et Ecclesia* 36, no. 1 (2015). https://doi.org/10.4102/VE.V36I1.1389.

O'Mathúna, "Christian Theology and Disasters."

Ross, "Talking About God with Trauma Survivors."

Wiegand, Katherine E., Howard M. Weiss. "Affective Reactions to the Thought of 'God': Moderating Effects of Image of God." *Journal of Happiness Studies* 7 (2006): 23–40. https://doi.org/10.1007/s10902-005-0930-6.

277. Seamands, *Healing of the Memories*.

278. Seamands, *Healing of the Memories*.

279. Wong-Mcdonald, Ana, and Richard L. Gorsuch. "A Multivariate Theory of God Concept, Religious Motivation, Locus of Control, Coping, and Spiritual Well-being." *Journal of Psychology and Theology* 32, no. 4 (2004): 318–334. https://doi.org/10.1177/009164710403200404.

280. Kennedy, James E., Robert C. Davis, and Bruce G. Taylor. "Changes in Spirituality and Well-being Among Victims of Sexual Assault." *Journal for the Scientific Study of Religion* 37, no. 2 (1998): 322–328. https://doi.org/10.2307/1387531.

281. Cheston, Sharon E., Ralph L. Piedmont, Beverly Eanes, and Lynn Patrice Lavin. "Changes in Clients' Images of God Over the Course of Outpatient Therapy." *Counseling and Values* 47, no. 2 (2011): 96–108. https://doi.org/10.1002/j.2161-007X.2003.tb00227.x.

282. Gall, Basque, Damasceno-Scott, and Vardy. "Spirituality and the Current Adjustment of Adult Survivors of Childhood Sexual Abuse."

283. Kwon, Soo-Young. "'God May NOT Be a Person!': A Case of Cultural Construction of God Representations." *Pastoral Psychology* 53 (2005): 405–421. https://doi.org/10.1007/s11089-005-2584-z.

284. O'Mathúna, Dónal P. "Christian Theology and Disasters: Where Is God in All This?" In *Disasters: Core Concepts and Ethical Theories*. Edited by Vilius Dranseika, Bert Gordijn, and Dónal P. O'Mathúna. Vol. 11 of *Advancing Global Bioethics*. Springer, 2018. 27–42.

285. Derouchie, Jason. "Is Every Promise 'Yes'? Old Testament Promises and the Christian." *Themelios*

42, no. 1. https://www.thegospelcoalition.org/themelios/article/is-every-promise-yes-old-testament-promises-and-the-christian/.

286. O'Mathúna, "Christian Theology and Disasters."

287. O'Mathúna, "Christian Theology and Disasters."

288. Ross, "Talking About God with Trauma Survivors."

289. Ross, "Talking About God with Trauma Survivors."

290. Hill, Clara E. *Helping Skills: Facilitating Exploration, Insight, and Action.* 4th edition. American Psychological Association, 2014. First published in 1999.

291. Keyes, Underwood, Snyder, Dailey, and Hourihan, "Healing Emotional Affective Responses to Trauma (HEART)."

292. Holeman, Virginia Todd. "10 Theological Ideas for Better Counseling." The Table. July 7, 2019. https://cct.biola.edu/10-theological-ideas-for-better-counseling/.

293. Matsakis, *I Can't Get Over It.*

294. Seamands, *Healing of the Memories.*

295. Silk, Kenneth R. "Object Relations and the Nature of Therapeutic Interventions." *Journal of Psychotherapy Integration* 15, no. 1 (2005): 94–100. https://psycnet.apa.org/buy/2005-02680-008.

296. Turell, Susan C., and Cassandra R. Thomas. "Where Was God? Utilizing Spirituality with Christian Survivors of Sexual Abuse." Women and Therapy 24, no. 3–4 (2002): 133–147. https://doi.org/10.1300/J015v24n03_08. Also in *The Invisible Alliance: Psyche and Spirit in Feminist Therapy.* Edited by Ellyn Kaschak. Psychology Press, 2002.

297. Turell and Thomas, "Where Was God?"

298. Hobson, George. *Imago Dei: Man/Woman Created in the Image of God: Implications for Theology, Pastoral Care, Eucharist, Apologetics, Aesthetics.* Wipf and Stock, 2019.

299. Exline, Julie Juola, Ann Marie Yali, and Marci Lobel. "When God Disappoints: Difficulty Forgiving God and its Role in Negative Emotion." *Journal of Health Psychology* 4, no, 3 (1999): 365–379. https://doi.org/10.1177/135910539900400306.

300. Worthington, Everett L., Jr. *Moving Forward: 6 Steps to Forgiving Yourself and Breaking Free from the Past.* WaterBrook, 2013.

301. Worthington, *Moving Forward.*

302. McGee, *The Search for Significance.*

303. Brende, Joel. Personal communication. 1986.

304. May, Rollo. *Man's Search for Himself.* W. W. Norton, 1953.

305. Rama, Swami, Rudolph Ballentine, and Swami Ajaya. *Yoga and Psychotherapy: The Evolution of Consciousness.* Himalayan Institute Press, 1976.

306. Perls, Frederick S. *Gestalt Therapy Verbatim*. 2nd revised edition. Gestalt Journal Press, 1992.

307. Seamands, David A. *Healing for Damaged Emotions*. Victor Books, 1981.

Seamands, *Healing of Memories*.

308. Schreiber, Flora Rheta. *Sybil: The Classic True Story of a Woman Possessed by Sixteen Separate Personalities*. Henry Regnery, 1973.

309. Dickstein, Leah J. "Images in Psychiatry: Cornelia Burwell Wilbur, M.D." *American Journal of Psychiatry* 155, no. 9 (1998): 1,274. https://doi.org/10.1176/ajp.155.9.1274.

310. Thigpen, Corbett H., and Hervey M. Cleckley. *The Three Faces of Eve*. McGraw-Hill, 1957.

311. Putnam, "Pierre Janet and Modern Views of Dissociation."

312. Putnam, "Pierre Janet and Modern Views of Dissociation."

313. Putnam, "Pierre Janet and Modern Views of Dissociation."

314. Steele, Kathy, Suzette Boon, and Onno van der Hart. *Treating Trauma-Related Dissociation: A Practical Integrative Approach*. W. W. Norton, 2016.

315. Putnam, "Pierre Janet and Modern Views of Dissociation."

316. Perls, Frederick S., Ralph Hefferline, and Paul Goodman. *Gestalt Therapy: Excitement and Growth in the Human Personality*. Gestalt Journal Press, 1994. First published by Julian Press.

317. Bradshaw, John. *Healing the Shame That Binds You*. Health Communications, 1988.

318. Ross, *Multiple Personality Disorder*.

319. Ross, *Multiple Personality Disorder*.

320. Watkins and Watkins, *Ego States*.

321. Watkins and Watkins, *Ego States*.

322. Polster, Erving, and Miriam Polster. *Gestalt Therapy Integrated: Contours of Theory and Practice*. Vintage Books, 1974.

323. Polster and Polster, *Gestalt Therapy Integrated*.

324. Perls, Frederick S. *In and Out the Garbage Pail*. Real People Press, 1969.

325. Polster and Polster, *Gestalt Therapy Integrated*.

326. Bradshaw, *Homecoming*.

327. Bradshaw, *Homecoming*.

328. Wright, H. Norman. *Self-talk, Imagery, and Prayer in Counseling*. Word Books, 1986. 108.

329. Wright, *Self-talk, Imagery, and Prayer in Counseling*.

330. Wright, *Self-talk, Imagery, and Prayer in Counseling*.

331. Maltz, Maxwell. *Psycho-cybernetics.* Simon and Schuster, 1960.

332. Rohr, Richard, and James Finley. *Intimacy: The Divine Ambush.* Center for Action and Contemplation, 2013. 10 compact discs. https://store.cac.org/products/intimacy-the-divine-ambush-cd.

333. Kanter, Jonathan W., Chauncey R. Parker, and Robert J. Kohlenberg. "Finding the Self: A Behavioral Measure and Its Clinical Implications." *Psychotherapy: Theory, Research, Practice, Training* 38, no. 2 (2001): 198–211. https://doi.org/10.1037/0033-3204.38.2.198.

334. Rivera, Margo. *More Alike Than Different: Treating Severely Dissociative Survivors.* University of Toronto Press, 1996.

335. Hassan, Steven. *Combating Cult Mind Control: The Guide to Protection, Rescue and Recovery from Destructive Cults.* 30th anniversary edition. Freedom of Mind Press, 2015. First published in 1988 by Park Street Press.

336. Halpern, James, and Mary Tramontin. *Disaster in Mental Health: Theory and Practice.* Thomas Brooks/Cole, 2007.

Neria, Yuval, Sandro Galea, and Fran H. Norris, eds. *Mental Health and Disasters.* Cambridge University Press, 2009. https://doi.org/10.1017/CBO9780511730030.

337. American Psychiatric Association, *Diagnostic and Statistical Manual of Mental Disorders: DSM-5.*

338. American Psychiatric Association, *Diagnostic and Statistical Manual of Mental Disorders: DSM-5.*

339. American Psychiatric Association, *Diagnostic and Statistical Manual of Mental Disorders: DSM-5.*

340. Kanter, Parker, and Kohlenberg, "Finding the Self."

341. ten Boom, Corrie, Sherrill, Elizabeth., Sherrill, John L. *The Hiding Place.* Chosen Books, 1971.

342. ten Boom, Sherrill, and Sherrill, *The Hiding Place.*

343. ten Boom, Sherrill, and Sherrill, *The Hiding Place.*

344. Bass and Davis, *The Courage to Heal.*

345. Rank, M. "Child, Adolescent and Traumatic Stress" (workshop). Greencross Academy of Traumatology, 2008.

346. Rank, "Child, Adolescent and Traumatic Stress."

347. Gabarino, James, Edna Guttmann, and Janis Wilson Seeley. *Psychologically Battered Child: Strategies for Identification, Assessment, and Intervention.* Jossey-Bass Publishers, 1986.

348. Rank, "Child, Adolescent and Traumatic Stress."

349. Rank, "Child, Adolescent and Traumatic Stress."

350. Herman, Judith Lewis. *Trauma and Recovery: The Aftermath of Violence—from Domestic Abuse to Political Terror.* Revised edition. Basic Books, 2015. First published in 1992.

351. Rank, "Child, Adolescent and Traumatic Stress."

352. Herman, *Trauma and Recovery*.

353. Rank, "Child, Adolescent and Traumatic Stress."

354. Rank, "Child, Adolescent and Traumatic Stress."

355. Diagnostic and Statistical Manual of Mental Disorders. 4th edition (DSM-4). APA, 2000.

Regarding the symptom of dysregulated mood: DSM. 5th edition (DSM-5). APA, 2023.

See also: DSM. 5th edition, Text Revision (DSM-5-TR). APA, March 2022.

356. Rank, "Child, Adolescent and Traumatic Stress."

357. Rank, "Child, Adolescent and Traumatic Stress."

358. Rank, "Child, Adolescent and Traumatic Stress."

359. Ross, Colin A. *Structural Dissociation: A Proposed Modification of the Theory*. Manitou Communications, 2013.

360. Ross, Colin A., and Naomi Halpern. *Trauma Model Therapy: A Treatment Approach for Trauma, Dissociation, and Complex Co-morbidity*. Manitou Communications, 2009.

361. Ross, Colin A. Personal communication. 1996.

362. Keyes, Underwood, Snyder, Dailey, and Hourihan, "Healing Emotional Affective Responses to Trauma (HEART)."

363. Harris, Anne Singer. *Living with Paradox: An Introduction to Jungian Psychology*. 1st edition. Wadsworth, 1995.

364. Seamands, *Healing for Damaged Emotions*.

365. Seamands, *Healing the Memories*.

366. Smith and Coloma, *Renting Lacy*.

367. Smith and Coloma, *Renting Lacy*.

368. Smith and Coloma, *Renting Lacy*.

369. Jones, Megan A. "Leaving 'the Life': The Recovery Journey of Sex Trafficking Survivors Using the HEART Model of Intervention." PhD diss. Regent University, 2014.

370. Herman, *Trauma and Recovery*.

371. Bradshaw, *Homecoming*.

372. Infographic by Vanessa Snyder and Benjamin B. Keyes.

373. Infographic by Vanessa Snyder and Benjamin B. Keyes.

374. Infographic by Vanessa Snyder and Benjamin B. Keyes.

375. Infographic by Vanessa Snyder and Benjamin B. Keyes.

376. Infographic by Vanessa Snyder and Benjamin B. Keyes.

377. Infographic by Vanessa Snyder and Benjamin B. Keyes.

378. U. S. Department of State. "2021 Trafficking in Persons Report" June 2021. https://www.state.gov/wp-content/uploads/2021/09/TIPR-GPA-upload-07222021.pdf.

379. Carter, Jimmy. *A Call to Action: Women, Religion, Violence, and Power.* Simon and Schuster, 2014.

380. International Labour Organization, and Walk Free Foundation "Global Estimates of Modern Slavery: Forced Labour and Forced Marriage." ILO Publications, 2017. http://www.ilo.org/global/publications/books/WCMS_575479/lang--en/index.htm.

381. International Labour Organization, and Walk Free Foundation, "Global Estimates of Modern Slavery."

382. U.S. Department of Justice. "Involuntary Servitude, Forced Labor, and Sex Trafficking Statutes Enforced." U. S. Department of Justice Civil Rights Division. Updated August 6, 2015. https://www.justice.gov/crt/involuntary-servitude-forced-labor-and-sex-trafficking-statutes-enforced.

383. Coloma, Cindy, and Linda Tuhiwai Smith. *Renting Lacey: A Story of America's Prostituted Children*. Revised edition. Shared Hope International, 2011. First published in 2009.

384. Coloma and Smith, *Renting Lacey*.

385. U. S. Department of Justice. "Human Trafficking." U. S. Attorney's Office District of Rhode Island. Updated August 10, 2016. https://www.justice.gov/usao-ri/human-trafficking.

386. International Labour Organization, and Walk Free Foundation, "Global Estimates of Modern Slavery."

387. International Labour Organization, and Walk Free Foundation, "Global Estimates of Modern Slavery."

388. These observations are derived from my personal experiences in Kenya, in 2012 and 2019.

389. O'Neill-Richard, Amy. "International Trafficking of Women to the United States: A Contemporary Manifestation of Slavery and Organized Crime." Center for the Study of Intelligence, 2000.

390. U. S. Department of State, "2021 Trafficking in Persons Report."

391. Department of Justice, "Human Trafficking."

392. U. S. Department of Justice. "Frequently Used Federal Drug Statutes." U. S. Attorney's Office District of New Hampshire. Updated May 21, 2020. https://www.justice.gov/usao-nh/frequently-used-federal-drug-statutes.

393. Lutheran Immigration and Refugee Service. "Our Work." https://www.lirs.org/our-work/.

United States Conference of Catholic Bishops. "Migration and Refugee Services: Human Trafficking." https://www.usccb.org/offices/migration-refugee-services/human-trafficking.

394. Hoy, Kevin (CEO and founder of The Smiles Foundation). Personal communication. 2009. Cihei, Romania.

395. Rogers, Carl R. *Client Centered Therapy: Its Current Practice, Implications, and Theory.* Houghton-Mifflin, 2021. First published in 1951.

Made in the USA
Middletown, DE
31 July 2024

58229636R00139